HARVARD ORIENTAL SERIES

EDITED BY MICHAEL WITZEL

VOLUME SEVENTY-EIGHT

BHĀVIVEKA ON SĀṂKHYA AND VEDĀNTA

THE SĀṂKHYA AND VEDĀNTA CHAPTERS
OF THE MADHYAMAKAHṚDAYAKĀRIKĀ AND TARKAJVĀLĀ

By

OLLE QVARNSTRÖM

(With Tibetological Assistance by Professor Per K. Sørensen)

PUBLISHED BY THE DEPARTMENT OF SOUTH ASIAN STUDIES

HARVARD UNIVERSITY

DISTRIBUTED BY HARVARD UNIVERSITY PRESS,

CAMBRIDGE, MASSACHUSETTS

AND LONDON, ENGLAND

2015

Printed in the United States of America

For information write to Editor, Harvard Oriental Series,
Department of South Asian Studies,
1 Bow Street, Cambridge MA 02138, USA
617-495 3295; email: witzel@fas.harvard.edu

Library of Congress Cataloguing in Publication Data
Bhāviveka on Sāṃkhya and Vedānta; the Sāṃkhya and Vedānta Chapters of the Madhyamakahṛdayakārikā and Tarkajvālā, translated and edited with introduction and notes by Olle Qvarnström.

Harvard Oriental Series; v. 78. ISBN 978-0-674-08849-8

I. Qvarnström, Olle 1953-
II. Title
III. Series: Harvard Oriental Series; 78
CIP

For my beloved mother,

Inga Qvarnström

Contents

Acknowledgements

First of all I would like to extend my profound gratitude to my dear friend and colleague, Professor Per K. Sørensen, Universität Leipzig, for his painstaking and untiring help with translating the Sāṃkhya chapter of the Tibetan *Tarkajvālā* and editing the Tibetan text of the Sāṃkhya and Vedānta chapters of the *Madhyamakahṛdayakārikā*. I am also deeply indepted to my equally dear friend and colleague, Professor Martin Gansten, Lund University, who substantially assisted me in translating the Sanskrit text of the Sāṃkhya chapter of the *Madhyamakahṛdayakārikā* as well as providing me with numerous critical remarks and suggestions. Martin Gansten was also generous enough carefully to proofread the entire manuscript. I would also like to extend my heartfelt appreciation to my learned friend Sven Ekelin, BA, Stockholm, in whose company I for many years had the pleasure of studying the Sāṃkhya chapter of the *Madhyamakahṛdayakārikā* as well as other relevant Sāṃkhya texts. I am most thankful to Allan Andersson, who significantly improved the English manuscript, successfully paraphrasing certain difficult passages in the commentary on the Sāṃkhya chapter. I extend my appreciation to Michael Witzel, Wales Professor of Sanskrit at Harvard University and editor of the Harvard Oriental Series, for kindly approving the publication. I express my great obligation to the Swedish Research Council for funding the entire project, and to Oscar och Signe Krooks stiftelse for kindly covering the printing costs.

Lund, April 2015
Olle Qvarnström

Introduction

> *On three separate occasions Karṇa fought against and was defeated by Ghaṭotkaca, the son of Bhīmasena and the forest demoness [Hidimbā]. Then, taking up the secret javelin that Indra had awarded him to kill his enemies, he hurdled it at Ghaṭotkaca. [To avoid the deadly javelin], Ghaṭotkaca transformed into a serpent, whereupon the javelin transformed into an eagle; Ghaṭotkaca then transformed into a mouse, whereupon the javelin transformed into an owl; finally, when Ghaṭotkaca transformed into fire, the javelin transformed into water. Every time Ghaṭotkaca transformed, the weapon continued to pursue him. No matter what form he assumed, the javelin transformed into a form that could defeat him until he was finally killed.*[1]

In this garbled version of the duel between Karṇa and Ghaṭotkaca on the 14th and 15th day of the great battle in the *Mahābhārata*, the Madhyamaka philosopher Bhāviveka (490/500-570 CE) cautions his imagined Sāṃkhya opponent that regardless of how many attempts he may make to modify the tenets of his system, Bhāviveka's relentless exposure of each modification's fallacy would eventually lead to entire defeat.[2] Just as Karṇa's javelin overtook and ultimately destroyed Ghaṭotkaca, Bhāviveka's logical arguments would overtake and ultimately destroy his opponent's point of view, regardless of the latter's various attempts to alter his doctrinal

[1] See MHK-TJ VI.40-41 with n.

[2] In accordance with Eckel (2008:88, n.1), I will use the name Bhāviveka. On the different names allotted to this author, see also Ames 1986:37; Gokhale 1958:165-166, n.1; La Vallée Poussin 1933:60-61; Krasser 2012:535, n.1. On the date of Bhāviveka, see Krasser 2012:580ff.

stance.[3] The adoption of such an attitude by competing philosophers in sixth century India was likely not uncommon.

In the centuries that followed the teachings of Nāgārjuna and Āryadeva, the philosophies of the Buddhist, Jain and Brāhmaṇical schools underwent significant development, resulting in an epoch of almost unrivalled intellectual activity and debate. For the Buddhists in particular, this period of philosophic flowering was especially productive, as indicated by the development of the Yogācāra school as well as advances in logic and epistemology, culminating in the establishment of Dignāga's logico-epistemological school. Outside the Buddhist tradition, improvements and innovations were achieved by the major schools of Brāhmaṇical and Jain philosophy, whose basic tenets were settled and provided with commentaries.[4]

Unlike their Greek and Roman counterparts, whose criticisms of Judaic and Christian theologies addressed worldviews that were fundamentally incompatible with their own and expressed in foreign idioms,[5] these Indian philosophers belonged to mutually influencing traditions that held common doctrines, a common

---

[3] TJ VI.40-41.

[4] Qvarnström 1989:9-13.

[5] I am here referring to the debate on reason and revelation, which had its roots in the Graeco-Roman tradition on the one side, and the Judaeo-Christian tradition on the other. Initiated in the 2nd and 3rd century of the Common Era by authors such as Celsus, Porphyrius and Emperor Julian, it came to dominate medieval scholasticism and was brought to the fore after the Renaissance as a result of the development of natural science and biblical criticism, among other things. This debate seems to have its Indian counterpart in the debate between Jains and Buddhists, on the one hand, and Mīmāṃsā on the other, as exemplified e.g. in the Mīmāṃsā chapter of Haribhadrasūri's *Śāstravārttāsamuccaya*. See Qvarnström 2005.

cognitive universe, and a common *lingua franca*. Like the students of medieval Europe's convent schools, whose curriculum included the seven liberal arts (*septem artes liberales*), these Indian philosophers, in addition to their respective confessional training, had studied the same basic elements consisting of grammar, dialectics and rhetoric as well as a number of arts and sciences. In other words, their agreement on more fundamental matters was sufficient to allow for a highly nuanced and informed debate on the particulars.[6]

For anyone interested in making a study of these 6th-century debates, Bhāviveka's *Madhyamakahṛdayakārikā* along with its auto-commentary the *Tarkajvālā* is an indispensible resource. The text was originally entitled the *Madhyamakahṛdaya, Tattvāmṛtāvatāra* or *Madhyamakahṛdayatattvāvatāra,* and contained both verses (in later transmissions, the *Madhyamakahṛdayakārikā* or *Tarkajvālāsūtra*) and a prose commentary (in later transmissions, *Tarkajvālā*). For purely practical purposes, I will refer to the verses as *Madhyamakahṛdaya-kārikā* (MHK) and the prose as *Tarkajvālā* (TJ).[7]

In this partially doxographical treatise, Hīnayāna (or Śrāvakayāna), Yogācāra, Saṃkhya, Vaiśeṣika, Vedānta and Mīmāṃsā are presented in a *pūrvapakṣa* and then subjected to critical examination in a collateral *uttarapakṣa*. The critique found in this section constitutes, as it were, a strengthening of the principles and methods expounded at great length by Bhāviveka in his crucial third chapter, the *Tattvajñānaiṣaṇa*, in which he explicitly propounds his own philosophy, including a revision of the doctrinal stance and methodology of Madhyamaka philosophy. A primary reason for

[6] Qvarnström 2005.

[7] Qvarnström 1989:25f.

such a revision was the immanent threat of being either absorbed or overshadowed by the Yogācāra school;[8] another concerned the challenge posed by various Brāhmaṇical systems to the Madhyamaka school. In order to avert these pitfalls and bring Madhyamaka philosophy into conformity with the prevalent philosophical requirements of India's 6th century intellectual *milieu*, Bhāviveka used logical devices originally formulated by Dignāga and others.[9] According to Bhāviveka, the mere depiction of a system's inherent contradictions was not enough to triumph in debate; a thorough refutation must include the presentation of one's own positive alternative as well. In other words, the *reductio ad absurdum* (*prāsaṅgika*)[10] approach is insufficient and requires the addition of independent propositions (*svatantra*) that both expound and validate one's own point of view. Employing both independent inferences (*svatantrānumāna*) and formal syllogisms (*prayogavākya*),

---

[8] With regard to the Buddhist systems criticized, Bhāviveka's refutation of the Yogācāra marks the definite split between the Madhyamakas and the Yogācāras, who prior to Bhāviveka tried to assimilate rather than oppose Madhyamaka Buddhism. For the Yogācāra chapter, see Eckel's brilliant study (2008) including a critical edition and annotated English translation of this and the *Śrāvakatattvaviniścayāvatāra* chapter.

[9] Bhāviveka's use of a threefold syllogism suggests, *inter alia*, the influence of Dignāga, especially the latter's *Pramāṇasamuccaya*, to which Bhāviveka frequently alludes in his TJ. Dignāga first reduced the five-fold syllogism of the *Nyāyasūtra* to a three-fold form and then incorporated and established the usage of syllogisms within the Buddhist tradition. The use of a five-fold syllogism at the very end of the *Prajñāpradīpa*, ch. XXVII, an independent essay on logic and *pramāṇa*, probably reflects the opponent's language, since Bhāviveka's reasons for not accepting the *pañcāvayava* doctrine are explicitly given in *Prajñāpradīpa* (*loc. cit.* 183b^{4}-184b^{1}); see Lindtner 1986:81, n. 33. It may also reflect another, later period of his scholarship in comparison to MHK-TJ. On Nāgārjuna's refutation of syllogisms, see Lindtner 1982b:89.

[10] On this debated term, see Dreyfus & McClintock 2003 (and the bibliography, na. s. v. Ruegg and Tillemans).

Bhāviveka considered himself not only well equipped to defeat all Buddhist, Brāhmaṇical and Jain propositions, but also fully capable of proving the validity of his own propositions and defending them against all counter-arguments.[11]

Bhāviveka, who was later classified as a Sautrāntika-[Svātantrika]-Madhyamaka by the Tibetan tradition,[12] was successful in influencing not only his contemporaries, but also later Mahāyāna philosophers. Within the Madhyamaka tradition, his *svātantrika* approach was followed and developed by such authors as Jñānagarbha, Śāntarakṣita and Kamalaśīla.[13] Nāgārjuna and Buddhapālita, on the other hand, used *prāsaṅgika* arguments to show that the opponent's position, with its implicit or explicit assumptions, had consequences unacceptable to the opponent himself. Bhāviveka's influence on the Madhyamaka tradition is also indicated by the opposition that he provoked. Candrakīrti's *prāsaṅgika* sub-school of Madhyamaka, which still dominates Tibetan Madhyamaka Buddhism through the *dGe-lugs-pa* branch of the Tibetan tradition, was actually formed in reaction to Bhāviveka's works.[14]

---

[11] Qvarnström 1989:14ff.

[12] See Ruegg 1980, 1981b, 1982; Mimaki 1982:27 sqq.; Qvarnström 1989:96-98; Lopez 1987:55-81. The term *svātantrika* (*raṅ-rgyud-pa*), applied to Bhāviveka, probably derives from passages in Candrakīrti's commentary on the *Madhyamakāvatāra* or from Jñānagarbha's *Satyadvayavibhāga/ °bhaṅga*, vv. 25-35. See Eckel 1987:92-99. The reason for classifying him as a Sautrāntika is most likely the fact that conventionally (*saṃvṛtitas*) he agrees with the Sautrāntikas at least on major ontological issues. This is evident from TJ VIII.66, where space (*ākāśa*) is regarded as merely the absence of a resistant substance (*sapratighadravyābhāvamātra*).

[13] See Ruegg 1981a:67-71, 87-100.

[14] Qvarnström 1989:96ff.

Bhāviveka's profound encyclopaedic knowledge is amply displayed in the MHK-TJ, which is one of the earliest surviving Sanskrit doxographical works.[15] As a doxographer, Bhāviveka actually initiated the comprehensive history-of-philosophy genre within Buddhism, an example of which would be the *Tattvasaṃgraha* by Śāntarakṣita (ca. 725-788).[16] The position held by Bhāviveka in Tibet relative to doxographical knowledge is as prominent as that held by Candrakīrti relative to the interpretation of Nāgārjuna.[17] The MHK-TJ is the earliest and most substantial work translated into Tibetan that seriously and in great detail presents and critically examines various heterodox schools. Thus Bhāviveka's work is of unique value in the attempt to identify a Madhyamaka approach to other schools. His encyclopaedic knowledge and philosophical innovations, formed in response to the challenges of his time, have given him an important place in the history of Buddhist philosophy.[18]

---

[15] See Qvarnström 1989, 1999; Eckel 2008:9ff.

[16] For the dates of Śāntarakṣita, see Frauwallner 1933:238-240; 1937:65-74. Haribhadrasūri refers in the auto-commentary on *Śāstravārtāsamuccaya* 296 to Śāntarakṣita's *Tattvasaṃgraha* 958 and 1083: *yad uktaṃ sūkṣmabuddhinā śānta-rakṣitena nāsato bhāvakartṛtvaṃ tadavasthāntaraṃ na saḥ* //. Bhattacharyya (ref. to in Winternitz 1983:460, n. 1) was, however, wrong in identifying Haribhadrasūri with an *ācārya sūri* alluded to in the *Tattvasaṃgraha* 124 and 126. The textual passage, which could refer to any Jain author, reads: *na hetur astīti vadan sahetukaṃ nanu pratijñāṃ svayam eva sād(h)ayet / athāpi hetuḥ praṇayālaso bhavet pratijñayā kevalayāsya kiṃ bhaved iti ācāryasūripādaiḥ.*

[17] On the Tibetan doxographical tradition, see Mimaki 1982; Hopkins 1996. For an example of a Tibetan doxographical text, see Hopkins' (2003) translation of *Grub-mtha'i rnam-par gźag-pa 'khrul-spoṅ gdoṅ-lṅa'i sgra-dbyaṅs; Grub-mtha'i rtsa-ba daṅ de'i tshig- 'grel bcas* (including chapters on Sāṃkhya and Vedānta).

[18] As far as the outline of Bhāviveka's reformative work of Madhyamaka philosophy and its historical presuppositions are concerned, I am indebted to the works of Ames (1986:28-58) and Eckel (1980:1-6; 1987:3-51; 2008:3-96).

Bhāviveka's major inspiration for the composition of a doxography may have been Dignāga's *Pramāṇasamuccaya*, which deals with Nyāya, Vaiśeṣika, Sāṃkhya and Mīmāṃsā within the *pramāṇa* tradition. Here it is of relevance to note that neither the *Pramāṇa-samuccaya* nor Dignāga's lost works (known to us from the *Pramāṇasamuccayavṛtti*[19]) include a refutation of Vedānta, possibly because this system did not at the time contain an independent theory of the "means of [valid] cognition" (*pramāṇa*). Bhāviveka's treatment of various schools within the *vāda* tradition can thus be viewed as a supplement to Dignāga's work.[20]

The value of a doxographical text is generally found not in its provision of new information, but rather in its manner of presenting opposing philosophical systems along with the doxographer's ideological stance relative to those views.[21] This notwithstanding, the MHK-TJ, in particular, contains obviously valuable information regarding Indian systematic philosophy, including what appear to be extracts from original sources that are otherwise unavailable. Due to his apologetic interests, however, Bhāviveka treats each philosophical tradition selectively rather than comprehensively, characterizing his opponents according to those of their propositions and arguments that he chooses to present. Thus Bhāviveka's selection, contextualization and organization of what are likely authentic arguments are aimed at refuting his opponents and establishing his own Madhyamaka point of view. In other words, whereas in the beginning stages of the doxographical tradition one's own ideological stance was defined in relation to hypothetical arguments, Bhāviveka defines his position

[19] Works in which he refuted adversaries from the Nyāya, Vaiśeṣika and Sāṃkhya traditions, among others.

[20] Qvarnström 1989:99f.

[21] Qvarnström 1999.

in relation to historically anchored arguments instead – arguments selected from various texts with various underlying ideologies that are assembled into a collage of ideas that facilitate his overarching purpose.

Against this background and as suggested by Eckel and Krasser, the MHK-TJ most probably served as a Madhyamaka debate manual for those engaged in argumentation with representatives of opposing philosophical schools. Indeed portions of this text may even have been written by students on the basis of a teacher's oral instructions or added at a later time by subsequent editors.[22] Here it should be noted that the outcome of these debates was of utmost importance to the disputants, who risked not only the prestige and potential patronage of their respective schools,[23] but also (and even more significantly) the omniscient status of their respective founders.[24]

Of the chapters dealing with Brāhmaṇical philosophy, the *Sāṃkhyatattvanirṇayāvatāra* (STNA) and *Vedāntatattvaviniścaya* (VTV) are of particular importance due to the scarcity of sources pertaining to the early formation and development of systematic Sāṃkhya and Vedānta philosophy. As far as Sāṃkhya is concerned, the only available texts from this period that have survived in their entirety are two summary compilations: the *Sāṃkhyakārikā* of

---

[22] Krasser 2011; Eckel 2008:9-17ff.

[23] Eckel 2008:12, 17.

[24] This is made plain by the implication of the following question, posed by the Jain philosopher Vidyānandin: "If [the Self] is intrinsically devoid of knowledge (*ajñāna*), Kapila would have nothing to say [about the nature of reality]?" (*yady ajñānasvabhāvaḥ syāt kapilo nopadeśakṛt*; *Tattvārthaślokavārttika*, ref. to by Tatia 1951:159).

Īśvarakṛṣṇa (350-450 CE)[25] and the *Yogasūtra* of Patañjali (350-450 CE) with their respective commentaries.

The earliest available *Sāṃkhyakārikā* commentary is likely the *Sāṃkhyavṛtti.*[26] This commentary, along with the slightly later *Suvarṇasaptati* and *Sāṃkhyasaptativṛtti*, may date from the 6th century CE and thus would have been available to Bhāviveka, although there is no explicit reference to these texts in the MHK-TJ.[27] The *Yuktidīpikā* is the only early commentary that substantially adds to our knowledge of the *Sāṃkhyakārikā's* content.[28] While this text of unknown authorship may date from the 6th century as well, Albrecht Wezler and Shujun Motegi have argued on good grounds

---

[25] Apart from the *Sāṃkhyakārikā* and its commentaries, there is the *Ṣaṣṭitantra*, an earlier, if limited, work containing a fully developed theory of epistemology and logic, known primarily through Frauwallner's (1958) reconstruction. More recently, Steinkellner (1999a, b) is known to have uncovered additional material for the reconstruction of the same, particularly as it relates to perception.

[26] Solomon 1973:6f.; 1974:111ff.

[27] According to Larson and Bhattacharya (1987:167f.), the overall content and specific wording of the *Sāṃkhyavṛtti, Suvarṇasaptati, Sāṃkhyasaptativṛtti*, Gauḍapāda's *bhāṣya* and *Māṭharavṛtti* are similar enough to suggest that they were involved in extensive borrowing or stem from a common original. Although Gauḍapāda's *bhāṣya* might have been of great interest to this study since the MHK quotes a number of *kārikās* from the *Gauḍapādīyakārikā*, it is most likely a later text that was not written by the author of the *Gauḍapādīyakārikā* (King 1995:15ff). Solomon (1973:171), however, believes that the author of Gauḍapāda's *bhāṣya* is the same as that of the *Gauḍapādīyakārikā*. Moreover, she places the composition of this commentary after the *Yuktidīpikā*; and given Wezler and Motegi's dating (see below), this implies that regardless of who authored this text, Bhāviveka could not have had access to it. With regard to the early *Sāṃkhyakārikā* commentaries, their relative chronologies and so forth, see Solomon 1974:111-181; Larson 1987:14f., 149ff.

[28] Harzer 2006:28.

that it originated around the late 7th century instead (680-720),[29] which would explain why it is not referenced in the MHK-TJ.

The only *Yogasūtra* commentary that would have been available when the MHK-TJ was composed is the *Yogasūtrabhāṣya*, which has been ascribed to Vyāsa (350-450 CE).[30] However, Philipp Maas has convincingly shown that rather than being two distinct texts, the *Yogasūtra* and *Yogasūtrabhāṣya* are the single work of a sole author, composed in the period between 325 and 425 CE and possibly going back to Patañjali himself: the *Pātañjalayogaśāstra*.[31] The philosophy of this text, with which Bhāviveka was familiar, is closely related to, if not identical with, the philosophy of Vindhyavāsin (350-400 CE),[32] which was an updated and revised version of Vārṣagaṇya's *Ṣaṣṭitantra*. The philosophy of Vindhyavāsin, most notably his epistemology, was in opposition to the philosophy of Īśvarakṛṣṇa's *Sāṃkhyakārikā*.[33] Both the *Sāṃkhyakārikā* and the *Pātañjalayogaśāstra*, representing two distinct traditions of interpretation of Vārṣagaṇya's *Ṣaṣṭitantra*, bear witness to a polemical encounter between Sāṃkhya and various Indic philosophical systems, most notably that of the Buddhists. However, with the possible exception of the *Yuktidīpikā*, not one Sāṃkhya treatise from this period exists that explicitly addresses this debate.

---

[29] Wezler and Motegi 1998:xxvii-xxviii, 434-435. As to the date of the *Yuktidīpikā*, suggestions by scholars range from the 6th to the 9th century CE (see Larson 1987:228). In her study of the epistemology of the *Yuktidīpikā*, Harzer (2006) places it in the latter half of the 6th century. For a summary account of the *Yuktidīpikā* see Larson 1987:227-269.

[30] Larson 2008:53.

[31] Maas 2006:xii-xix.

[32] Some scholars have even suggested that the *Yogasūtrabhāṣya* could have been composed by Vindhyavāsin, who then would be the same person as Vyāsa. See Larson 2008:36ff.

[33] Larson 2008: 38-41, 67.

As far as early systematic Vedānta philosophy is concerned, three complete texts have survived: the *Brahmasūtra*; the *Vākyapadīya*; and, the *Gauḍapādīyakārikā*.[34] From a historical perspective, these texts are the result of an assimilation of the Brāhmaṇical and the Buddhist traditions. As far as the *Gauḍapādīyakārikā* is concerned, it is clear that it is greatly indebted to Madhyamaka-Yogācāra philosophy.[35] The *Gauḍapādīyakārikā* quotes either fully, or partially, from Nāgārjuna's *Mūlamadhyamakakārikā*, Āryadeva's *Catuḥśataka*, Asaṅga's or Maitreyanātha's *Mahāyānasūtrālaṅkāra* and from several other works. With respect to the *Brahmasūtra*, the structure of some of the argumentation resembles the *prasaṅga* of the Madhyamaka school. It is therefore most likely that the *Brahmasūtra* in its final redaction was influenced by Madhyamaka philosophy in this respect.[36] As far as the Mahāyāna influence on the *Vākyapadīya* is concerned, the Madhyamaka-Yogācāra influence is not restricted only to terminology and formal structure, but penetrates to the very core of its doctrinal content.[37] The indebtedness of these three texts to Mahayana philosophy was probably not limited only to logic and epistemology. Even in an ontological sense the Madhyamaka-Yogācāra influence may be discernable. Despite the doctrinal differences, all postulate in one way or another the relative or illusory nature of the phenomenal world. The fundamental reason for such an ontological reflection is, however, com-

[34] MHK-TJ VIII.78-84 and IX.14, respectively. The *Vākyapadīya* is also quoted in the *Prajñāpradīpa*. As far as the *Paramārthasāra* of Ādiśeṣa is concerned, Rüping (1977:2) and Danielson (1980:1-2), dates it before CE 550 on the basis of the *Yuktidīpikā*, which quotes the *Paramārthasāra* 83 in the commentary on *Sāṃkhyakārikā* 2. This, however, does not provide sufficient evidence for such an early dating of the *Paramārthasāra* since, according to Wezler and Motegi (1998:xxvii-xxviii), the *Yuktidīpikā* dates from the 7th century at the earliest.

[35] King 1995:183ff

[36] Nakamura 1983:435-436.

[37] Nakamura 1973; Hacker 1953:199, 200-201.

pletely different in Mahāyāna and in Vedānta. Whereas the former postulates the illusory nature of the phenomenal world on the basis of its dependent origination, the latter tradition takes such a stand on the basis of the assumption that the world is produced by a single, all-pervading and self-containing reality. References to fragmentary accounts of early Vedānta philosophers are primarily found in the works of Śaṅkara, Bhāskara, Rāmānuja, Yāmunācārya, Sureśvara and Ānandagiri. The majority of these pre-Śaṅkara Vedānta philosophers appear, therefore, not as authors of independent systems but as interpreters of the Upaniṣads.[38]

Rather than providing a comprehensive, systematic description of one specific Vedāntic tradition, for educational and other purposes, Bhāviveka chose to present and then criticize a diversity of philosophical ideas from a variety of Vedāntic traditions; this makes it all the more difficult to identify the specific texts that were accessible to Bhāviveka at the time. This notwithstanding, the fact that Bhāviveka quotes from the *Śvetāśvatara Upaniṣad* indicates that he might have been familiar with certain pre-Śaṅkara commentaries on this and other Upaniṣads – a perspective that gains strength from the fact that his depiction of Vedānta philosophy is largely consistent with pre-Śaṅkara Vedāntic thought, for which the *Śvetāśvatara Upaniṣad* was important. Apart from this and a few stray references to the *Vākyapadīya*, it is clear from his discussion of the pot-space simile and the notion of *ajātisamatā*, that he was certainly familiar with the *Gauḍapādīyakārikā*.

---

[38] On the fragments of early Vedānta philosophy, see e.g. Hiriyanna 1924a, 1924b, 1925, 1928; Sastri 1924; Kane 1930; Ingalls 1952:9-11, 1954:291-294; Nakamura 1983:369-390; 2004.

The Sāṃkhyatattvanirṇayāvatāra Chapter

In the STNA, Bhāviveka provides us with a hypothetical debate between Madhyamaka and Sāṃkhya philosophy.[39] The overall description in both the *pūrvapakṣa* and the *uttarapakṣa* (where Bhāviveka occasionally gives voice to objections from his Sāṃkhya opponent) largely follows the *Sāṃkhyakārikā* and presumably its early commentaries. In addition, Bhāviveka describes Sāṃkhya doctrines that are referred to in neither the *Sāṃkhyakārikā* nor the *Yogasūtra*, nor in their respective commentaries. This indicates that they may have belonged to an older, currently unavailable, stratum of Sāṃkhya thought, or perhaps to 6th-century Sāṃkhya teachings that heretofore were known to us only through later Sāṃkhya, Buddhist and Jain texts.[40]

---

[39] Sāṃkhya philosophy is also discussed in both the MHK-TJ III and the *Prajñāpradīpa* (see, e.g., Ames 1986, ch. 1, pt. 2, p. 27; Kajiyama 1963:58), but not in an exhaustive and systematic manner. In addition, the **Karatalaratna* (*Ta tch'eng tchang tchen louen*) and *Madhyamakaratnapradīpa*, both most probably falsely ascribed to Bhāviveka (Krasser 2012:554f.), also portray and criticize classical Sāṃkhya philosophy. See Honda 1967; Iida 1980: 123ff., 200ff., 226ff. Within the Jain tradition, the *Vedavāda-* and *Sāṃkhyadvātriṃśikā,* ascribed to Siddhasena Divākara (see below), and probably contemporaneous with the MHK-TJ, portrays Sāṃkhya (and Vedānta) philosophy. Later on, we find prominent Jain authors dealing with Sāṃkhya philosophy, notably Haribhadrasūri (8th century), in his *Śāstravārttasamuccaya* (*puruṣaprakṛtivāda*) and *Ṣaḍdarśanasamuccaya,* and Vidyānandin (9th century), in his *Satyaśāsanaparīkṣā* (*Sāṃkhyaśāsanaparīkṣā*). Furthermore, Abhayadeva (11th cent.), Prabhācandra (11th cent.), Vādideva (12th cent.) and Mallisena (13th cent.) deal with Sāṃkhya philosophy in the *Tattvabodhavidhāyinī* (pp. 280ff.), *Prameyakamalamārtaṇḍa* (pp. 98ff., 285ff.), *Nyāyakumudacandra* (pp. 191ff.), *Syādvādaratnākara* (pp. 233ff.) and *Syādvāda-mañjarī* (esp. ch. 15) respectively (see Qvarnström 2012).

[40] MHK-TJ shows that Bhāviveka was also familiar with Jainism, even though he does not explicitely mention his sources. The list of 363 given in TJ IX.19 is only to be found in Jain sources, and MHK-TJ chapter X, dealing with the omniscience of the Buddha, also reports the critique of this notion by the Jains/Nirgranthas.

The fact that these particular doctrines deviate from what Gerald Larson has labeled Kārikā- and Pātañjala-Sāṃkhya[41] indicates that they might represent yet another attempt to update Sāṃkhya philosophy, one that differed from that found in the *Sāṃkhyakarikā* and *Yogasūtra* and their respective commentaries. The most salient of these doctrines concern the Sāṃkhya understanding of how and where knowledge arises and how the Self is able to experience knowledge without undergoing change and deviating from its intrinsic nature. This epistemological question occupies a good portion of the discourse found in the Sāṃkhya chapter of MHK-TJ, as does Bhāviveka's criticism of the concept Primordial Matter (*mūlaprakṛti*) and the notion that the effect preexists in its cause (*satkāryavāda*).

The historical background of this debate is linked to fundamental notions of classical Sāṃkhya philosophy, the seeds of which can be found in such proto-Sāṃkhya texts as the *Mahābhārata* (*Mokṣadharma*), *Bhagavadgītā* and *Carakasaṃhitā,* wherein there are discussions about whether the Self should be defined as a knower (*jña*), whether pure consciousness (*caitanya*) constitutes the Self's intrinsic nature, whether the manifest world is derived from primordial nature rather than from eight creative principles and so forth.[42] With the composition of the *Sāṃkhyakārikā* and the *Yogasūtra*(*bhāṣya*), an insurmountable philosophical chasm was established between a non-active Self or consciousness and active non-conscious Primordial Matter. In these works, the Self is viewed as the knower and the process by which the Self knows is said ultimately to belong to the material faculty of knowledge. Although the Self *per se* is considered to be outside the process of knowledge,

---

41 Larson 1987:18-29.

42 Malinar 1999:619ff.; Johnston 1937:53ff., n.2; Kent 1982:265.

it nonetheless remains connected to it in a fundamentally interdependent way. Other schools of thought readily detected the contradictions involved in this radically dualistic stance, and thus Sāṃkhya philosophy was challenged by a diversity of critics, including those representing the Vaiśeṣika and Buddhist traditions, which emphasized the transformational as opposed to the enduring nature of the knowledge-acquiring process. With regard to the Buddhist tradition, Bhāviveka and his predecessor Āryadeva (3rd century)[43] argued against Sāṃkhya from within the *vāda* tradition, whereas Dignāga (480-540), the most vigorous of the critics, argued from within the *pramāṇa* tradition of logic and epistemology in his *Pramāṇasamuccaya*.[44] These arguments were later used and developed by Śāntarakṣita and Kamalaśīla in the *Tattvasaṃgraha* and *Pañjikā* respectively.

Bhāviveka ascribes to the Sāṃkhya tradition two different theories concerning the process of knowledge. These theories are presented in a manner that is reminiscent of the doctrine of two truths (*dvisatya*), which was introduced into Buddhist systematic philosophy by Nāgārjuna. More precisely, Sāṃkhya philosophy as described by Bhāviveka teaches that the process of acquiring knowledge takes place in one way for those that exist in the cycle of

---

[43] In **Śataka* II and *Catuḥśataka* X, Āryadeva criticizes the Vaiśeṣika and Sāṃkhya views on the nature of the Self as consciousness (*caitanya*), and in **Śataka* VII (and briefly *Catuḥśataka* XI.15) he criticizes the *satkāryavāda* (see Lang 1986:11-13, 94f). Dharmapāla, a contemporary of Bhāviveka, wrote a commentary on the second half of the *Catuḥśataka* (see Honda 1968). *Tattvasaṃgraha* VII.35 uses the same argument as CŚ 10.

[44] Dignāga also wrote the now extinct *Sāṃkhyaparīkṣā*; Hattori 1968:9, 52-62, 148-160.

birth and death (*saṃsāra*) and in another way for those that exist in the liberated state (*mokṣa*).[45]

According to the first of these epistemological theories, the senses (*indriya*) apprehend a given object (*artha*) by coming into mutual conformity with it, after which it is apprehended by the mind (*manas*). Then the object is ascertained and fully comprehended by the intellect or faculty of knowledge (*buddhi*),[46] which grasps its image (*ākāra*).[47] The Self (*puruṣa*), although non-active and without content, is somehow in proximity to, and thus connected to, the faculty of knowledge. Because of this, the Self comes to understand the object by following the activity of the faculty of knowledge. In this way the cognitive process of the Self (*abhijñavṛtti*) is said to become non-different from that of the faculty of knowledge (*buddhivṛtti*).[48]

The second theory conforms to the first theory up to the point where it is stated that the object of knowledge is ascertained and fully comprehended by the faculty of knowledge. It diverges, however, in stating that when the mind is elevated to the point where it becomes dominated by *sattvaguṇa*, the Self acquires knowledge of the object by way of imitating, through reflection (*pratibimba*), the operations of the intellect or the faculty of knowledge (*buddhivṛtti*).[49] The description runs as follows in the MHK (VI.2): "When *sattva* [*guṇa*] predominates in the mind (*manas*), the Self imitates the operations of the intellect (*buddhivṛtti*) either

---

[45] See MHK-TJ VI.2-3, TJ VI.7, MHK-TJ VI.8, TJ VI.12, MHK-TJ VI.13.

[46] The text of the TJ VI.2 is corrupt, but this seems to be the core idea, collaborating it with TJ VI.8.

[47] MHK VI.8. Cf. *Yogasūtrabhāṣya* II.20 (=IV.22).

[48] MHK VI.13.

[49] On *pratibimba* in MHK-TJ VIII, see also Saito 2011.

through the arising of a reflection (*pratibimba*) or by means of a transformation (*pariṇāma*)." According to the TJ, this verse provides two alternative ways of explaining how this imitation is effected: the first in terms of a reflection of the *buddhi's* understanding in the *puruṣa*; and the second in terms of a transformation of consciousness that, nonetheless, brings about no real change (*vikṛti*) to the intrinsic nature of the Self – i.e., consciousness. The transformation is likened to the reflection in a mirror, and thus most probably constitutes an alternative explanation of the theory of reflection or *pratibimba*. This conclusion is made more plausible by the fact that in the third chapter of the MHK-TJ, it is pointed out that the Self transforms when the object is reflected in it.[50]

According to Bhāviveka, the theory that the cognitive process of the Self becomes non-different from that of the *buddhi* undermines the notion of an independent or contentless Self or consciousness that is intrinsically different from the *buddhi*. It is possible to establish non-difference between separate substances by way of their own distinctions, he says, but not between a substance (i.e., *buddhi*) and a metaphorical entity (*upacāra*) (i.e., *puruṣa*).[51] As to the theory that the Self experiences knowledge by imitating the operations of the intellect via reflection, this is criticized by Bhāviveka as follows: even if the Sāṃkhyas are correct in concluding that the Self remains unchanged by the process of reflection, their own argument nonetheless demands that it would have to be involved as its facilitating cause (*upakārihetu*) – a notion that contradicts the Sāṃkhya view that the Self is fundamentally *outside* the realm of cause and effect. Moreover, the notion that the imitation involves a process of transformation is considered to be contradictory as well,

[50] See MHK-TJ III.53.

[51] See TJ VI.13.

despite the Sāṃkhya claim that it brings about no real change to the Self: if the *puruṣa* is said to undergo a transformation, it cannot simultaneously be said to possess an intrinsic nature. Thus by introducing the idea of transformation, the Sāṃkhyas contradict their own notion of a permanent, uncaused and omnipresent consciousness or Self.[52]

In more general terms, Bhāviveka's Buddhist criticism of these theories rests upon the assumption that the Self (*puruṣa*) or consciousness (*caitanya*) is fundamentally non-existent and his arguments concerning the locus and process of knowledge ultimately aim at proving this ontological point.[53] For Bhāviveka, since consciousness is said to be identical to the knowing of an object, and to be the result of *buddhi's* conformity with that object, consciousness cannot logically exist in the absence of an object. As such, in the state of liberation, where cause and effect are no longer factors, knowing (and therefore consciousness) cannot exist. It is logical to define *(ava)bodha* as a knowing of "something else" that manifests the property (*dharma*) of change (*pariṇāma*), but since the Self is said to be eternal and non-changing, it cannot simultaneously be said somehow to take on the changing feature of that "something else" (*anyarūpa*); in other words, the Sāṃkhyas cannot have it both ways. Bhāviveka concludes that a consciousness that is distinct from that which is called *(ava)bodha* cannot possibly exist.[54] Moreover, he continues, since the Self or consciousness is said to be devoid of activity (*kriyā*), it cannot possibly be a "knower" (*jña*).

---

[52] TJ VI.22-23. The text is corrupt, but this seems to be the main idea.

[53] On Sāṃkhya, etc., notions of *caitanya*, see, e.g., Murakami 1999.

[54] MHK-TJ VI.9.

If we are to take Bhāviveka at his word, the above discourse suggests that during the 6th century CE Sāṃkhya epistemology included two theories relating to the process of knowledge. The first, which had been previously established, describes the process of knowledge within cyclic existence and the second describes it outside that framework in the state of liberation. Like the Madhyamaka school, it presupposed that the *buddhi's* mental operations consisted of an imprinted image of the form of the external object (*sākārajñāna-vāda)*. The first of these theories is mentioned in both the *Yogasūtra-bhāṣya* (attributed to Pañcaśikha)[55] and the *Yuktidīpikā* (ascribed to Vārṣagaṇya);[56] the second has been hitherto associated with Vācaspatimiśra (9th/10th century), although it must have been formulated several centuries earlier since it is described first by Bhāviveka and later by Śāntarakṣita (in the *Tattvasaṃgraha*) and Kamalaśīla (in the *Tattvasaṃgrahapañjikā*). The *Yogasūtrabhāṣya* ascribed to Vyāsa[57] documents a different version of this second theory, according to which the Self or *puruṣa* is reflected in the *buddhi* and not vice versa. Such a theory also appears in fragments attributed by various Jain authors (including Haribhadrasūri) to either Vindhyavāsin or the mythical Āsuri.[58] It is therefore

---

[55] *Yogasūtrabhāṣya* II.20 (=IV.22).

[56] *Yuktidīpikā* (p. 171, l. 15-18): *arthākāra ivābhati yathā buddhis tathā pumān / ābhāsamāno buddhyāto boddhā maṇivad ucyate // yathā yathā manovṛttiḥ puruṣo 'pi tathā tathā / buddhirūpam avāpnoti cetanatvāt parāśrayam //*.

[57] *Yogasūtrabhāṣya* II.20=IV.22; IV.23.

[58] The following two quotes are ascribed to Vindhyavāsin and Āsuri, respectively, in Haribhadrasūri's *Yogabindu* (449-450): "By means of [sheer] proximity, the Self, the essence of which is unchanging [consciousness], makes the mind (*manas*), which is devoid of consciousness (*acetana*), a reflection of itself (*svanirbhāsa*), just as an adjunct (*upādhi*), [e.g., a flower, makes] a crystal [a reflection of itself]." "It is said [by Āsuri and others] that the highest pleasure (*bhoga*) of the [Self (*puruṣa*)] arises when the intellect (*buddhi*) has undergone such a change whereby it has become separated [from the Self, and whereby the Self is reflected in the *buddhi*],

reasonable to assume that Vindhyavāsin formulated the earliest known version of the doctrine of reflection (*pratibimbavāda*) within the classical Sāṃkhya tradition in order to defend the position that the Self retains its unchanging status while simultaneously experiencing knowledge.

Thus Bhāviveka's doxographical account of Sāṃkhya philosophy seems to provide us with unique information about the Sāṃkhya tradition during the 6th century CE since it had been previously unknown that such an epistemological theory existed in complete form prior to the 8th century. Indeed, this theory cannot be found even in such central Jain and Buddhist texts as the *Yuktidīpikā* and the *Pramāṇasamuccaya*, which are from the same period as the MHK-TJ. Also conspicuous in Bhāviveka's account is the purported attempt by the Sāṃkhyas to synthesize both conceptions of the process of knowledge into one general theory.

To my knowledge, the merging of these two theories into a two-truth framework is not found elsewhere in the Sāṃkhya tradition, despite its strong Vedāntic affiliation. Of course, it is also possible that Bhāviveka himself fabricated this synthesis of what appear to be two competing epistemological theories. Then, however, we would have to inquire as to what would impel an adherent of Buddhist ideology to effectively rescue Sāṃkhya from its own logical dilemma. As such, the more likely explanation is that Bhāviveka's depiction of Sāṃkhya philosophy represents some sort of transitional phase in the history of the Sāṃkhya tradition, in

---

just like the appearance of the reflection of the moon in clear water." See Qvarnström 2012 (including a discussion of Haribhadrasūri's critique of Sāṃkhya in his *Śāstravārttāsamuccaya* and *Yogabindu*, as well as a translation of *Yogabindu*, vv. 444-457). On Jain critique of Sāṃkhya, see also Granoff 1999. For a translation of the Sāṃkhya chapter of the *Śāstravārttāsamuccaya*, see Bossche 2010.

which there was a need to place two competing epistemological theories within a doctrine of two truths to avoid further criticism. Later, when theories of reflection were undisputed and well established, the epistemological device of two truths was apparently no longer needed. Thus, over the course of time, the theory of the old Sāṃkhya school was gradually replaced by different versions of the *pratibimbavāda*, most notably those documented by Śāntarakṣita, Kamalaśīla and Haribhadrasūri, and advocated by Vācaspatimiśra and Vijñānabhikṣu. Vijñānabhikṣu criticized Vācaspatimiśra and introduced a theory of mutual reflection (*anyonyapratibimba*). This theory states that just as consciousness becomes reflected in the *buddhi*, so do the intellect's operations become reflected in pure consciousness.[59]

Apart from the above debate on epistemology, Bhāviveka introduces another major subject of discussion, which he had inherited from his predecessors, notably Āryadeva, and which was to be accentuated in future debates between Sāṃkhya and Buddhism in the works of Śāntarakṣita and others. This discussion concerned two interrelated matters that have already been mentioned above: the existence of Primordial Matter and the doctrine that the effect exists within its cause (*satkāryavāda*), which finds its classical expression in the *Chāndogya Upaniṣad*[60] and which Sāṃkhya shared with Yoga and Vedānta.[61] With one striking exception,[62] this critique takes as its point of departure the classical arguments of SK supporting the existence of *prakṛti*.[63]

---

[59] Larson 1987:36, 82; Ram 1988; Rukmani 1988.

[60] *Chāndogya Upaniṣad* VI.1.4.

[61] *Sāṃkhyakārikā* 9; *Brahmasūtra* II.1.7.

[62] See MHK-TJ VI.25-26 with n.

[63] *Sāṃkhyakārikā* 15-16.

Generally speaking, Bhāviveka agrees with Sāṃkhya that everything is caused, but disagrees that all things are transformations of one underlying, primordial substance. Sāṃkhya attempts to establish that all things have a common origin on the one hand and distinctive properties such as pleasure, pain or delusion on the other by comparing the conception of *prakṛti* and its qualities with the Buddhist notion of an aggregate of sensation (*vedanāskandha*) and its qualities. Bhāviveka conters this attempt by pointing out that the qualities of the aggregate of sensation are not intrinsic because they alternate between one another individually; within the aggregate of sensation, for example, delusion can be replaced by happiness.[64] The conclusion is that since all things lack intrinsic qualities and since Sāṃkhya claims a logical connection between all things and Primordial Matter, Primordial Matter must likewise lack intrinsic qualities.[65] According to Bhāviveka, even if one disregards the fact that happiness, etc., alternate, the notion that a connection exists between cause and effect seems to contradict the notion that cause and effect are of opposite natures.

Moreover, if the effects have different qualities, how can they originate from a common source? And if these different qualities already exist in Primordial Matter, then it cannot be homogenous, as Sāṃkhya claims. Furthermore, the identity of cause and effect is also contradicted by common knowledge and stands in opposition to the basic methodology of Sāṃkhya, according to Bhāviveka. The claim of some followers of Sāṃkhya that previous thoughts exist in the present[66] invalidates the making of inferences from preceding thoughts. If one thought cannot give rise to another thought, logical

[64] See MHK-TJ VI.28-30.

[65] VI.31-32ab.

[66] MHK-TJ VI.38.

reasoning (*anumāna*) – the core of Sāṃkhya epistemology – is rendered impossible. Moreover, the oneness of cause and effect would make it impossible for a new object or thought to occur, since its occurrence would negate the continuity between cause and effect, thus negating the idea that they are one. Bhāviveka's criticism here continues with his opposition to the Sāṃkhya simile of a sandalwood tree and its splinters, which are likened to Primordial Matter and its effects. According to Sāṃkhya, the sandalwood tree still exists even when it transforms into splinters, just as Primordial Matter still exists even when it transforms into effects; in other words, it does not cease to exist, but only disappears from view (*tirobhāva*).[67] While Sāṃkhya considers this possible because Primordial Matter intrinsically has six states of temporal transformation, Bhāviveka considers this to be contradicted by the Sāṃkhya notion of identity between cause and effect, past and present. In other words, and once again, the Sāṃkhyas cannot have it both ways.

The Vedāntatattvaviniścaya Chapter

To our knowledge, Bhāviveka's treatment of Vedānta in MHK-TJ is the earliest extant systematic Buddhist presentation and criticism of Vedānta philosophy (*vedāntadarśana*).[68] Moreover, the fact that

---

[67] MHK-TJ VI.40-41.

[68] The MHK-TJ is the earliest known text in the Buddhist tradition to list the terms *vedāntavādin* (VIII.1) and *vedāntadarśana* (MHK IV.7, TJ VIII.1). Bhāviveka defines *vedānta* and *vedāntavādin* in TJ VIII.1: (P. 282b7) || *rig pa'i mthar phyin pa ni rig byed mtha' ba ste* | *chags pa med par ṅes par rig pa'o* || *de smra ba'i ṅaṅ tshul ga la yod pa'am* | *tshig de gaṅ la yod* (P. 282b[8]) *pa ni rig byed kyi mthar smra ba'o* || " 'Vedānta' means the end of [all] knowledge, which certainly should be known as [a knowledge with] non-attachment (*asaṅga*). One who discusses it or maintains it as his own theory is a 'Vedāntavādin'." On the term *darśana*, see Halbfass 1979, 1981. Bhāviveka's usage of *darśana* (TJ VIII.1, MHK IV.7), as a designation of a philosophical system, is to be noticed as an early occurrence of such a connotation.

this work includes separate chapters on Vedānta and Mīmāṃsā supports the conclusion that the Mīmāṃsā school was divided into two mutually exclusive philosophies long before Kumārila and Śaṅkara.[69] This view is further confirmed by the fact that the *Dvātriṃśikā* (ascribed to Siddhasena Divākara)[70] dedicates an entire chapter to Vedānta (*Vedavāda*).[71] The *Vedavāda,* which may be contemporary with MHK-TJ, describes Vedānta philosophy in a more or less systematic manner, predating the *brahmādvaitavāda* chapter of Haribhadrasūri's *Śāstravārttasamuccaya* (8th century). In addition, leaving aside the question of authorship, an intriguing possibility is that the *Dvātriṃśikā's* Vedānta chapter constitutes an

---

The title of MHK ch. III is perhaps Bhāviveka's term for "philosophy": *Tattva-jñānaiṣaṇā* ("The Search for Knowledge of Reality"), cf. Greek *philosophia.* The Buddhists, more precisely: the Mahāyānists, are designated with the rare and interesting term *śūnyasaṃskāravādinaḥ* (MHK-TJ VIII.1).

[69] According to Parpola (1981:155), who subscribed to the view of Jacobi (1911), the Mīmāṃsā school was divided into two mutually exclusive philosophies, Mīmāṃsā and Vedānta, *subsequent* to Kumārila and Śaṅkara. On the *Dvātriṃśikā* ascribed to Siddhasena Divākara, see Qvarnström 2003 (*Vedavāda*), 2014 (*Niyati*).

[70] Originally, the *Dvātriṃśikā* is said to have comprised 32 minor texts of which 22 are still extant, including the *Nyāyāvatāra.* The doctrinal content ranges from Jain philosophy and religion to doxographical accounts of non-Jain systems, labelled by the copyists in the colophons as *Vedavāda-* (IX), *Nyāya-* (XII), *Sāṃkhya-* (XIII), *Vaiśeṣika-* (XIV), *Bauddha-* (XV) and *Niyativādadvātriṃśikā* (XVI). The references to the *Dvātriṃśikā* as a homogenous text comprising 32 minor texts are late and occurs in hagiographies on Siddhasena Divākara (Krause 1999:127, 169 n. 96). Internal and external criteria also negate the assumption that the *Dvātriṃśikā* and its doxographical texts were written by a single author. Apart from possibly being emic accounts, the *Vedavāda* and *Sāṃkhya* texts are interesting since they presumably stem from a period of which our historical knowledge is fragmentary or simply lacking. Their style and content suggest that they may date from the 5th/6th century CE, even though this assumption rests on weak grounds. See Qvarnström 1999:177-179, 2003, 2014. On Jain criticism of Sāṃkhya, see Granoff 1999; Qvarnström 2012.

[71] Qvarnström 2003.

emic account that was merely edited (and possibly altered) by one or several individuals serving as Jain conveyers of non-Jain knowledge systems.[72]

As with the chapter on Sāṃkhya philosophy, it is likely that the doctrines contained within the Vedānta chapter of MHK-TJ were selectively extracted from various (largely unidentifiable) Vedāntic texts, representing a variety of philosophical ideologies, and formulated into a coherent whole by Bhāviveka himself.[73] Accordingly, like his portrayal of Sāṃkhya philosophy, his depiction of Vedānta is not in keeping with any one surviving early text on this philosophy. Thus Bhāviveka's particular presentation of Vedānta has no single historical counterpart, although its provision of a form of difference-non-difference (*bhedābheda*) philosophy does appear to be generally consistent with pre-Śaṅkara Vedānta philosophy. Like the 6th-century portrayal of pre-Śaṅkara Vedānta in the *Vedavādadvātriṃśikā,*[74] Bhāviveka seems more or less to model

[72] Qvarnström 2003, 2014.

[73] Cf. King 1995:42, 267 n. 68; Qvarnström 1989:111. That Bhāviveka had different texts in front of him while compiling the Vedānta chapter is seen, e.g., in TJ VII.54, where various interpretations of the nature of the Self within the Vedānta school are referred to.

[74] See, e.g., *Vedavādadvātriṃśikā* 2, 16, 25cd, 28, 31 (Qvarnström 2003). Reality according to Vedānta as described in the *Vedavāda* consists of two diametrically opposite aspects forming one inseparable and undifferentiated synthesis. The first aspect is identical to everything created, moving and unmoving, and encompasses gods, human beings, the cosmos as well as moral principles. The second aspect is identical to the Self or essence of everything created, and constitutes as such its creator and sole experiencer. The first aspect is associated with the Veda, the second is maintained to lie beyond the Veda. In order to illustrate this oneness consisting of two aspects, various symbols are employed, such as that of the cosmic Person (*puruṣa*) or tree (*aśvattha*), both with Vedic roots (cf. *Śvetāśvatara Upaniṣad).* This two-in-one reality is further described in terms of homologies modelled on the *Puruṣasūkta.* It is depicted as both personal and

his depiction on the *Puruṣasūkta* and the early metrical Upaniṣads, especially the *Śvetāśvatara*.

One salient feature of Vedānta philosophy as construed by Bhāviveka is the attempt to synthesize religio-philosophical concepts of different historical and semantic settings into a consistent framework. MHK-TJ VIII.17 explains:

> [Various] words are applied to it (i.e. the Self) by those whose cognition is led astray by difference. [The term Brahman is used to describe it, as well as other terms like: Self (*ātman*), Person (*puruṣa*), Lord (*īśvara*), the All-pervasive (*sarvatraga*), the Eternal (*nitya*) and so forth. The meaning of other such terms is to be understood just like the meaning of the Self. Its nature being inexpressible, the Vedas have called it: "self-born, actionless, immeasurable", "the Person beyond darkness" (and further) "I have known that great Seer, radiant like the sun and living beyond darkness. Having known Him, one surpasses death. There is no other way leading to the place of non-birth".

The above and other textual passages of VTV provide an anthropomorphic description of *puruṣa* ("Person"), probably originating from the *Puruṣasūkta* of the *Ṛgveda* (X.90). *Puruṣa* is conceived as an

---

impersonal, of all genders and forms, and including a variety of gods all viewed as expressions of the one reality and consequently serving as its alternative designations. Ultimately, reality is beyond expression, not reproducible, and defying any classification. Through ritual purification and other religious practices, the inferior Self (*durātman*) may, however, acquire knowledge of this ultimate reality, and thus rise to a supreme state or *parātman* in which there is neither suffering nor ignorance.

embodied being (*dehin*) whose individual bodily parts (*deha*) correspond with the various phenomenal elements of relative existence.[75] In VTV this idea is combined with a purely philosophical notion of *puruṣa* that is identical to the notion of *ātman*. Thus, on a macrocosmic level, Absolute and relative existence are comprehended as being encompassed within a "Person" that is conceived as an embodied being. The microcosmic counterpart consists of a human embodied being that is comprised of a Self[76] and a psychophysical constitution (*dehādi*). These two aspects of "embodied being": the Absolute/Self and the relative existence/psychophysical constitution are illustrated in the "pot-space" simile as "space" (*ākāśa*) and "pot" (*ghaṭa*) respectively.[77] With regard to this simile, it is most likely that Bhāviveka draws on the *Gauḍapādīyakārikā*.[78] As far as we know, Gauḍapāda is the one who introduced this simile into the Vedānta tradition, perhaps under Buddhist influence.[79] This assumption is further strengthened

---

[75] See TJ VIII.4.

[76] The proofs for the existence of a Self (*ātman*): remembrance (*smṛti*), recognition (*pratyabhijñāna*), knowledge (*jnana*), etc., found in MHK-TJ, chs. III and VIII, are similar to those stated in the *Nyāyasūtra*.

[77] For a discussion of the pot-space simile in VTV and the *Gauḍapādīyakārikā*, see Bhattacharya 1943:50-53, Qvarnström 1989:108-127, King 1995:35ff.

[78] Walleser (1910:18), followed by Bhattacharya (1943:50-53), was the first scholar to establish the relationship between VTV and the *Gauḍapādīyakārikā*: MHK VIII.10 resembled *Gauḍapādīyakārikā* III.3; MHK VIII.11, 12 resembled *Gauḍapādīyakārikā* III.6cd. However, Walleser (*ibid.* p. 18) and Bhattacharya (*ibid.* p. 52) maintained incorrectly that MHK VIII.13 was a *verbatim* quotation of *Gauḍapādīyakārikā* III.5. This inaccuracy was due to the fact that these scholars could not benefit from having access to the Sanskrit Ms of VTV. On the possibility of Gauḍapāda borrowing from Bhāviveka, see King 1995:35-43.

[79] On *ghaṭākāśadṛṣṭānta*, see the *Prasannapadā ad* XVIII.9 (B 374.14 sqq., Vaidya 1960: 31, 105-106). Here, an early Mahāyānasūtra, the *Āryasatyadvayāvatārasūtra*, is quoted, which apparently already knows this example. (For a translation, see de Jong 1949:31.) Since Bhāviveka frequently refers to this *sūtra* in his works, the

by Bhāviveka's criticism of the *ajātisamatāvāda of the Gauḍapādīya-kārikā found in VTV.[80]

Bhāviveka's criticism of Vedānta revolves around the doctrine of a Self and its inherent properties and is linked to the very notion of an intrinsic nature. If the Self has an intrinsic nature, then opposites such as manifoldness and oneness, bondage and liberation, suffering and happiness could not inhere within it. The statement by the Vedāntavādins that the Self has properties such as being simultaneously one and many thus contradicts the very notion of an intrinsic nature. In this way, both the existence of the Self and the notion that the Self is the cause of the world are disproven.[81] For Bhāviveka, then, to say that the Self exists is like saying that there can be a son of a barren woman,[82] a flower growing in the sky[83] or a

---

"pot-space" simile was probably familiar to him even from Buddhist *Āgama.* Although it is not historically established, Gauḍapāda may also have benefitted from this Mahāyānasūtra in his discussion of the "pot-space" simile.

[80] The concept of *ājatisamatā* is not to be found prior or posterior to the *Gauḍapādīyakārikā* in the Vedānta tradition (see *Gauḍapādīyakārikā* III.2, 38; IV.80, 93, 95, 100). This strengthens our assumption that the criticism of *ājatisamatā* in MHK VIII.78-84 must be directed towards the *Gauḍapādīyakārikā* (e.g. MHK VIII.81 seems to be a critique of *Gauḍapādīyakārikā* III.2, 38). Furthermore, since Gauḍapāda, according to our present knowledge, was the one to introduce the *ghaṭākāśa* simile in the Vedānta tradition (*Gauḍapādīyakārikā* III.3, 4, 5), description (MHK VIII.10, 11, 13) and criticism of this *dṛṣṭānta* (MHK VIII.63-67) may also prove the relationship Bhāviveka's between MHK and the *Gauḍapādīyakārikā.* This leads us to assume that even MHK VIII.78-84 are by the same author who was criticizing the *Gauḍapādīyakārikā*, and that these verses have once been a part of the original work of Bhāviveka. In the Buddhist tradition, the above mentioned *Āryasatyadvāyāvatāra,* quoted in the *Prasannapadā* and known to Bhāviveka, also knows the concept of *ājatisamatā* (see B 374.14 sqq., Vaidya 1960:31, 105-106). On *ājatisamatā*, see also Lindtner 1985a.

[81] MHK-TJ VIII.19.

[82] MHK-TJ VIII.49.

horn protruding from the head of a hare.[84] In other words, there is no intrinsic nature or Self but only emptiness (*śūnyatā*) – the one all-pervasive and permanent "nature" of all entities.[85] Absence of intrinsic nature is then equal to absence of Self, and that, in Bhāviveka's opinion, cannot to be properly regarded some type of "Self", which would be a logical contradiction.[86]

The Vedāntavādins, on their side, regard the question of whether or not the Self has an intrinsic nature as a mere matter of epistemology, and in this way sidestep the argument that the Self actually changes its status and thus cannot have an intrinsic nature. In their view, the true nature of the Self can be realized only when the individual has fully awakened (*prabodha*) and become absorbed in the immortal (*amṛta*) Person (*puruṣa*), as a result of having eliminated all karma. In terms of the pot-space simile, they state that the space within a pot that is covered by dust, smoke and so forth is like the Self that possesses qualities such as pleasure, pain and so forth – i.e., an "individual", "mortal" and "bound" Self. The transformation of the mortal[87] individual Self (*antarātman*)[88] into the immortal supreme Self (*paramātman*),[89] located beyond this relative existence, does not change the ontological status of the Self.

---

[83] MHK-TJ VIII.50.

[84] TJ VIII.67.

[85] MHK VIII.90.

[86] MHK VIII.100.

[87] TJ VIII.3, 43.

[88] MHK-TJ VIII.50-53, 71, 98, 101. Bhāviveka uses the term *antarātman* connotating an "individual [mortal] Self". This rare usage of the term *antarātman* is also found, e.g., in the *Manusmṛti* VI.73, XII.13, and in the *Catuḥśataka* X.1 (see Lang 1986:95 with n. 1). The Upaniṣads use it consistently for an "inner/internal Self".

[89] MHK-TJ VIII.50-53.

Bhāviveka dismisses the attempt by the Vedāntavādins to combine the notion that the Self has an intrinsic nature with the notion of a "twofold" Self. According to him, the Self, in the strict sense of the word, cannot be arranged under, or subordinate to, the device of different epistemological theories, since, according to the Vedāntavādins, the Self has the intrinsic nature of cognition (*jñāna*).[90] The Self and the cognition of the Self are therefore non-different. Thus, the distinction between an individual [mortal] Self (*antarātman*) and a supreme [immortal] Self (*paramātman*), or a Self that is bound up with the so-called body (*deha*) and a liberated (*mukta*) Self that rests in the supreme (*parameṣṭhātman*),[91] is not merely an epistemological difference but one that pertains to the Self's ontological status. In other words, it is a distinction that would conflict with the very concept of an "intrinsic nature". This leads Bhāviveka to conclude that supreme reality as described by the Vedāntavādins does not have an intrinsic nature and thus cannot be a "Self" by definition.[92]

Bhāviveka proceeds with his critical examination (*parīkṣā*) through an analysis of the very concept of "space", since this was the correlate of the Self in the "pot-space" simile. Bhāviveka states in TJ VIII.65 that the example of space that was put forward has not at all been established because "that object which is empty of substance is relative space. There is movement for those who move; there is room for those demanding room."[93] Here Bhāviveka argues that since space is dependent on the non-existence of substance (*dravya*),

---

[90] MHK-TJ VIII.40, etc.

[91] In MHK VIII.24, Bhāviveka seems to have coined (*metri causa?*) the term *pareṣṭhātman* (*mchog na gnas pa grol pa'i bdag*) (P. *fol. Dza*: 289a4-289a5; D. *fol. Dza*: 256b1), which is short for *parameṣṭhātman*.

[92] MHK VIII.65.

[93] MHK VIII.66.

it has no definite status. Space neither exists nor subsists as a substance and a support (*ādhāra*)[94] containing an intrinsic nature (*svabhāva*), and thus it is similar in nature to a non-existent Self. To this the Vedāntavādins object by quoting *sūtra* passage, the origins of which remain unknown, which frequently recurs in the polemics between Buddhist and Vedāntic philosophers:[95]

> If space is totally non-existent,[96] as you suggest, why has your own teacher, the Buddha, taught that it supports the wind? Is not the following passage there? "O Gautama, on what does earth rest? O Brahmin, earth rests upon water. And on what does water rest? Water rests upon wind. And on what does wind rest? Wind rests upon space." In the same *sūtra* it is further stated: "O Gautama, on what does space rest? O Brahmin, now you go too far! It is difficult to understand the limit of this question, [because] if space is formless, invisible and unchecked, on what can it rest?"[97]

---

[94] Cf. MHK-TJ VIII.60.

[95] It is quoted in Yaśomitra's *Sphuṭārthāvyākhyā* (I.5) and alluded to in Śaṅkara's *Brahmasūtrabhāṣya* (II.2.24), Bhartṛhari's *Vākyapadīya* III.7.151 (III.407) as well as in the *Ratnagotravibhāga* Cf. also the *Ratnagotravibhāga* I.55 and prose (ed. Johnston, p. 44, 10, and n. 6, p. 44). On references to *a-nidassana* ("which cannot be characterized"/"invisible") in relation to *vijñāna, ākāśa* and *nirvāṇa*, see *A Critical Pāli Dictionary* (CPD) I:173. See also Norman 1987:23-25.

[96] The Upaniṣads as well as the *Vākyapadīya, Brahmasūtra, Gauḍapādīyakārikā, Brahmasūtrabhāṣya* by Śaṅkara, etc., regard space (*ākāśa*) as a positive entity. On space and substance as a theme in Madhyamaka-Vedānta polemics, see Qvarnström 1989:96-130.

[97] P. 299a^{8}-299b^{3}.

In order to cope with the grand edifice of Buddhist dogma handed down and codified in the Abhidharma, and to substantiate his criticism of the Vedāntadarśana, Bhāviveka refers to the views of the Sautrāntikas[98] and the Vaibhāṣikas.[99] In TJ VIII.67, the Vedāntavādin's view on space is linked to that of the Vaibhāṣikas, who considered space to be an unconditioned (*asaṃskṛta*) *dharma*[100] in contrast to empirical entities (*bhāva*) that are only nominally existent (*prajñaptisat*). For these two schools, then, space is considered to be a substance possessing existence (*dravyasat*) and intrinsic nature (*svabhāva*).[101] And as an existing substance with an intrinsic nature, space (*ākāśa*) is further considered by the Vaibhāṣikas to be a substance that is unchecked (*anāvṛti*) and that provides room (*avakāśa*).[102]

Even if the existence of a relationship between the Vaibhāṣikas and the Vedāntavādins can be questioned from a historical and/or philosophical point of view, Bhāviveka seems to base his

---

[98] TJ VIII.66.

[99] TJ VIII.67.

[100] See *Abhidharmakośa* I.5a-c. Bhāviveka refers to the major text (*grantha*) of the Vaibhāṣikas in TJ III.128. From the enumeration of *asaṃskṛtadharmas* found in MHK III.129cd: *asaṃskṛtā nirodhau dvāv ākāśaṃ tathatā tathā //*, it is clear that Bhāviveka does not rely upon the Sarvāstivāda teaching as reported in the *Abhidharmakośa* by Vasubandhu. Cf. the **Karatalaratna* on *ākāśa,* etc. (See La Vallée Poussin 1933:105-116).

[101] See, e.g., *Abhidharmakośa* V.25, VI.4. The intentionality of consciousness (*vijñāna*) expressed for example in the *Abhidharmakośa* V.25 (*sati viṣaye vijñānaṃ pravartate nāsati* / "consciousness occurs [only] if the object exists, not if it does not exist"), along with the notion of the intentional object's *a priori* existence, may explain the Vaibhāṣika position.

[102] TJ VIII.67. See *Abhidharmakośa* I.5d: *tatrākāśam anāvṛtiḥ.*

comparison upon the fact that they both consider space a substance that exists by virtue of an intrinsic nature.[103]

By referring to the Vaibhāṣikas and the Sautrāntikas, Bhāviveka demonstrates his firm ideological affiliation with Buddhist tradition (*āgama*) when applying his reason (*yukti*)[104] to Vedānta philosophy. Whereas the overall Madhyamaka critique of the Vaibhāṣika doctrine is used by Bhāviveka to reject the notion of space and Self held by the Vedāntadarśana, the reference to the Sautrāntika system is meant to consolidate his own view of space. As we have seen, Bhāviveka conventionally (*saṃvṛtitas*) agrees with the Sautrāntika view of space as the mere absence of a resistant substance (*sapratighadravyābhāvamātra*).[105] Bhāviveka's view on space, however, is not unique in the Madhyamaka tradition.[106] The fact that such Madhyamaka masters as Nāgārjuna, Āryadeva and Bhāviveka criticize the very concept of "space" as a designation for something that is said to possess existence and an intrinsic nature does not, however, prevent them from using space as a symbolic representation of their own fundamental reality (*tattva*),[107] which is regarded as empty (*śūnya*), devoid of an intrinsic nature (*niḥsvabhāva*) and so forth.[108]

---

[103] On the rather complex picture of space given in both the unsystematic and systematic texts of early Vedānta philosophy, see Qvarnström 1989:96-130.

[104] On *āgama* and *yukti* in the works of Bhāviveka, see Iida 1966.

[105] See TJ VIII.66; *Abhidharmakośa* II.55d.

[106] Nāgārjuna states for instance in the *Ratnāvalī* I.99ab: "Space is a mere designation because it is a mere absence of form (*rūpasyābhāvamātratvād ākāśaṃ nāmamātrakam*). See also Āryadeva's *Śataka* IX.3. For further references on the refutation of space (*ākāśa*), see Lang 1986:89, n. 5.

[107] See also Nāgārjuna's *Bodhicittavivaraṇa* (vv. 46, 47, 51) and Bhāviveka's MHK III.11, 28, 275, etc.

[108] See, e.g., Nāgārjuna's *Acintyastava* 37-39.

One of the main reasons for Bhāviveka to incorporate the Vedānta notion of a "Self" (*ātman*) into the framework of his theory of "intrinsic nature" (*svabhāva*) is that he maintains that the Vedāntavādins have actually adopted or stolen some of their notions from Mahāyāna Buddhism.[109] MHK VIII.86 states:

> Being convinced that this infallible system of the Tathāgata is good (*śubha*), here [in the Vedānta system] the heterodox sectarians (*tīrthika*), being desirous (*spṛhā*) of [that doctrine], have therefore [even] made it their own, [saying: "This is our system". But that is eclecticism, endowed with the fault that consists in the contradiction of former and latter parts, and it is therefore to be classified as a mental construction (*vikalpa*).]

This explains Bhāviveka's reply in the *Śrāvakatattvaniścayāvatāra* chapter of MHK. Here the Hīnayānists maintain that Mahāyāna does not represent the teaching of the Buddha since it is not included in the doctrinal scriptures (*sūtrāntādi*) and since it teaches heterodox paths to liberation, as does the Vedāntadarśana. Bhāviveka answers in MHK IV.56ab: "Whatever is well said in the Vedānta has [already] been said by the Buddha."[110] Instead of taking this to mean that

---

[109] See MHK VIII.86. with n. (TJ VIII.86).

[110] *Vedānte ca hi yat sūktaṃ tat sarvaṃ buddhabhāṣitam*. Already Mātṛceṭa seems to say much the same. Bhāviveka is clearly reflecting Mātṛceṭa: The *Varṇārhavarṇastotra* VII.19 states: *ito bāhyeṣu yat sūktaṃ ghuṇākṣaravad īk[ṣy]ate / tat tatrātulyajātīyaṃ jātarūpam ivāyasi //* "Was bei denen, die außerhalb [dieser Lehre stehen], an Wohlgesprochenem – gleichsam wie ein von einem Holzwurm [hervorgebrachter] Buchstabe – gefunden wird, das ist dort von so ungleicher Natur wie Gold zwischen Eisen." (Hartmann 1987:228). *Varṇārhavarṇastotra* VII.20ab: *kaḥ śraddhāsyati tat tasmin pūrvāparaparāhatam /* has clearly inspired Bhāviveka in MHK VIII.87ab: *kaḥ śraddhāsyati tāṃ tatra pūrvāparavirodhinīm /*.

Bhāviveka had a favourable attitude towards Vedānta philosophy, the intention may be quite the reverse: all that is well said in Vedānta is actually nothing but Buddhism that the followers of Vedānta have stolen or borrowed! Śāntarakṣita, quoting the *Gauḍapādīyakārikā*,[111] exclaims in his *Madhyamakālaṃkāravṛtti*: "What they state has already been said by the Tathāgata!"[112] Consequently, Bhāviveka felt "obliged" in his MHK-TJ to explain the "stolen goods" thoroughly for the Vedāntavādins. Having done this, he says in MHK VIII.95, with respect to the notions of a "Self" or an "intrinsic nature":

> Obviously, if such a Self [or intrinsic nature] is accepted even by you, [then] that [Self or intrinsic nature, which is the general characteristic of non-origination] is infallible and completely proper, because of extensive conceptual correspondences with regard to name, etc.

Bhāviveka explains in the commentary to this verse that if the followers of Vedānta also maintain that the Self is the general characteristic (*sāmānyalakṣaṇa*) of non-origination then the dispute concerns a mere name. The Vedānta adherents say "supreme Self" (*paramātman*) and we Buddhists say "non-origination" (*ajātitva*), so there is no contradiction. Therefore, Bhāviveka invites his opponents to satisfy themselves with the supreme nectar of reality (*tattvāmṛta*) offered by the friends of the world, the Buddhas. Consequently, as far as Bhāviveka himself is concerned, the apologetic purpose is not admitted. Instead he wants us to accept his didactic purpose.

---

[111] *Gauḍapādīyakārikā* II.31f., 35.

[112] *de dag gis gaṅ brjod pa de ni bde bar gśegs pas gsuṅs pa*. See Lindtner 1982b:280.

Irrespective of Bhāviveka's confessional theories of assimilation, the historically established doctrinal assimilation of Buddhist thought into Vedānta systematic philosophy did not result in the eradication of the fundamental difference between Buddhism and Brāhmaṇism that had existed from the time of the early scriptures of the respective traditions and of which these traditions had been well aware.[113] The affirmation and negation of a "Self" (*ātman*) or an "intrinsic nature" (*svabhāva*) still constituted the line of demarcation between the two traditions. In this context, the *Vedāntatattvaviniścaya* is interesting because it is the first Buddhist text to distinguish Madhyamaka philosophy from purely Vedānta systematic philosophical notions. As we have seen, Bhāviveka maintains that the notion of a "Self" – or in his terminology, an "intrinsic nature" – actually was borrowed from the Madhyamaka school. Thus Bhāviveka considers it his duty not only to refute the Vedānta interpretation of this notion, but also to outline his own view on this matter at great length. Bhāviveka can thus be said to have initiated the first systematic discussion on this primary controversy, which even continues down to the present day.[114]

The Text

Bhāviveka himself uses no less than four different titles to refer to his own work: *Madhyamakahṛdaya, Tarkajvālā, Tattvāmṛtāvatāra* and *Madhyamakahṛdayatattvāvatāra.* He does not refer to the verse section and the prose section under separate titles, indicating that he did not consider them to be separate works. At some point in the line of transmission, the verses seem to have been separated out from the entire work and subsequently titled *Madhyamakahṛdaya-kārikā* or *Tarkajvālāsūtra.* Gokhale, and later Ruegg, held that

---

[113] See *Majjhima Nikāya* 22 (I:137) and *Kaṭha Upaniṣad* IV.14 (II.4.14-15).

[114] A systematical account of these *ātman*-controversies is presented by Claus Oetke (1988).

Chapters I-III originally constituted an independent work that was later expanded with the addition of Chapters IV-XI. The title of this work was *Tattvāmṛtāvatāra*, derived from the colophon to Chapter Three.[115]

Most scholars appear to agree that the author of the *Prajñāpradīpa* – the commentary on Nāgārjuna's *Mūlamadhyamakakārikā* – also wrote MHK. However, the authenticity of the *Tarkajvālā* has been called into question. Textual interpolations in TJ have led scholars such as Ejima to assume that an 8th-century author had written portions of the text. According to Krasser, however, these interpolations are best explained by assuming that students had written them on the basis of the teacher's oral instructions, as with the digressions in the *Prajñāpradīpa*.[116] This would also explain the problematic phrase *ācārya āha*, which led previous scholars to assume that TJ and MHK had been written by different authors.[117] Today, however, the majority of scholars (including myself) consider these works to have been written by the same author, apart from the above referenced interpolations and digressions as well as one puzzling doctrinal deviation discovered in this study.[118]

---

[115] See Gokhale 1958:165-166, n. 1; 1972:41-42; Gokhale/Bahulkar 1985:78. Cf. Eckel's discussion (2008:18f.).

[116] Krasser 2011:50-60. See also Eckel 2008:22f.

[117] TJ VIII.67. See Walleser 1910:17, n. 1; Gokhale 1985:76; and Ejima as cited in Lindtner 1982a:182-184.

[118] See n. *ad* MHK VI.25-26. On the authenticity of the TJ, see Eckel 2008: 17-27; Krasser 2011:60ff., 2012: 569ff. There are, to be sure, also two Tantric texts, ascribed to a certain Bhavyakīrti, but these are unlikely to have been written by Bhāviveka. See Ruegg 1981a:106, n. 339. The *Nikāyabhedavibhaṅgavyākhyāna*, treated as a separate work of Bhāviveka in the *bsTan-'gyur*, is identical with parts of TJ, ch. 4. See Iida 1980:13-14; Ruegg 1981a:63. The *Madhyamakabhramaghāta* ascribed to Āryadeva is in fact nothing but an extract from TJ. This has been pointed out by Per K. Sørensen.

For the study of MHK-TJ, the following source materials have been at our disposal:

1. A unique (if incomplete) 11th-century Sanskrit manuscript (Ms)[119] written in Northern India's so-called proto-Bengali-cum-Maithili (or *rañjanā*) script[120] and consisting of 24 palm leaves, each measuring 22 1/2 x 2 inches, with 5 or 6 lines on recto (a) and verso (b).[121] It was discovered in 1936 by Rāhula Sāṅkṛtyāyana at Tibet's Źa lu monastery and contains approximately 928 *anuṣṭubh* verses, divided into 11 chapters of uneven length. It is a copy of an unknown number of antecedents that have an uncertain relationship with the original, which (as far as we know) is no longer extant.

Being unable to photograph the manuscript, Sāṅkṛtyāyana rapidly copied it by hand. This copy was later given to Prof. V.V. Gokhale, who then transcribed it with the help of G. Tucci's partly illegible photographs of the very same manuscript. Up to the spring of 1987, the only available source material consisted of these photographs and Gokhale's transcription, later published by S. S. Bahulkar and referred to herein as (Msc).[122] The situation changed, however, when professor Jiang Zhongxin, from Beijing's Institute of South and Southeast Asian Studies, revealed at a Copenhagen conference that during the 1960s Chinese researchers had discovered the *Ms* and other manuscripts in the libraries of different Tibetan monasteries. Among the large number of palm leaf manuscripts,

---

[119] Ejima 1980:263. Cf. Gokhale 1958:165, n. 1 (10th century).

[120] Ejima 1980:263. Cf. Gokhale 1958:165, n. 1.

[121] The Ms is described by Sāṅkṛtyāyana in JBORS XXIII, pt. I, 1937, p. 48, and registered as: VII Źa lu Monastery, XXXVII, 1.311: *Tarkajvālā* (*Madhyamakahṛdaya*), or as: 11. *Tarkajvālā* (p. 55).

[122] Bahulkar 1994.

only a handful were considered capable of being transported intact to Beijing; the others were in such fragile condition that they had to be photographed on the finding site. Today the palm leaves can be found in the China Library of Nationalities (*Zhongguo Minzu Tushuguan*) and the microfilm can be found in the China Center of Tibetology (*Zhongguo Zangxue Xueyuan Zhongxin*).[123]

The *Sāṃkhyatattvanirṇayāvatāra* chapter consists of 2 palm-leaves, extending from fol. 16b[4]-17b[6], 5 or 6 lines on recto and verso. Some verses found in the Tibetan translations of MHK and TJ (i.e. vv. 49-64) are absent in *Ms*. These verses were most likely part of the lost leaf (18) that covered portions of the Sāṃkhya (and Vaiśeṣika, vv. 1-26) chapters, and were probably not genuine but inserted later by students on the basis of a teacher's oral instructions.[124] Some of *Ms*'s verses are not to be found in the Tibetan translations of MHK and TJ, although they are paraphrased in TJ (i.e. 12cd, 30, 33ab, 35ab, 38ab, 39ab). All Tibetan translations of MHK include an almost verbatim quotation of *Sāṃkhyakārikā* 3 as the second verse (VI.2).[125] This verse is absent in *Ms*, and in TJ it forms part of the commentary *ad* VI.1. From the perspective of TJ, the quotation from the *Sāṃkhyakārikā* fits well, dividing the commentary on the first verse into two substantively logical parts. However, given its metre (*āryā*), which explains the extra line in the Tibetan translations of MHK, it is unlikely that it was once part of the MHK, all of its ca. 928 verses being in the *anuṣṭubh* metre.

---

[123] For a synoptic list of titles of earlier inventories of Sanskrit Manuscripts in Tibet, see Harrison 2014.

[124] See Krasser 2011.

[125] *rtsa ba'i raṅ bźin mi 'gyur ba | | chen po la sogs rnam pa bdun | | raṅ bźin 'gyur ba bdun ñid do | | 'gyur ba rnam pa bcu drug kyaṅ | | raṅ bźin 'gyur ba min skyes bu |.*

The *Vedāntatattvaviniścaya* Chapter consists of 3 palm leaves, extending from fol. 19a¹-21b¹, 6 lines on recto (a) and verso (b).[126] Some verses of VTV found in *Ms* are not to be found in the Tibetan translations (i.e., 78-84). These verses contain a criticism of the **ajātisamatāvāda* of the *Gauḍapādīyakārikā* and were likely *antaraślokas* that were inserted at that time (or a bit later) by Bhāviveka himself.[127] A few verses contained in the Tibetan translations, but not in *Ms*, are also considered genuine (i.e., vv. 8, 12cd, 23, 52cd, 53cd).

2. The *dBu ma'i sñiṅ po'i 'grel pa rtog ge 'bar ba* (*Madhyamakahṛdayavṛtti Tarkajvālā*) consists of a Tibetan translation of TJ that incorporates MHK. The original copy of this translation – the joint work of Atiśa (981/982-1054 A.D) and Lotsawa Jayaśīla (Tshul khrims rgyal ba) – is only indirectly available in later editions printed in Narthang, Peking, Derge and Cone. Gokhale has pointed out that a previous Tibetan translation of MHK and TJ existed in the early 9th century.

3. The *dBu ma'i sñiṅ po'i tshig le'ur byas pa* (*Madhyamakahṛdayakārikā*) consists of a Tibetan translation of MHK. Translators and available editions are the same as for the above.

This critical edition of the Sāṃkhya and Vedānta chapters of MHK is based on a comparison of the unique palm leaf manuscript *Ms* with the generally reliable Peking and Derge editions of MHK and TJ,[128] since Narthang and Cone possess only a number of faulty readings

---

[126] The 18th folio of Ms is missing. The numbering of the folios is according to the Libary of Nationalities, Beijing: 17b-17a-19a-19b-20a-20b.

[127] On *antaraśloka*, see Mimaki 1980.

[128] The present edition and translation of the *Vedāntatattvaviniścaya* is a thoroughly revised version of Qvarnström 1989, 1990.

and thus do not contribute to the Sanskrit edition of MHK.[129] In editing the Tibetan text, minor variant readings that do not enhance our understanding of either the Tibetan or the Sanskrit texts have been tacitly ignored.[130] The photographs of the Vedānta chapter were made available by professor Jiang Zhongxin in 1987, and the Sāṃkhya chapter through the reproduction of the complete *Ms* by Zhongxin (published as an appendix to the first of two volumes of *Papers in Honour of Prof. Dr. Ji Xianlin on the Occasion of His Eightieth Birthday*, Bejing 1991). The process of editing the Sāṃkhya and Vedānta chapters has also benefitted from available editions.[131]

Orthographical peculiarities are noted in the *apparatus criticus* only if a different grammatical structure is possible; otherwise they are tacitly normalized. The same applies to the irregular and awkward punctuation (single and double *daṇḍa*) of *Ms*., which also does not provide verse numbers.

---

[129] *Sāṃkhyatattvanirṇayāvatāra*: (MHK) Peking bsTan-'gyur [Vol. 96]. (No. 5255) (fol.: Dza 27a^{5}-29b^{4}), sDe-dge bsTan-'gyur (No. 3855) (fol.: Dza 24b^{1}-26b^{4}); (TJ) Peking bsTan-'gyur: [Vol. 96]. (No. 5255) (fol.: Dza 253b^{7}-272b^{2}), sDe-dge bsTan-'gyur (No. 3855) (fol.: Dza 227a^{7}-242a^{7}). *Vedāntatattvaviniścaya*: (MHK) Peking bsTan-'gyur [Vol. 96]. (No. 5255) (fol.: Dza 30b7-34a8), sDe-dge bsTan-'gyur (No. 3855) (fol. : Dza 27b5-31a7); (TJ) Peking bsTan-'gyur: [Vol. 96]. (No. 5256) (fol.: Dza 282b6-306a2), sDe-dge bsTan-'gyur (No. 3856) (fol. : Dza 251a1-271a2).

[130] E.g., VIII.2b pa: ba P; VIII.5c de yi: de'i PK, P.

[131] Nakada (1972, 1983) edited MHK-TJ VI.1-4 (*pūrvapakṣa*) and VI.5-7 based on Msc. Gokhale (1958:165-180) edited MHK VIII.1-17 (*pūrvapakṣa*) on the basis of Msc and Nakamura's edition of TJ VIII.1-17 (1958:181-190). Nakamura (1975, 1981=2004) also presented a rather incomplete edition of MHK VIII based on Msc. Qvarnström (1989, 1990) presented an improved edition relative to the attempts by Gokhale and Nakamura, who did not have access to Ms. Lindtner (2001) presented a critical edition of the entire MHK, including chapters VI and VIII, based on Ms, and Huanhuan He (2013) edited MHK-TJ VI-VIII based on Ms.

The Translation

Due to the elliptical nature of Sanskrit prose, a vigorous and clear English translation has to identify parts of the sentence that are omitted in the Sanskrit. These parts will be inserted in brackets. Concerning the present translation,[132] it is not only necessary to include brackets containing words or sentences carried down from a preceding verse (as a result of the distinctive style of Sanskrit philosophical prose), but also to insert brackets comprising paraphrases of the main content of TJ. Thus the information contained within the brackets should not be viewed as a literal translation, but rather as a summary of the doctrinal content of TJ that is crucial for understanding the verse in question. This particularly applies to the chapter on Sāṃkhya due to its corrupt state.[133] As for verses 49-63 of the Sāṃkhya chapter, as noted above, they are most likely later interpolations containing either unnecessary repetitions of doctrines that have been already dealt with in preceding verses or simplified and unstructured explanations containing themes that have been randomly selected.

---

[132] The Sāṃkhya chapter has never been translated into a Western language. The present translation of the Vedānta chapter is an updated version of a 1989 translation, which was also made by the present author. Prior to that, Walleser (1910) had translated MHK VIII.1-3, 5. 10-13 = VIII.1-3, 5, 11-14, and Gokhale (1958) had translated MHK-TJ VIII.1-17, based on Msc and Nakamura's edition of MHK-TJ VIII.1-17 (1958). With the exception of MHK-TJ VIII.1-17, which partly follows Gokhale's translation (1958), the inserted summaries of TJ are based on the *Peking* and *sDe-dge bsTan-'gyur*. A Japanese translation of MHK-TJ VIII is found in Nakamura (1981) and a Chinese translation of MHK-TJ VI and VIII in He (2013). For editions, studies and translations of the different chapters of MHK-TJ, see Heitmann 1997:106-154,
Eckel 2008:450-451.

[133] In an attempt to bring out the meaning of the verses more clearly, I have treated verses VI.31-32ab and VI.32cd-33 as syntactical units rather than as discrete entities.

Thus, rather than providing literal translations of these verses, I have attempted to provide interpretations based on the respective commentaries as well as thematically related passages.

In Bhāviveka's original work, verses and prose commentaries were presented together. In other words, the verses cannot – *and should not* – be understood without the commentary and vice versa. In an attempt to indicate the narrative structure of the text, subheadings are inserted in brackets. It should be noted, however, that the subheadings do not exhaust the content discussed beneath them.

Sigla

DK The Tibetan version of *Madhyamakahṛdayakārikā* in the sDe-dge bsTan-'gyur
D The Tibetan version of *Tarkajvālā* in the sDe-dge bsTan-'gyur
ex con. T my conjecture based on PK, P, DK, D
Gok Gokhale's edition of the *pūrvapakṣa* of the Vedāntatattvaviniścaya based on Msc
H Huanhuan He's critical edition of the *Madhyamakahṛdaya-kārikā* and *Tarkajvālā* of the *Sāṃkhyatattvāvatāra* and *Vedānta-tattvaviniścaya*
illeg illegible
L Lindtner's edition of the *Madhyamakahṛdayakārikā*
Ms Photographs of a unique Sanskrit manuscript of Bhāviveka's *Madhyamakahṛdayakārikā* preserved in the Sanskrit Manuscript Collection of the China Library of Nationalities (Zhongguo Minzu Tushuguan), Beijing, China
Msc Gokhale's transcription of Sāṅkṛtyāyana's hand copy of Ms
Nak Nakamura's edition of the *uttarapakṣa* of the *Vedāntatattva-viniścaya* based on Msc
omit omitted
PK The Tibetan version of *Madhyamakahṛdayakārikā* in the Peking bsTan-'gyur
P The Tibetan version of *Tarkajvālā* in the Peking bsTan-'gyur
T Tibetan

Text

Sāṃkhyatattvanirṇayāvatāra

acetanā hi prakṛtis triguṇā prasavātmikā / 16b4
viparītaḥ pumān asmād ity abhyāsavataḥ sadā //1//

| raṅ bźin gaṅ źig rtogs pa med |
| yon tan gsum daṅ bskyed bdag ñid |
| de las bzlog pas skyes bu ñid |
| 'di dag rtag tu goms par bya |

udbhūtasattve manasi buddhivṛttyanukāritā /
pratibimbodayāt puṃsaḥ pariṇāmād athāpi vā //2//

| yid la sñiṅ stobs skyes pa can |
| skyes bu'i gzugs brñan 'byuṅ ba'am |
| de bźin yoṅs su gyur nas ni |
| blo 'jug pa yi rjes su byed |

1d sadā *ex con T.* rtag tu: yataḥ *Ms*
2a udbhūta° *ex con T.* skyes pa can: tadbhūta° *Ms*, H, L
2b °anukāritā: °anukāriṇaḥ *Ms*, H, L Tibetan rjes su byed corresponds to Sanskrit *anukāraḥ*, which is metrically incorrect. It may, however, be *metri causa* for rjes su byed (pa) ñid.

anyo ’ham anyā prakṛtir ity evaṃ tattvadarśanāt /
nivṛttakāryakaraṇo mukta ity ucyate pumān //3// 16b[5]

| bdag kyaṅ gźan źiṅ raṅ bźin gźan |
| ’di ltar de ñid mthoṅ ba yi |
| byed daṅ bya ba ldog pa yi |
| skyes bu grol ba yin źes brjod |

nāhaṃ mameti saṃbuddheḥ kṛtārthā cety anugrahāt /
mucyate prakṛtir veti tattvaṃ sāṃkhyāḥ pracakṣate //4//

| bdag daṅ bdag gi med rtogs pa’am |
| don byas pa na rjes bzuṅ ba |
| raṅ bźin gyis ni grol yin phyir |
| de ñid yin par graṅs can smra |

tatra pradhānapuruṣau yathāyuktau tathoditau /
mīmāṃsyete punaś cāpi nātmā caitanyam iṣyate //5//

| de la gtso bo skyes bu ni |
| ci ltar mi rigs las sṅar bstan |
| de yaṅ yaṅ ’dir brtag bya ste |
| bdag ni rtogs pa ma yin no |

3a źiṅ: la PK and DK
3d ity ucyate *ex con T.* źes brjod: omit. *Ms*
5c mīmāṃsyete: mīmāṃsye te H, L

jñeyāvabodhaś caitanyaṃ jñeyābhāve na cāstitā /
kaś cedānīṃ bhaved ātmā cetano vāpy acetanaḥ /6//

| śes bya rtogs pas rtogs yin na |
| śes bya med pas de yaṅ med |
| rtogs pa can nam rtogs med pa |
| 'dir ni bdag tu gaṅ gis 'gyur |

nādagdhaṃ dahati yuktyā dāhyābhāvāt sa pūrvavat / 17a[1]
nāto dahanadṛṣṭāntāc cetanātmā prasidhyati //7//

| ma bsregs sreg par mi rigs te |
| bsregs pa med phyir de sṅon bźin |
| des na sreg byed dpe yis ni |
| rtogs pa'i bdag ñid grub ma yin |

bodhyākāraṃ dadhāno hi buddhibodha itīṣyate /
dravyāśrayatvād bhāvasya sa cāyaṃ puruṣāśrayaḥ //8//

| śes bya'i rnam pa 'dzin byed pas |
| śes la rtogs pa źes 'dod de |
| dṅos po byed pa la brten phyir |
| de yaṅ skyes bu 'di la brten |

6d gis: źig PK, DK
7a nādagdhaṃ *ex con T.* ma bsregs: nādahaṃ *Ms*
7b sa pūrvavat *ex con T.* de sṅon bźin: [ ]vat *Ms*
8b dadhāno *ex con T.* 'dzin byed pas: dadhānā *Ms*

puruṣe 'vikṛtau svārthe sa cāyaṃ vidhuro vidhiḥ /
bodhād anyan na caitanyaṃ kiṃ tad anyat prakalpyate //9//

| skyes bu 'gyur med raṅ gi yul |
| de daṅ de ni lugs 'dis 'gal |
| śes las rtogs pa gźan min pas |
| ci źig gźan du brtag par bya |

caitanyaṃ na matir yuktā hetumattvād yathā ghaṭaḥ /
ato na buddhiś caitanyam ity evaṃ cen matir bhavet //10// 17a[2]

| rtogs pa blo gros ma yin te |
| rgyu daṅ ldan phyir bum pa bźin |
| des na rtogs pa śes pa min |
| gal te blo la de sñam na |

caitanyād anyatā buddheḥ sādhyā cen na nidarśanam /
buddhau hi tadabhāvaś ced abhyupetena bādhyase //11//

| rtogs las śes pa gźan yin par |
| sgrub byed ce na dpe yaṅ med |
| śes pa'aṅ de dṅos med ce na |
| khas blaṅs pa yis gnod pa yin |

9c anyan na: anyac ca *Ms*
10d matir: mater H

ajātasya ca caitanyam ajātatvān na yuktimat /
asti ced asatas tasmād buddhir eva hi tan matam //12//

| xx xx xx xx xx xx xx |
| xx xx xx xx xx xx xx |
| ma skyes pa ni rtogs min te |
| ma skyes phyir ni rigs ldan min |

buddhivṛttyaviśiṣṭābhijñavṛttir yata iṣyate /
bhede saty aviśeṣaḥ syāt sa ca nāstīti so 'py asan //13//

| blo yi 'jug pa'i khyad par ni |
| gaṅ phyir śes la 'jug 'dod na'aṅ |
| tha dad khyad can ñid 'gyur gyi |
| de med pas na de yaṅ med |

12a ca: na H
12ab *omit.* T
13a buddhivṛtty° *ex con T.* śes la 'jug pa: °buddhivṛtya° *Ms*,
13b °abhijñavṛttir *ex con T.* śes la 'jug (pa): °abhijñabuddhir *Ms*:
°aviśiṣṭābhijñavṛttir L: °aviśiṣṭābhir jñavṛttir H
13c saty aviśeṣaḥ: satyaviśeṣaḥ H, L

atha syād ātmadhīr yāpi yathārthāsau kvacin matā / 17a[3]
kvacit tadviparītatvāt sthāṇau sthāṇumatir yathā //14//

| gal te bdag gi blo gaṅ yaṅ |
| la lar ji bźin don du 'dod |
| la lar de las bzlog ñid de |
| mtho la mtho yi blo bźin no |

yatra kvacid yathārthā cet saṃvṛtyā siddhasādhanam /
yathārthā cittaviṣayā yasmān nātmeti no matā //15//

| la lar ji ltar ji bźin don |
| źe na kun rdzob grub pa sgrub |
| ji bźin don gyi sems kyi yul |
| bdag ces bya bar bdag cag 'dod |

atha sarvagatatvādilakṣaṇe dhīyathārthatā /
na tattvato na saṃvṛtyā kiṃcid asti nidarśanam //16//

| ci ste kun la khyab sogs kyi |
| mtshan ñid can blo don bźin na |
| de ñid du'am kun rdzob tu'aṅ |
| dpe ni yod pa ma yin no |

14a yāpi *ex con T.* gaṅ yaṅ: yap[ ] *Ms*
15c yasmān nātmeti: yasmāc cātmeti H
16b °lakṣaṇe: °lakṣaṇai *Ms*

nācetanāyāś caitanyaṃ vikṛtiś cetanasya vā /
tattvajñānodayaḥ kasya yasya muktir bhaviṣyati //17// 17a[4]

| rtogs pa med pas rtogs pa ni |
| raṅ bźin rtogs pa med pa'am |
| gaṅ gi de ñid śes skye bas |
| gaṅ źig grol bar 'gyur ba yin |

caitanyānugrahe 'py asyā nāhamityādiniścayaḥ /
acaitanyād ayuktaḥ syāt kiṃ punas tadasaṃbhave //18//

| rtogs pas 'dzin par byed pa na |
| bdag ni 'di ltar źes sogs ṅes |
| rtogs pa med phyir gźan mi rigs |
| de med gyur na yaṅ ci źig

nivṛttir nāpi yuktāsyā bahusādhāraṇatvataḥ /
yathā mṛtaikajārāyās parṣaddāsyā itīṣyate //19//

| 'di yi ldog pa'aṅ rigs min te |
| maṅ po dag daṅ thun moṅ phyir |
| ji ltar rje gcig śi gyur kyaṅ |
| tshogs pa dag gi bran bźin 'dod |

17c gi: gis P, D
18b nāhamityādiniścayaḥ: cāham ityādiniścayaḥ H
19c tathā *ex con T.* bźin: yathā *Ms*
19d parṣad°: *ex con T.* tshogs pa dag: parṣa° *Msc*: tathā *Ms*, L

katham ātmāntaraiḥ puṃso deśābhedād anāvṛteḥ /
udbhūtasattve manasi tattvadṛṅniyamo mataḥ //20//

| tha dad yul la ma bsgribs phyir |
| ji ltar bdag gi dbye ba las |
| skyes bu'i yid la sñiṅ stobs dag
| lhag pas de ñid mthoṅ bar 'dod |

śabdādipratipattau ca dharmādharmādayas tathā / 17a[5]
tulyaparyanuyogatvād adṛṣṭo niyamo 'py asan //21//

| sgra la sogs pa rtogs pa daṅ |
| de bźin chos daṅ chos min dag
| skyon ni rjes su mtshuṅs pa'i phyir |
| ma mthoṅ ṅes pa med pa'aṅ yin |

acetano na vāhetur naiva sarvagataḥ pumān /
pariṇāmād yathā dadhnaḥ puṃsaḥ pariṇatir yadi //22//

| gal te skyes bu 'gyur źe na |
| skyes bu rtogs pa med pa daṅ |
| rgyu med khyab pa ma yin te |
| skyes bu 'gyur phyir 'o ma bźin |

20b deśābhedād: deśabhedād *Ms*, L
21d adṛṣṭo: adṛṣṭā *Ms*: adṛṣṭe H
22a vāhetur: cāhetur H: vā hetur L
22c dadhnaḥ *ex con T.* 'o ma: dadhyāt *Ms*
22c yathā dadhnaḥ: payovat syāt H

pratibimbasya hetutvāc citer avikṛter api /
yathoktadoṣasaṃsargo jāyate mukhabimbavat //23//

| sems ni ’gyur ba med na yaṅ |
| gzugs brñan gyi ni rgyu yin phyir |
| ji skad smras pa’i skyon ldan par |
| ’byuṅ ste gdoṅ gi gzugs brñan bźin |

akalpakatvāt puṃsaś ca nānyo ’ham iti yujyate /
upacārād adoṣaś cen muktiḥ syād aupacārikī //24// 17a[6]

| skyes bu rtog pa med pa’i phyir |
| bdag daṅ gźan źes mi rigs so |
| brtags na skyon med ce na yaṅ |
| grol ba btags pa ñid du ’gyur |

asti pradhānaṃ bhedānām anvayāt pariṇāmataḥ /
kāryakāraṇabhāvāc ca śaktito vaiśvarūpyataḥ //25//

| gtso bo yod de sna tshogs kyi |
| rjes su ’gro phyir yoṅs gyur phyir |
| bya daṅ byed pa’i ṅo bo’i phyir |
| nus phyir sna tshogs ṅo bo’i phyir |

yad yathoktaṃ tathoktaṃ tat karparāṇāṃ kalādivat /
tathā ca bhedās tadvattas tasmād bhedāḥ sakāraṇāḥ //26//

| ji skad smras pa de bźin te |
| snod chag pa yi dum sogs ltar |
| de bźin dbye ba de daṅ ldan |
| des na dbye ba rgyu daṅ bcas |

bhedānāṃ cet sahetutvaṃ sādhyate siddhasādhanam /
samanvayasya cāsiddher hetoś ca syād asiddhatā //27//

| dbye rnams rgyu daṅ bcas ñid du |
| sgrub byed ce na grub pa sgrub |
| kun la chags par ma grub ste |
| 'di ni gtan tshigs ma grub phyir |

sāmānyapūrvakatvaṃ ced iṣṭaṃ sāmānyavattvataḥ / 17b[1]
sāmānyato viśeṣād vā prāgvan na vā nidarśanam //28//

| spyi ni sṅon du soṅ 'dod de |
| spyi daṅ ldan pa'i phyir źe na |
| spyi ñid dam ni khyad par la |
| sṅa ma bźin du dpe yaṅ med |

26b tat karparāṇāṃ: tatkarparāṇāṃ H
26c tadvattas: tadvantas H
27a cet sahetutvaṃ *ex con T.* rgyu daṅ bcas ñid: bhedānān te 'sya *Ms*

na sukhādisvabhāvatvaṃ vedanāskandhavan matam /
skandhatvāt sukhaduḥkhādyaiḥ pratyekaṃ vyabhicārataḥ //29//

| bde la sogs pa'i ṅo bo'i phyir |
| tshor ba'i phuṅ po bźin mi 'dod |
| phuṅ po yin phyir bde sdug sogs |
| so sor ma ṅes pa ñid yin |

mohasya vā vedanatvād dṛṣṭāntanyūnatā bhavet /
hetumattvāc ca tatsiddhir neṣṭā duḥkhasukhādivat //30//

| xx xx xx xx xx xx xx |
| xx xx xx xx xx xx xx |
| xx xx xx xx xx xx xx |
| xx xx xx xx xx xx xx |

vyabhicārasyāpahater evam apy akṛtātmatā /
anvayādyanumānāc ca pratijñādoṣabhāvanāt //31 //

| ma ṅes pa yi spaṅs pas na |
| de ltar don byed bdag ñid yin |
| rjes 'gro sogs kyi rjes dpag gi
| dam bcas skyon gyis gnod pa yin |

30a mohasya: mohasyā *Ms*
30c tatsiddhir: tatsiddher *Ms*
31b akṛtātmatā: akṛtārthatā H
31d pratijñādoṣabhāvanāt: pratijñādoṣabhā... *Msc*:
pratijñādoṣabādhanāt *Ms*, L

ajātānantavattvāditadviśeṣanirākṛteḥ / 17a[2]
prādhānikaguṇaiś ceṣṭā hetavo vyabhicāriṇaḥ //32//

| skye med mtha' med ñid sogs kyi |
| de yis khyad par spaṅs pas na |
| gtso bo'i yon tan 'dod pa yi |
| gtan tshigs ma ṅes pa ñid yin |

ekakāraṇapūrvatve syāc ca teṣāṃ viruddhatā /
tathā vibhaktahetutve vidyate na nidarśanam //33//

| xx xx xx xx xx xx xx |
| xx xx xx xx xx xx xx |
| de bźin tha dad rgyu las kyaṅ |
| 'byuṅ bar 'dod ba'i dpe yod min |

candanaṃ śakalotpattau na dhvastam iti gamyate /
balarūpapramāṇādipratyāsattes tadātmavat //34//

| tsandan dum bur gyur pa na |
| ñams pa min par rtogs bya ste |
| stobs daṅ gzugs daṅ tshad la sogs |
| ñe bar gnas te bdag ñid bźin |

32b °tadviśeṣa° *ex con T.* de yis khyad par: °tvaviśeṣa° *Ms*

ato vibhaktahetutve dṛṣṭāntāsiddhatā na cet/
śaktyātmanā tadastitve pūrvavan na nidarśanam //35// 17a[3]

| xx xx xx xx xx xx xx |
| xx xx xx xx xx xx xx |
| nus pa'i bdag ñid ñid du de |
| yod na snar bźin dpe mi 'grub |

vyaktātmanā tadastitve kṛtāntatyāgitā bhavet /
kāryakāraṇayor aikyasādhane 'py uktanītivat //36//

| gsal ba'i ṅo bor de yod na'aṅ |
| grub pa'i mtha' ni spaṅ bar 'gyur |
| bya daṅ byed pa gcig ñid du |
| sgrub na'aṅ smras pa'i tshul ñid yin |

ekajātinayaikatvasādhane siddhasādhanam /
tadanyārthavikalpe ca pūrvavad doṣasaṃplavaḥ //37//

| rigs mthun ñid la gcig ñid du |
| sgrub na'aṅ grub pa sgrub pa yin |
| de las don gźan rtog na yaṅ |
| sṅa ma bźin du skyon kun 'byuṅ |

36cd aikyasādhane: aikyaṃ sādhane Ms, H

etena pūrvabuddhīnāṃ niṣiddhāpy anumānatā /
sarvadā sukhaduḥkhādyair hetavo vyabhicāriṇaḥ //38//

| xx xx xx xx xx xx xx |
| xx xx xx xx xx xx xx |
| bde daṅ sdug bsṅal sogs kun tu |
| gtan tshigs ma ṅes pa ñid yin |

yatas tattvena nānyatvaṃ [...]na coktavat / 17a[4]
kālābhedād ananyatve rūḍhyāgamavirodhitā //39//

| xx xx xx xx xx xx xx |
| xx xx xx xx xx xx xx |
| dus dbyer med pas gźan min na'aṅ |
| grags daṅ luṅ daṅ 'gal ba ñid |

38b niṣiddhāpy anumānatā: niṣiddhā vartamānatā H
38c sogs kun tu: la sogs kun P, D
39a tattvena nānyatvaṃ [...]na: tattve nānyatvaṃ [...] na *Ms,* L: tattve vānyatvaṃ svasvato vā H
39ab yatas tatvo nānanyatve svator vā na coktavat *Msc*
39b [...]na: svasvato vā na H
39c kālābhedād *ex con T.* dus dbyer med: kālabhedād *Ms,* L

na candanatirobhāve 'bhāvaś cet sa prasādhyate /
ṣaṣṭhakāle na cāpy ukte vartamānakṣaṇo yathā //40//

| tsandan ṅo bo mi mṅon pas |
| med par sgrub pa ma yin te |
| dus daṅ drug pas bstan pa'i phyir |
| da ltar skad cig bźin źe na |

nanv evam api notsāhaḥ svanīticchidraguptaye /
noktadoṣo 'nubadhnāti ghaṭa utkacam uktivat //41//

| de lta na yaṅ spro gyur nas |
| raṅ gi lugs kyi skyon sbed kyaṅ |
| smra ba'i skyon rnams med min te |
| gyen du skra 'greṅ bum 'dra bźin |

tādrūpyād iti hetvarthavikalpe vyabhicāritā /
abhedarūpatāyāṃ ca syād vā hetor asiddhatā //42// 17b[5]

| des gzugs śe na gtan tshigs don |
| rnam par rtog pa ma ṅes ñid |
| dbyer med ṅo bo yin na yaṅ |
| gtan tshigs ma ṅes pa ñid yin |

40c ṣaṣṭha°: ṣeṣṭa° *Ms*, L: ṣaṣṭhyā° H
40cd cāpy ukte: cāpyukter H, L
41a notsāhaḥ: notsāhaṃ *Ms*, H, L
41d ghaṭa utkacam uktivat: ghaṭotkacaśaktivat H

sabhoktṛtvaṃ ca śrotrāder acaitanyād yadīṣyate /
anirdiṣṭaviśeṣeṇa bhoktā cet siddhasādhanam //43//

| rna sogs spyad bya ma yin te |
| rtogs pa med phyir gal te 'dod |
| khyad par dag ni ma bstan par |
| spyad bya'o źe na grub pa sgrub |

athodāsīnanityādiviśeṣānunayaḥ kutaḥ /
bhoktṛtvaṃ na nirīhatvāc caitanye saty apīṣyate //44//

| ci ste gyo ba med sogs kyi |
| khyad par can na rjes 'gro gaṅ |
| rtogs par bden yaṅ rtsol med phyir |
| spyod pa por ni mi 'dod do |

niṣkriyatvaṃ tu bhāvānāṃ prameyatvāt pramīyate /
yad yathoktaṃ tathā tac ca pratītaṃ sukhamohavat//45//

| dṅos rnams bya ba med ñid du |
| rab tu rtogs te gźal bya'i phyir |
| smras pa ci ltar de de ltar |
| rtogs te bde daṅ gti mug bźin |

43c anirdiṣṭaviśeṣeṇa *ex con T.* khyad par dag ni ma bstan par: nanirdiṣṭāṣeṇa *Ms: anirdiṣṭaviśeṣāṇāṃ* L
43c bhoktā: bhīkṣya *Ms:* bhakṣaś L
44ab °viśeṣānunayaḥ: °viśeṣeṇānvayaḥ H
45c tathā tac *ex con T.* de de ltar: yathoktaṃ *Ms; Ms* add: *dṛṣṭāntanyūnatā caiva ghaṭṭasya dravyasattvataḥ*

duḥkham apy avasetavyaṃ niṣkriyaṃ hetumattvataḥ / 17b[6]
acetanatvād vācyatvān meyatvād vāpi mohavat //46//

| bya ba med par sdug bsṅal yaṅ |
| śes par bya ste rgyud ldan phyir |
| rtogs pa med phyir brjod bya'i phyir |
| gźal bya yin phyir gti mug bźin |

hetutvam anvayādīnāṃ bhedatve sati vāñchataḥ /
prādhānikaguṇais teṣāṃ satyaṃ na vyabhicāritā //47//

| rjes 'gro la sogs gtan tshigs rnams |
| tha dad ñid du 'dod pas na |
| gtso bo'i yon tan la de rnams |
| ma ṅes ma yin pa de bden |

siddhaṃ kāraṇakāryādi hetumattvānumānataḥ /
saviśeṣaṇahetūnāṃ syād evaṃ te viruddhatā //48//

| bya daṅ byed pa sgrub bcas phyir |
| rgyu daṅ ldan par rjes dpag ñid |
| gtan tshigs rnams kyaṅ khyad bcas pas |
| de ltar 'gal ba ñid du 'gyur |

46a avasetavyaṃ: avasātavyaṃ
48a bcas: byas P
48ab siddhaṃ kāraṇakāryādi hetumattvānumānataḥ:
sat sakāraṇakāryādihetumattvānumānataḥ H
48c saviśeṣaṇahetūnāṃ: saviśeṣeṇa hetūnāṃ H

xx xx xx xx xx xx xx xx /
xx xx xx xx xx xx xx xx //49//

| de ma bzuṅ bar mi ’dzin pas |
| gzugs sogs gźan min de dṅos bźin |
| tha dad dṅos phyir gźan min min |
| gaṅ de rtogs bya rtogs byed phyir |

xx xx xx xx xx xx xx xx /
xx xx xx xx xx xx xx xx //50//

| des na mi mṅon ma yin la |
| bya ba yod pa’aṅ mi ’dod do |
| da ltar gyi ni skad cig kyaṅ |
| rdzas su yod par ma grags ñid |

xx xx xx xx xx xx xx xx /
xx xx xx xx xx xx xx xx //51//

| spyod daṅ bcas pa’i spyad bya ’di |
| spyad bya yin phyir mal sogs bźin |
| rtogs pa po ni spyod pa ñid |
| de yi sgrub par byed pa min |

51a daṅ bcas pa’i: bcas pa yi PK

xx xx xx xx xx xx xx xx /
xx xx xx xx xx xx xx xx //52//

| rtogs pa ṅes par rtogs yin na |
| de ni gaṅ gi yin pa smros |
| dṅos po byed pa la brten te |
| gos sogs tshon du btsos pa bźin |

xx xx xx xx xx xx xx xx /
xx xx xx xx xx xx xx xx //53//

| sgra sogs śes par mi 'gyur ba |
| yin yaṅ śes pa ji ltar yin |
| sgra sogs śes par 'gyur ba ñid |
| yin na'aṅ śes pa ji ltar yin |

xx xx xx xx xx xx xx xx /
xx xx xx xx xx xx xx xx //54//

| byed pa med pa ma skyes phyir |
| byed bo ñid du ji ltar 'dod |
| ma skyes pa la 'dogs na yaṅ |
| skyes bu btags pa pa ru 'gyur |

xx xx xx xx xx xx xx xx /
xx xx xx xx xx xx xx xx //55//

| byed po'i sgra yi brjod bya'i phyir |
| me bźin khyod kyi skyes bu yaṅ |
| rgyu bcas bya bcas spyad bya daṅ |
| bya ba rab tu bskyed pa'aṅ yin |

xx xx xx xx xx xx xx xx /
xx xx xx xx xx xx xx xx //56//

| kun khyab ma yin raṅ bźin las |
| gźan pa ma yin skyes bu min |
| de yi raṅ dṅos khyad par ni |
| de yis 'di ltar spoṅ bar 'gyur |

xx xx xx xx xx xx xx xx /
xx xx xx xx xx xx xx xx //57//

| des na khas blaṅs pa de la |
| gnod phyir dam bcas skyon bcas phyir |
| ji ltar dbaṅ phyug rgyur smar bźin |
| rtogs pa la sogs spaṅs pa yin |

55a yi: yis DK
55b kyi: kyis PK
56c yi: yis PK
57b skyon bcas phyir: skyon med min PK, DK: skyon med phyir P, D

xx xx xx xx xx xx xx xx /
xx xx xx xx xx xx xx xx //58//

| bdag daṅ bdag gi min rtogs pa |
| blo yi rjes su rtogs pa yi |
| lta ba log pas grol bar ni |
| khyod kyi skyes bur 'gyur mi rigs |

xx xx xx xx xx xx xx xx /
xx xx xx xx xx xx xx xx //59//

| skyes bu tha dad mthoṅ ba yis |
| thar pa 'thob pa ma yin te |
| blo gźan yin phyir spyad bya daṅ |
| skyes bu gźan ñid mthoṅ ba bźin |

xx xx xx xx xx xx xx xx /
xx xx xx xx xx xx xx xx //60//

| ji ltar rnam rtog bcas pa'i phyir |
| mi ni tha dad mthoṅ ba ltar |
| skyas bu tha dad mthoṅ ba yis |
| de bźin grol bar mi 'dod do |

59a yis: yi PK

xx xx xx xx xx xx xx xx /
xx xx xx xx xx xx xx xx //61//

| de ltar graṅs can de ñid ni |
| sṅon daṅ phyi mar ’gal ba daṅ |
| rigs pa daṅ ni mi ldan la |
| mkhas pa rnams kyi blo mi ’jug

xx xx xx xx xx xx xx xx /
xx xx xx xx xx xx xx xx //62//

| nya gro dha yi sa bon gyi |
| naṅ na yod pa’i nya gro daṅ |
| bud med skyes pa ’grogs la bu |
| rṅa yi naṅ na sgra gnas daṅ |

xx xx xx xx xx xx xx xx /
xx xx xx xx xx xx xx xx //63//

| zas kyi naṅ nya phyis sogs |
| śiṅ la ’bar yod mi mthoṅ źes |
| gaṅ źig mṅon sum spoṅ byed pa |
| de ni bden smra ji ltar yin |

62a dha: da PK, P, DK, D
63a nya: na PK, P, DK, D

xx xx xx xx xx xx xx xx /
xx xx xx xx xx xx xx xx //64//

| de ni yod kyaṅ mi gsal bas |
| des na bya ba sṅon ma mthoṅ |
| źe na mi gsal med min pas |
| e ma'o bstan bcos śin tu legs |

64b mngon: sngon PK, D

Vedāntatattvaviniścaya

vedāntavādinaḥ prāhur ātmavid durlabho bahiḥ / 19a[1] 19a[2]
kuta ātmadviṣāṃ mokṣaḥ śūnyasaṃskāravādinām //1//

| rig byed mthar smra smras pa ni |
| 'dus byas stoṅ par smra ba yi |
| phyi rol pa la bdag rig dkon |
| bdag sdaṅ thar pa ga la yod |

tamaḥparastāt puruṣaṃ mahāntaṃ sūryavarcasam /
mṛtyum atyeti matimān matvātmānaṃ maheśvaram //2//

| mun pa las gźan skyes bu ni |
| chen por gyur pa ñi ma'i 'od |
| dbaṅ phyug chen po bdag de ñid |
| mkhas pas śes na 'chi med 'gyur |

1c kuta: kutaḥ *Ms*
1d sdaṅ: daṅ PK
2a °parastāt *ex con T.* las gźan: °purastāt *Ms*
2a bu: bus D
2c mṛtyum atyeti *ex con T.* 'chi med 'gyur: mṛtyubhyeti *Ms*

rukmavarṇaṃ yadā paśyaḥ paśyet kartāram īśvaram /
vihāya pāpaṃ puṇyaṃ ca paraṃ sāmyaṃ tadāpnuyāt //3//

| byed po dbaṅ phyug gser mdog tu |
| gaṅ źig mthoṅ źiṅ lta ba de |
| sdig daṅ bsod nams las 'das nas |
| mchog tu źi ba thob par 'gyur |

bhūtaṃ bhavad bhaviṣyac ca sarvaṃ puruṣa iṣyate /
so 'ntar bahiś ca dūre ca so 'ntike sa ca karmakṛt //4// 19a[3]

| byuṅ gyur byuṅ daṅ 'byuṅ ba dag
| thams cad skyes bu yin 'dod de |
| de ni phyi naṅ riṅ ba daṅ |
| de ni ñe daṅ de las byed |

viśve bhāvās tato jātā ūrṇanābhād ivāṃśavaḥ /
tasmin pralīnā vidvaṃso nāpnuvanti punarbhavaṃ //5//

| srid pa sna tshogs de las skyes |
| dar gyi srin bu'i skud pa bźin |
| mkhas pa de yi char thim pa |
| yaṅ srid len par mi 'gyur ro |

3a paśyaḥ: paśyan *Ms*, H
3b źig: gis PK, DK; lta: blta PK, DK
3d sāmyaṃ *ex con T.* źi ba: sātmyaṃ *Ms*
4a 'byuṅ: byuṅ P
4d de: des PK
5a srid pa sna tshogs (*citra), T. *dṅos po thams cad
5b srin: srid PK

amṛtatvaṃ na martyasya vahneḥ śaityam iveṣyate /
tasmād amṛtatāyuktāprabodhāt puruṣe 'mṛte //6//

| 'chi bcas rnams la bdud rtsi med |
| me la graṅ ba ji bźin no |
| des na bdud rtsi skyes bu ñid |
| ma rtogs bdud rtsi yod mi rigs |

yataḥ paraṃ paraṃ nāsti yato jyāyān na vidyate /
aṇīyān vāpi tenedaṃ viśvam ekena saṃtatam //7//

| gaṅ las mchog gyur gźan med phyir |
| gaṅ las dam pa gźan med la |
| 'di las phra gyur gźan med pas |
| sna tshogs 'di dag rgyu gcig ñid |

xx xx xx xx xx xx xx xx /
xx xx xx xx xx xx xx xx //8//

| de ni phra daṅ rags daṅ ldan |
| yaṅ ldan gtso bo dbaṅ sgyur ba |
| rab phye 'dod pa'i mthar thug gaṅ |
| rnal 'byor ji ltar 'dod par 'gro |

6a na martyasya *ex con T.* 'chi bcas ... med: tam abhyasya *Ms*
6d 'mṛte *ex con T.* bdud rtsi: mṛte *Ms*
7c vāpi: nāpi H
7d sna tshogs (*citra/nānā): *Ms* viśvam: T. *kun thams cad
8 omit. *Ms*
8b sgyur: bsgyur DK

tasmin sarvāṇi bhūtāni bhavanty ātmaiva paśyataḥ / 19a[4]
bālapaṇḍitacaṇḍālaviprādīnāṃ ca tulyatā //9//

| der ni 'byuṅ ba thams cad kyaṅ |
| bdag ñid du ni 'dus par mthoṅ |
| byis daṅ mkhas daṅ gdol pa daṅ |
| bram ze sogs rnams mñam pa ñid |

ghaṭotpattau vināśe vā nākāśasya tadātmatā /
tadātmatātmano 'pīṣṭā na dehādyudayavyaye //10//

| bum pa 'byuṅ źiṅ 'jig pa ltar |
| nam mkha' de yi bdag ñid min |
| lus can 'byuṅ źiṅ 'jig pa ltar |
| de bdag yin pad bdag mi 'dod |

ghaṭākāśavad ekasya nānātvaṃ ced abhedataḥ /
ghaṭabhedena caikatvaṃ sāmyaṃ sarvasya yan matam //11//

| bum pa'i nam mkha' bźin du gcig
| du ma'o źe na bum pa dag
| chag na dbyer med gcig ñid du |
| thams cad mñam par 'gyur bar 'dod |

9b bhavanty: bhavaty *Ms*
9c mkhas: mkhas pa P
10d °vyaye *ex con T.* ltar: 'vyayaṃ *Ms*
11b ced *ex con T.* źe na: deh° *Ms*
11c caikatvaṃ *ex con T.* gcig ñid du: caikasya *Ms*
11d sāmyaṃ *ex con T.* mñam par: sāmye *Ms*; yan: jan *Ms*
11d mñam: ñams PK

yathā ghaṭādibhede ’pi mṛdbhedo nāsti kaś cana /
xx xx xx xx xx xx xx xx //12//

| ji ltar bum sogs tha dad kyaṅ|
| sa la tha dad ’ga’ yaṅ med |
| de bźin lus ni tha dad kyaṅ |
| bdag la tha dad ’ga’ yaṅ med |

ghaṭākāśe yathaikasmin rajodhūmādibhir vṛte / 19a[5]
tadvattā na hi sarveṣāṃ sukhāder na tathātmanaḥ //13//

| ji ltar bum pa’i nam mkha’ gcig
| rdul daṅ du bas bsgribs pa na |
| thams cad de bźin ma yin ltar |
| bde sogs de bźin bdag la min |

aprabodhād anātmajñaḥ svapne bhogābhimānavat /
cinoti karma bhuṅkte ca tatphalaṃ yac chubhāśubham //14//

| bdag ma źes źiṅ ma rtogs pas |
| rmi lam loṅs spyod ṅa rgyal bźin |
| las rnams sogs śiṅ dge ba daṅ |
| mi dge’i ’bras bu spyod pa yin |

12cd omit. *Ms*; *tathaiva dehabhede ’pi nātmabhedo ’sti kaś cana // (Gokhale 1958:17); *tathā deheṣu bhinneṣu na kaścid bheda ātmani // (Bhattacharya 1943:53)
13d sukhāder: sukhādair *Ms*
14b °mānavat: °mānivat *Ms*

dehasaṃstho 'py asaṅgatvād bhuñjāno nopalipyate /
rājavat kāmacārī ca pāpenānaparādhy asau //15//

| lus la gnas kyaṅ ma chags daṅ |
| spyod par byed kyaṅ mi gos te |
| 'dod bźin spyod kyaṅ rgyal po bźin |
| sdig pas gnod par mi 'gyur ro |

ekaṃ sarvagataṃ nityaṃ paraṃ brahmācyutaṃ padam /
yogī yuñjan yadā vetti na tadaiti punarbhavam //16// 19a[6]

| gcig pu kun khyab rtag pa ste |
| tshaṅs mchog 'chi ba med pa'i gnas |
| rnal 'byor pa yis goms byas na |
| de ni yaṅ srid len mi 'gyur |

nityaṃ tad avikalpaṃ ca yatra vācām agocaraḥ /
giras tatra prayujyante bhedāpahṛtabuddhibhiḥ //17//

| de ni rtag par rtog med pa |
| ṅag gi spyod yul gaṅ ma gyur |
| blo ni dbye bas phrogs rnams kyis |
| de la tshig tu sbyor bar byed |

16a pu: po DK
16b brahmācyutaṃ: brahmācchutaṃ (?) *Ms*
16c yuñjān yadā vetti cum Gok: yuñjāna[ ]tti *Ms*
16c yis: yi P; goms (byas) *abhyāsa, rtogs, (s)goms pa, usually for -bhū meaning understand, perceive, cf. e.g. *Yuktiṣaṣṭikā* no. 1, *Ms* vetti, i.e. *rig (byas), *śes (byas); na: nas P
17b ṅag: gaṅ P, DK, D
17c phrogs: phrog P

atrāpīdaṃ parīkṣante pakṣapātānapekṣiṇaḥ /
pakṣarāgāvṛtamatiḥ satyaṃ yathāpi nekṣate //18// 19b[1]

| phyogs su lhuṅ ba ma yin pas |
| 'dir ni 'di yaṅ 'di ltar dpyad |
| phyogs la chags pas bsgribs pa'i blos |
| ji ltar bden pa'aṅ rtogs mi 'gyur |

niṣiddham ātmano 'stitvaṃ jagatkāraṇatā tathā /
atas taddarśanān muktir abhūtaiva prakalpitā //19//

| bdag yod pa ni bkag pas na |
| 'gro ba'i rgyu yaṅ de bźin te |
| des na de mthoṅ grol ba ni |
| mi bden par ni rab brtags ñid |

satkāyadṛṣṭiḥ sahajā paśūnām apy aśāntaye /
sarvasaṃkleśamūlatvāt saiva tvayā vivardhitā //20//

| byol soṅ rnams la 'jig tshogs lta |
| lhan cig skyes yod źi ma gyur |
| kun ñon moṅs kun rtsa ba'i phyir |
| de ñid khyod kyis śin tu spel |

18c °vṛta° *ex con T.* bsgribs pa: °vikala° *Ms*
18d satyaṃ yathāpi *ex con T.* ji ltar bden pa'aṅ: saty[ ]pi *Ms*
19a pa: pas PK, DK; pas: pa PK, DK
20d tvayā *ex con T.* khyod kyis: bhūyā *Ms*
20d kyis: kyi PK

satkāyadṛṣṭyāviṣṭānāṃ mamāhaṃkārakāriṇām /
yato bhavati saṃsāro muktir apy uditā tataḥ //21// 19b[2]

| 'jig tshogs lta la źen pa yi |
| bdag 'dzin bdag gir ' dzin pa dag
| gaṅ las 'khor ba 'byuṅ 'gyur ba |
| de ñid grol ba yin par smra |

taddṛṣṭau ced bhavec chāntir madād iva madātyaye /
ajīrṇāt saṃnipannasya bhojanāt svasthatā bhavet //22//

| myos par gyur la myos 'gyur bźin |
| de lta ba yis źi 'gyur na |
| źin tu ma źu'i nad ldan la |
| kha zas zos pas phan par 'gyur |

21a la: ba P
21b °kāriṇāṃ: °kāriṇā[ ] *Ms*
21b gir: gis PK; dag: de P
21c yato bhavati *ex con T.* gaṅ las ... 'byuṅ bar 'gyur: [ ]ha (h[i]?)[ ] *Ms*: bhāvitaḥ L, H (non-metrical: *pañcamaṃ laghu sarvatra*!).
21d muktir: muktid *Ms*
21d yin par smra[s]; *Ms* uditā, i.e. "denoted", better ud + √i, "emerged", T *byuṅ bar gyur
22b yis: yi PK; 'gyur: gyur PK, DK

xx xx xx xx xx xx xx xx /
xx xx xx xx xx xx xx xx //23//

| rig byed smra bas bdag de ni |
| rnam pa gñis su 'dod byed de |
| lus źes bya ba bciṅs bdag daṅ |
| mchog na gnas pa grol pa'i bdag

na pareṣṭhātmaviṣayā yathārthātmeti dhīr matā /
ātmany evaṃ parāmarśād dehādāv ātmadhīr yathā //24//

| mchog tu 'dzin pa bdag gi yul |
| bdag blo ji bźin don ma yin |
| bdag ni 'di źes mchog 'dziun phyir |
| lus la bdag gi blo bźin no |

23 omit. *Ms*
24a pareṣṭhātma°: pareṣṭātma° L, H. Cf. 23d, mchog na gnas pa grol pa'i bdag: pareṣṭātma° *Ms*, T. mchog tu 'dzin pa bdag corroborates *Ms* (para+iṣṭa+ātman); °viṣayā *ex con T.* yul: °viṣayād *Ms*, H
24c °ād *ex con T.* phyir: °parāmarśā *Ms*
24d cet tan: cetan *Ms*

parikalpitasattvo ’pi kim ātmā kurute tava /
rūpaśabdādiviṣayāṃ buddhiṃ cet tan na yujyate //25//

| yoṅs su brtags pas yod na yaṅ |
| khyod kyis bdag gis ci źig byed |
| gzugs daṅ sgra sogs yul rnams la |
| blo’o źe na de mi rigs |

dhiyo rūpādiviṣayā jāyante nātmakartṛkāḥ / 19b^{3}
pratyayāyattajanmatvāt sūryakāntād ivānalaḥ //26//

| gzugs sogs yul la blo dag ni |
| byed po bdag ni med kyaṅ skye |
| rkyen la bltos pa’i skye yin phyir |
| me śel gyis ni me bźin no |

25 Between vv. 25 and 26, 12 syllables are deleted: (19b2)rūpādiviṣ[ ](19b^{3}) cetannayujya *Ms*
25a brtags: btags PK, DK; pas: pa PK, DK; na yaṅ: na’aṅ PK
25b kyis: kyi PK, DK; gis: gi PK
25d cet tan: cetan *Ms*
26b skye: ste PK
26c °janmatvāt *ex con T.* skye yin phyir: °janmatvā *Ms*
26d źel: źes P; gyis: gyi PK, DK, D

dhvanir varṇātmako yaś ca so 'pīṣṭo nātmakartṛkaḥ /
śrāvaṇatvād dhvanitvād vā tadyathā pratiśabdakaḥ //27//

| gaṅ yaṅ yi ge'i bdag ñid sgra |
| de yi byed po bdag mi 'dod |
| mñan bya'i phyir daṅ sgra yin phyir |
| dper na brag ca ji bźin no |

etena śeṣāḥ pratyuktā gamanāgamanādikāḥ /
hastapādādivispandalakṣaṇā dehajāḥ kriyāḥ //28//

| 'dis ni lus kyi bya ba gźan |
| 'oṅ ba daṅ ni 'gro ba daṅ |
| lag pa rkaṅ pa gyo ba ni |
| mtshan ñid lhag ma rnams kyaṅ bkag

vyavacchedena saṃjñāyā saṃjñānaṃ smaraṇaṃ smṛteḥ / 19b[4]
prajñānaṃ ca prakāreṇa prajñāto vedanaṃ vidaḥ //29//

| rnam par bcad nas kun śes las |
| kun śes dran pa ñid las dran |
| so sor rnam par rab śes las |
| śes rab ñams su myoṅ las tshor |

27a dhvanir: dhvani *Ms*
27b mi: min DK
27d ca: cha PK, P
28b gamanāgamanādikāḥ: gamānāgamanādikāḥ *Ms*
28d dehajāḥ: dehajā *Ms*; kriyāḥ: kriyā *Ms*
29b saṃjñānaṃ *ex con T.* kun śes: [ ]jñānaṃ *Ms*
29d las: la D

na cānyad ātmanaḥ kāryaṃ svabhāvo nāvadhāryate /
khapuṣpavad atas tasya na sattāpy avadhāryate //30//

| xx xx xx xx xx xx xx |
| xx xx xx xx xx xx xx |
| xx xx xx xx xx xx xx |
| xx xx xx xx xx xx xx |

jñānādeḥ karaṇokteś cet karaṇatvaṃ prasādhyate /
tadanyakartṛkatvaṃ vā dātṛvat tan na yuktimat //31//

| śes sogs byed par smra źe na |
| byed pa ñid du sgrub pa 'am |
| de las gźan pa'i byed po ñid |
| gcod byed bźin du rigs ldan min |

kartari pratyayotpatter naiṣāṃ karaṇatā yataḥ /
ato 'siddhārthatā hetor anekāntikatāpi vā //32//

| byed pa po la rkyen ldan gyis |
| gaṅ phyir byed pa la min pas |
| des na gtan tshigs ma grub pa'am |
| ma ṅes pa ñid yin par 'gyur |

30a ātmanaḥ: ātmana *Ms*
31a karaṇokteś: karaṇoktaś *Ms*
31d dātṛvat *ex con T.* gcod byed bźin: dātūvat *Ms*
32a la: ni P; gyis: gyi P, D: źiṅ PK, DK
32c 'siddhārthatā *ex con T.* ma grub pa [ñid]: siddhārthatā *Ms*
32d vā: va *Ms*

jñānādīnāṃ hi kartṛtvaṃ kartṛśabdābhidhānataḥ / 19b[5]
devadattaś chinattīti yathā dṛṣṭātra kartṛtā //33//

| śes la sogs pa byed po ñid |
| byed po'i sgra yis brjod pa'i phyir |
| lhas byin gyis ni gcod do źes |
| ji ltar byed por mthoṅ ba bźin |

nirīha eva saṃskārarāśau syāt kartṛvācyatā /
kāraṇatvād yathā dīpe dīpo dyotayatīti te //34//

| 'dus byas phuṅ po byed bral ñid |
| 'di la byed por brjod bya ste |
| byed pa yin phyir mar me yis |
| gsal bar byed pa yin ba bźin |

na mukhyas tattvataḥ kartā naiko hi ghaṭakṛd yataḥ /
naupacārikakartṛtvaṃ dīpāder iṣyate tataḥ //35//

| yaṅ dag gtso gcig byed po min |
| gaṅ phyir gcig gis bum mi byed |
| des na mar me sogs byed po |
| gdags pa par ni mi 'dod do |

33b sgra yis: sgra'i PK
33c byin: sbyin DK
34a byed: bye PK, P
34b por: par PK
34c yis: yi PK
35c naupa°: na upa° H
35d dīpa° *ex con T.* mar me: dvīpa° *Ms*
35d pa par: ba bar P: pa bar D; *Ms* upacārika°, T *ñe [bar] gdags par

cittaṃ rāgādivaśagaṃ saktaṃ rūpādigocare /
pratibaddhaṃ ca nirmokṣe baddhaṃ saṃsāracārake //36// 19b[6]

| 'dod chags sogs kyi dbaṅ phyug sems |
| gzugs sogs yul la mṅon źen pa'i |
| thar pa mi mthun phyogs kyis phrogs |
| 'khor ba'i btson rar bciṅs pa yin |

pāṇyādisamudāyo 'yaṃ sacittaḥ sattvasaṃjñakaḥ /
tyāgādicetanotpatter dātetyādi nigadyate //37//

| lag pa la sogs tshogs pa ni |
| sems bcas sems can źes bya ste |
| gtoṅ ba la sogs sems 'byuṅ ba |
| yod pa gtoṅ por la sogs brjod |

vidyotpattāv avidyādisaṃyojananivṛttitaḥ /
rāgādibandhanān mukto mukta ity abhidhīyate //38//

| rig pa skyes pas ma rig sogs |
| kun sbyor ldog par gyur pa'i phyir |
| chags sogs 'chiṅ ba las grol ba |
| grol ba śes ni brjod pa yin |

36a °vaśagaṃ: °vaśaga *Ms*
36c pratibaddhaṃ: pratibaddhaḥ *Ms*; nirmokṣe *ex con T.* thar pa: [ ]mokṣe *Ms*; ca: omit. *Ms*: ca nirmokṣe: nirmokṣe ca H
36d baddhaṃ: baddhaḥ *Ms*

ātmani vyomakalpe tu sarvam etat sudurvacaḥ /
khapuṣpam astu vāpy ātmā yady ātmātīva vallabhaḥ //39//

| nam mkha' 'dra ba'i bdag la ni |
| 'di dag thams cad brjod par dka' |
| gal te bdag la lhag chags na |
| nam mkha'i me tog bdag 'dod kyis |

svabhāvato hi yady ātmā jñānabhāva itīṣyate / 20a[1]
na tarhy asyaikatā yuktā karaṇādivyapekṣaṇāt //40//

| gal te bdag ni raṅ bźin gyis |
| śes pa'i ṅo bor 'dod na ni |
| byed pa la sogs bltos pa'i phyir |
| de ni gcig tu mi rigs so |

39c vāpy ātmā *ex con T.* vāpy omit. T. bdag la: vāryāte *Ms*
39d yady ātmātīva *ex con T.* gal te bdag la lhag chags na: yadyātīva *Ms*
40a gal te, *Ms* yadi: gaṅ phyir PK, P, DK, D, reading *yasmāt, yataḥ; gyis: gyi PK
40ab ātmā jñānabhāva *ex con T.* bdag ni ... (40a) śes pa'i ṅo bor: ātmā[ ]bhāva *Ms*
40c asyaikatā: asyekatā *Ms*
40d karaṇādi° *ex con T.* byed pa la sogs: kāraṇādi° *Ms*

sati vātmādike jñeye jñānaṃ tan na nivartate /
kṛtārthasyāpi dīpasya dṛṣṭaṃ janma svakāraṇāt //41//

| bdag sogs śes bya yod pas na |
| śes pa ldog par mi 'gyur te |
| don byas zin pa'I mar me yaṅ |
| raṅ gi rgyu las skye bar mthoṅ |

sato jñānodayo yāvat tāvad bījaṃ pracīyate /
ārāvaprabhavo yāvat tāvat pratiravo yathā //42//

| ji srid yod la śes 'byuṅ ba |
| de srid sa bon sogs 'gyur te |
| ji srid sgra ni yod gyur pa |
| de srid sgra brñan 'byuṅ ba źin |

41b tan na *ex con T.* tan omit. T. mi: tadva *Ms*
41d rgyu: rgyud D
42a sato *ex con T.* yod la: ato *Ms*
42a ji srid: ci srid PK, P, DK, D; yod la: yin la PK; yid la P, DK, D; *Ms* [s]ato, T *yod la, T yid la, *mateḥ, a *lectio facilior* prompted by the adjacent śes and sa bon?

saṃsāraś ca kathaṃ jñasya jñānaṃ ca karaṇaṃ vinā /
sarvadā vāviśiṣṭatvād bandhamokṣau kutaḥ katham //43// 20a[2]

| byed pa med par źes pa ni |
| 'khor ba ji ltar śes pa yin |
| kun tu khyad med yin pa'i phyir |
| gaṅ las ji ltar bciṅs daṅ grol |

na duḥkhenāpi nirmokṣo mokṣe 'py ekātmavādinaḥ /
ātmanas tadananyatvād yathoṣṇena vibhāvasoḥ //44//

| sdug bsṅal las kyaṅ thar min te |
| thar daṅ gcig tu smra ba'i phyir |
| bdag las de ni gźan min phyir |
| ji ltar me daṅ tsha ba bźin |

43a jñasya: jñāsya *Ms*
43c °aviśiṣṭatvād *ex con T.* kun tu khyad med yin pa'i phyir: °aviśiṣṭa *Ms*
43c khyad: khyab PK, P, DK, D
43d bandhamokṣau *ex con T.* bciṅs daṅ grol: mokṣau *Ms*
44c °ananyatvād: °atanyatvād *Ms*
44d vibhāvasoḥ: vibhāvayoḥ *Ms*

līnānutpannabuddhiś ca kathaṃ jñaḥ karaṇaṃ vinā /
yathā hi pūrṇakaś chettā na yuktaḥ paraśuṃ vinā //45//

| ñams daṅ ma skyes pa yi blo |
| byed pa med par ji ltar yin |
| gaṅ pos gcod par byed pa yaṅ |
| sta re med par ji ltar rigs |

agninā dahatīty ukte dahaty agnir na rādhakaḥ /
tadvad vetti dhiyety ukte jñānaṃ vetti na vaḥ pumān //46//

| me yis sreg ces smras pa na |
| me yis sreg kyi byed pas min |
| de bźin blo yis rig smras pas |
| śes pas rig gi skyes bus min |

45b par: pa P, D; yin: min PK
45c pūrṇakaś chettā *ex con T.* gaṅ pos gcod par byed pa: pūrvakaś cittān *Ms*: pūrṇakaśchettā H
45c gaṅ pos, "filler, filled", *Ms* pūrṇaka, "woodpecker", T *śiṅ rgon
45d sta re, "axe", *Ms* paraśu, "beak", T *rva mchu, *bya mchu
46a yis: yi PK; sreg: bsreg DK: bsregs PK; ces: byed P
46b dahaty *ex con T.* bsregs: na dahaty *Ms*
46b sreg: bsregs PK, P, DK, D
46c yis: yi P; rig: rigs D
46d pas: par D

kulālavan na tatsiddhis tatsvabhāvo yato na saḥ / 20a[3]
neṣṭā dahanavat siddhir dāhyābhāve 'gnyasaṃbhavāt //47//

| rdza mkhan bźin du de mi 'grub |
| de yi ṅo bo med pa'i phyir |
| sreg byed bźin du'aṅ 'grub mi 'dod |
| bsreg bya med pas me med phyir |

na cājño jñaḥ kathaṃ kartā bhoktā ca sa bhavet tava /
vyomakalpo 'vikalpaś ca kiṃ kalpyaḥ kevalāgamāt //48//

| gal te mi śes byed po daṅ |
| za po khyod kyis śes ji ltar |
| mkha' 'dra rtog pa med pa yaṅ |
| luṅ 'ba' źig gis brtags ci bya |

47a na tatsiddhis *ex con T.* de mi 'grub: na ta[ ]ddhis *Ms*
47c dahanavat siddhiḥ *ex con T.* sreg byed bźin du'aṅ 'grub: dahanavad asmin *Ms*
47c sreg: sred DK
47d dāhyābhāve *ex con T.* bsreg bya med pas: bāhyābhāve *Ms*; 'gnyasaṃbhavāt *ex con T.* me med phyir: agnisambhavāt *Ms*
48a cājño jñaḥ *ex con T.* mi śes...daṅ...śes (48b): cājñājñaḥ *Ms*, H
48c 'vikalpaś *ex con T.* rtog pa med pa: vikalpaś *Ms*
48d kalpyaḥ *ex con T.* brtags...bya: kupta *Ms*
48d brtags: btags P, D

na cājñajñaḥ svabhāvo vā niḥsvabhāvo bhaved asau /
niḥsvabhāvaś ca nātmā syād vandhyātanayavat sa ca //49//

| mi śes pa 'am śes dṅos min |
| 'di ni dṅos po med par 'gyur |
| dṅos med bdag du mi 'gyur te |
| 'di ni mo gśam bu bźin no |

yatpīḍānugrahe yasya na duḥkhānugrahodbhavaḥ /
na tasyātmā hy asau yukto yathākhaṃ devaśarmaṇaḥ //50// 20a[4]

| gaṅ la gnod daṅ phan pa las |
| gaṅ la gnod daṅ bde mi 'byuṅ |
| de de'i bdag tu mi rigs te |
| nam mkha' de ba śar ma'i bźin |

49a cājñajñaḥsvabhāvo: cājñājñaḥ svabhāvo *Ms*, L, H
50a °pīḍānugrahe: °pītānugrahe *Ms*
50b na duḥkha° *ex con T.* gnod...mi: tad duḥkha° *Ms*
50b bde: bdi DK
50c hy asau: [ ]sau *Ms*
50c de'i: yi PK
50d amṛtaḥ *ex con T.* mi 'chir: na mṛtaḥ *Ms*

dhyānajñānādi ced iṣṭaṃ muktaye ’rthāntarātmanaḥ /
anātmārthaḥ prayatnaḥ syān martyaḥ syād amṛtaḥ katham //51//

| ñi tshe’i bdag daṅ grol bar ni |
| bsam gtan śes sogs kyis ’dod na |
| bdag med don la ’bad pa yis |
| śi ba mi ’chir ji ltar ’gyur |

antarātmātmano ’nyaś cet pratijñā te ca hīyate /
xx xx xx xx xx xx xx xx //52//

| ñi tshe’i bdag ni bdag las gźan |
| źe na thams cad skyes bu yin |
| de ni ñi tshe gñis bdag daṅ |
| phyi źes dam bcas ñams pa yin |

51a daṅ: gaṅ P, D
51c yis: yi PK
51d ’chir: ’chi P, D
52 one hemistich (cd or ab) is lacking in *Ms*
52b hīyate *ex con T.* ñams pa: dīyate *Ms*
52c bdag: dag PK, DK

nāntarātmātmano 'nyaś cet pratijñā te ca hīyate /
xx xx xx xx xx xx xx xx //53//

| bdag las ñi tshe'i bdag de ni |
| gźan min źe na'aṅ dam bcas ñams |
| gaṅ yaṅ bdag gi bde sdug sogs |
| 'gro bas mi śes gtso bo min |

yadi sūkṣmo mahān nāyaṃ mahāṃś cen nāsya sūkṣmatā /
na caiko rūpidharmaś ca katham ātmany arūpiṇi //54//

| gal te phra yin 'di che min |
| chen po yin na phra ba min |
| gcig kyaṅ ma yin gzugs kyi chos |
| ji ltar gzugs med bdag gi yin |

na yuktā hastidṛṣṭāntād ekasyānekarūpatā / 20a[5]
karaḥ karī yato neṣṭaḥ karādīnāṃ na caikatā //55//

| gcig ñid du ma'i ṅo bo ru |
| glaṅ po'i dpe 'di mi rigs te |
| sna ni glaṅ du mi 'dod phyir
| sna sogs rnams kyaṅ gcig ñid min |

53 one hemistich (cd or ab) is lacking in *Ms*
53b hīyate *ex con T.* ñams pa: dīyate *Ms*
53b źe: źi PK
54a yadi *ex con T.* gal te: ati° *Ms*
55a hasti° *ex con T.* glaṅ po: h[ ]sti° *Ms*

sūryādivarṇo yady ātmā syād avarṇaḥ kathaṃ ca saḥ /
neṣṭā palāśadṛṣṭāntād ātmano ’nekarūpatā //56//

| gaṅ yaṅ bdag ni ñi sogs mdog
| yin na mdog bral ji ltar yin |
| bdag de du ma’i ṅo bo yi |
| dper na pa la śa mi ’dod |

yataḥ palāśo naiko ’sti sarvadā vikṛtātmakaḥ /
mūlādayo yato naike pratyayaiś cāpi bhedinaḥ //57//

| gcig pu pa la śa med de |
| kun tu ’gyur ba’i bdag ñid daṅ |
| ji ltar rtsa ba sogs du mar |
| rkyen la sogs pas ’byed pa’i phyir |

jyāyastā ca paratvaṃ ca tadanyāpekṣam iṣyate /
saṃbhavo ’muṣya ca vidher ekatve katham iṣyate //58// 20a[6]

| gtso bo ñid daṅ dam pa ñid |
| de las gźan la bltos nas ’dod |
| gcig ñid yin na tshul ’di ñid |
| yod par ji ltar ’dod par bya |

56d ’neka° *ex con T.* du ma: neka° *Ms*
57c naike: naikai *Ms*
57c du: su P
58b bltos: ltos DK, D
58c saṃbhavo ’muṣya *ex con T.* ’di ñid yod par: [ ]mbhavo muṣya *Ms*

dravyaṃ yadi bhaved ātmā dravyatvāt sarvago na saḥ /
ghaṭavan nāpi nityaḥ syāt tena pūrṇaṃ kuto jagat //59//

| gal te bdag de rdzas yin na |
| rdzas yin phyir na kun khyab min |
| bum pa bźin du rtag mi 'gyur |
| des na 'gro ba rgyas ji ltar |

dravyasyādhāratā yuktā dravyaṃ cātmā na yujyate /
khapuṣpavad ajātatvān nādhāratvaṃ yatas tataḥ //60//

| rdzas ni rten du rigs 'gyur na |
| bdag ni rdzas su mi rigs te |
| nam mkha'i me tog ji lta bar |
| de bźin ma skyes phyir rdzas med |

kasmin sarvāṇi bhūtāni bhavanty ātmaiva paśyataḥ /
ātmatānātmano neṣṭā yathābhāvasya bhāvatā //61//

| thams cad byuṅ gyur byuṅ ba daṅ |
| 'byuṅ 'gyur bdag med ji ltar mthoṅ |
| bdag med bdag tu mi rigs te |
| ji ltar dṅos med ṅo bo bźin |

60cd ji lta bar | de bźin, *yathā tathā, *Ms* yataḥ tataḥ, *gaṅ phyir de'i phyir
61a kasmin: kesmiṃ *Ms*
61b bdag med (*anātman)! ātmā *Ms*
61c ātmatānātmano *ex con T.* bdag med bdag tu: ātmatādyātmano *Ms*

na bālādyaviśeṣo 'to nirādhāro 'nidarśanaḥ / 20b[1]
ekatvenātmano naikadoṣopaplavasaṃbhavaḥ //62//

| byis sogs khyad par med ma yin |
| rten med pa daṅ dpe med phyir |
| bdag gcig yin na du ma yi |
| skyon rnams 'byuṅ bar 'gyur ma yin |

maitrātmā caitrakaraṇaiś caitrātmavad apīkṣyatām /
caitrād abhinnamūrtitvād deśābhedād athāpi vā //63//

| tsai tra'i bdag de mai tra'i byed |
| mai tra'i bdag gi'aṅ de bźin te |
| tsai tra tha dad min dṅos phyir |
| yaṅ na [ ] yul la dbye med phyir |

62a na bālādyaviśeṣo 'to *ex con T.* byis sogs khyad par med ma yin...phyir:
na[ ] viśeṣā to *Ms*
62b nirādhāro *ex con T.* rten med pa: nidhādhār/n)o *Ms*; 'nidarśanaḥ *ex con T.* dpe med: nidarśanaḥ *Ms*
62c ekatvenātmano: ekatve nātmano L
63a caitra° *ex con T.* tsai tra'i: caikatra° *Ms*
63a tsai: tse PK, DK; mai: me PK, DK
63b apīkṣyatām: apīkṣatām *Ms*, L, H
63b mai: me PK, DK
63c tsai: tse PK, DK

sukhaduḥkhopabhoktā ca tanmuktau cāpi mucyatām /
tadbandhe cāpi bandho 'sya tadduḥkhe vāstu duḥkhitaḥ //64//

| bde daṅ sdug bsṅal spyod pa daṅ |
| de grol bas kyaṅ grol ba daṅ |
| de bciṅs kyaṅ bciṅs pa daṅ |
| de sdug pas kyaṅ sdug ñid 'gyur |

na ghaṭākāśadṛṣṭāntāt sarveṣāṃ tadasaṃbhavaḥ /
ākāśasya yato 'siddham ekatvaṃ bhāvatāpi ca //65// 20b[2]

| bum pa'i nam mkha' dper bstan pa |
| kun la de ni 'byuṅ ma yin |
| gaṅ phyir nam mkha' gcig ñid du |
| khyod kyis de ni ma grub ste |

64b °muktau: °mukto *Ms*
64d tadduḥkhe: taduḥkhe *Ms*
65a °dṛṣṭāntāt: °dṛṣṭāntā *Ms*
65c ākāśasya: ākāśa[ ] *Ms*
65d kyis: kyi PK, P, DK, D

mukto dravyasya yo bhāvas tad ākāśaṃ hi sāṃvṛtam /
gatir gatimatāṃ tatra so 'vakāśo 'vakāśinām //66//

| rdzas kyi ṅo bos gaṅ stoṅ pa |
| de ni kun rdzob nam mkha' yin |
| de la 'gro ldan 'gro ba daṅ |
| de ni skabs 'dod skabs can no |

nāto 'nāvṛtir ākāśaṃ nāvakāśasya dātṛ ca /
taddhetūktau tadastitve hetos tu syād asiddhatā //67//

| des na nam mkha' sgrib med min |
| skabs sbyin pa yaṅ ma yin te |
| de yod gtan tshigs smras pa yis |
| gtan tshigs 'di yaṅ ma grub ñid |

66a mukto: mukta *Ms*
66a kyi: kyis P
66d 'vakāśinām: vakāśitāṃ *Ms*
67a 'nāvṛtir *ex con T.* sgrib med: nāvṛ[ ]r *Ms*
67a mkha': mkha'i PK, DK
67b nāvakāśa° *ex con T.* skabs...ma yin: tāvakāśa° *Ms*

nāpi hetvanupādānād ākāśaṃ bhāva iṣyate /
vandhyātanayavan nāpi tad ekam ata eva hi //68//

| rgyu las ñe bar ma byuṅ ba |
| nam mkha' dṅos por mi 'dod do |
| de ni gcig kyaṅ ma yin te |
| mo gśam gyi ni bu bźin no |

mṛdo ghaṭādirūpāyā mṛjjātīyatayaikatā / 20b[3]
anyā cānyā ca kuṇḍādāv ato naikatvam ātmanaḥ //69//

| bum sogs gzugs kyi sa rnams ni |
| sa yi rigs su gcig na yaṅ |
| rdza sogs gźan daṅ gźan yin ltar |
| des na bdag ni gcig ma yin |

68ab °upādānād ākāśaṃ: °upādānnākāśaṃ *Ms*
68c vandhyātanayavan: vandhyāt anayavan H
69c rdza: sa P, D
69d ātmanaḥ *ex con T.* bdag ni: ānataḥ *Ms*

jñatve saty aviparyāsān neṣṭā jñasyābhimānitā /
ajñatve cāviparyāsān neṣṭājñasyābhimānitā //70//

| śes ñid phyin ci ma log pas |
| śes 'di ṅa rgyal mi rigs so |
| mi śes ñid na'aṅ log med pas |
| mi śes ṅa rgyal mi 'dod do |

vyomavac cāvikāritvād asaṅgatvād athāpi vā /
nātmanaḥ kartṛtā yuktā yuktā nāpi ca bhoktṛtā //71//

| nam mkha' bźin du 'gyur med phyir |
| de bźin chags pa med pa'i phyir |
| bdag ni byed por mi rigs la |
| za ba po yaṅ mi rigs so |

kartā cel lipyate nātmā kartur iṣṭaṃ phalaṃ katham /
na yukto rājadṛṣṭāntaḥ pāpabhāṅ nṛpatir yataḥ //72// 20b[4]

| byed po bdag yin mi gos pa |
| byed po'i 'bras bu 'dod ji ltar |
| mi dbaṅ sdig daṅ bcas pa'i phyir |
| rgyal po'i dpe ni mi rigs so |

70a log: logs P
70d 'jña° *ex con T.* mi śes: jña° *Ms*
70d do: pas P
72b ji: ci DK, D
72c °dṛṣṭāntaḥ: °dṛṣṭānta *Ms*

na caikatādvitīyasya yuktā bāhyānapekṣaṇāt /
ekatvayogād ekaś ced yogas tasyaiva netaraḥ //73//

| phyi rol la ni ma bltos par |
| gcig ñid ṅo bo ñid mi rigs |
| gcig ñid daṅ ldan pas śe na |
| de ni de daṅ ldan ma yin |

anekaṃ kalpayitvā ced ekatā tadapohataḥ /
ekatvaṃ tattvato na syāt kalpanā sāṃvṛtī yataḥ //74//

| du ma ñid du brtags pa daṅ |
| bsal ba gcig ñid yin źe na |
| ji ltar brtags pa kun rdzob phyir |
| des na gcig de don dam min |

73a bltos: ltos DK, D
73b bāhyānapekṣaṇāt *ex con T.* phyi rol la ni ma bltos par: pohyānapekṣaṇāḥ *Ms*
73b gcig ñid ṅo bo ñid: *Ms* ekatādvitīyasya, T *gcig ñid ṅo bo gñis
73c śe: źe P, DK
73d netaraḥ *ex con T.* de...ma yin: tenannaḥ *Ms*
74a brtags: btags N, P, D, C; daṅ: dag PK, P, DK, D
74b ced: caid *Ms*
74b bsal: gsal PK, P, DK
74c brtags: btags P, D
74d de: ste DK

nityaikatvādirūpeṇa tattvataś cet sa vidyate /
ekādiśabdadhīvṛttir arthe sati niratyayā //75//

| rtag daṅ gcig sogs ṅo bo yis |
| don dam de yod yin źe na |
| gcig sogs sgra daṅ blo 'jug pa |
| don yod na ni skyon med 'gyur |

ekatvādivikalpāc ca katham asyāvikalpatā / 20b[5]
vikalpaviṣaye cārthe vācāṃ vṛttir avāritā //76//

| gcig la sogs par rnam rtog pa |
| 'di ni ji ltar mi rtog ñid |
| rnam par rtog pa'i yul don la |
| tshig 'jug pa ni ma bkag go |

dhiyām aviṣayo hy evaṃ kathaṃ vāgocaro girām /
avācyo nirvikalpo 'pi vitathaḥ pūrvanītivat //77//

| 'di ltar blo yi yul min daṅ |
| ṅag gi spyod yul min ji ltar |
| brjod med rtog pa med pa yaṅ |
| sṅar bstan rigs pas brdzun pa ñid |

76a rnam: rnam par N, P
76b asyāvikalpatā *ex con T.* 'di ni...mi rtog ñid: as[ ]vikalpatā *Ms*
76b ji: ci P, DK, D; rtog: rtag PK, DK
77a aviṣayo (cāviṣayo, vāviṣayo?) *ex con T.* yul min: ca viṣayo *Ms*
77c rtog: rtogs P, D
77d rigs: rig PK

buddhyā ced darśanān muktis tadbhedāt katham ekatā /
nānātvadhīvat sā ca syād vitathā pūrvavad grahāt //78//

|xx xx xx xx xx xx xx|
|xx xx xx xx xx xx xx|
|xx xx xx xx xx xx xx|
|xx xx xx xx xx xx xx|

ajātisamatāṃ yāte jñāne 'bhedāt kva darśanam /
adarśanād vimuktiḥ syān muktir vā nāsti kasyacit //79// 20b[6]

|xx xx xx xx xx xx xx|
|xx xx xx xx xx xx xx|
|xx xx xx xx xx xx xx|
|xx xx xx xx xx xx xx|

78-84 lacking in all Tibetan recensions
78a buddhyā: budhyā *Ms*
79a ajātisamatāṃ cum Lindtner 1985a
79b 'bhedāt: bhedāt *Ms*
79c vimuktiḥ: vimukti *Ms*
79d nāsti: nā[ ]i *Ms*

bodhe sati tadutpādād ajātisamatā kutaḥ /
saty abhāvād anutpāde tadvikalpasamo 'pi saḥ //80//

|xx xx xx xx xx xx xx|
|xx xx xx xx xx xx xx|
|xx xx xx xx xx xx xx|
|xx xx xx xx xx xx xx|

ajātir jātivad dharmas tadabhāve ca sā satī /
naivātmasamatā tasya yuktā nāpi na tatsthatā //81//

|xx xx xx xx xx xx xx|
|xx xx xx xx xx xx xx|
|xx xx xx xx xx xx xx|
|xx xx xx xx xx xx xx|

ajasya ko na bhedo 'sti mato yena samarthanam /
na jātājātayor iṣṭam ajatvaṃ tattvato yataḥ //82//

|xx xx xx xx xx xx xx|
|xx xx xx xx xx xx xx|
|xx xx xx xx xx xx xx|
|xx xx xx xx xx xx xx|

80a bodhe: bodhye *Ms*
80c saty abhāvād: satyabhāvād L, H
80d °samo: °kṣayo (?) *Ms*
82a ajasya cum Nak.: ajaś ca *Ms*, H; bhedo 'sti cum Nak.: ced asti *Ms*
82b mato: matā *Ms*, H

khapuṣpāt tadabhedaś ced asatpakṣaparigrahaḥ /
parinișpattibhedaś ced advaitaṃ na prasidhyati //83// 21a[1]

|xx xx xx xx xx xx xx|
|xx xx xx xx xx xx xx|
|xx xx xx xx xx xx xx|
|xx xx xx xx xx xx xx|

nāto bhāvo na cābhāvo na pṛthaṅ nāpṛthak pumān /
na nityo nāpy anityaś ca na buddhidhvanigocaraḥ //84//

|xx xx xx xx xx xx xx|
|xx xx xx xx xx xx xx|
|xx xx xx xx xx xx xx|
|xx xx xx xx xx xx xx|

jñeyasya sarvathāsiddher nyāyyo buddher agocaraḥ /
dhīgocaranivṛttau ca syād girām apy agocaraḥ //85//

| śes bya ye nas ma grub pas |
| blo yi yul du mi rigs so |
| blo yi yul las log pas na |
| ṅag gi yul las log pa'aṅ yin |

83b parigrahaḥ: parigraha[ ] *Ms*
83c parinișpatti: [ ]ṣpātta *Ms:* parinișpattibhedaś L: parinișpatte bhedaś H
84d ca na: cāto *Ms*
85a jñeyasya: jñeya *Ms*
85b nyāyyo *ex con T.* rigs: nyāyo *Ms*, H
85c °nivṛttau *ex con T.* las log pas na: °nirvṛttau *Ms*
85d agocaraḥ: agocara *Ms*

tāthāgatīm avitathāṃ matvā nītim imāṃ śubhām /
tasmāj jātaspṛhais tīrthyaiḥ kṛtaṃ tatra mamāpi tat //86//

| de bźin gśegs pa'i mi brdzun pa'i |
| lugs 'di dge bar śes nas ni |
| de phyir mu stegs 'dod skyes te |
| de la bdag gir byas pa yin |

kaḥ śraddhāsyati tāṃ tatra pūrvāparavirodhinīm / 21a^{2}
atyantātulyajātīyaṃ maṇiratnam ivāyasaḥ //87//

| sṅon daṅ phyi mar 'gal ba yi |
| de yi lugs la su źig dad |
| śin tu rigs mi gcig pa'i phyir |
| lcags las nor bu rin chen bźin |

deśanāyās tu vaicitryād ihaivaṃ syād ayaṃ nayaḥ /
ākarṣaṇārtham ekeṣāṃ śeṣagrāhanivṛttaye //88//

| 'di ltar 'di ni lugs 'di la |
| kha cig dag ni draṅ phyir daṅ |
| lhag ma 'dzin las bzlog pa'i phyir |
| sna tshogs dag tu bstan pa yin |

86a avitathāṃ: avitathā *Ms*
86c tīrthyaiḥ: tīrthaiḥ *Ms*
86d tat: taṃ *Ms*
87a kaḥ *ex con T.* su źig: [ ] *Ms*
87b dad: daṅ P, D
88b ihaivaṃ: ihaiva *Ms*
88c las: la P

ajātatā hi bhāvānāṃ svabhāvo ’kartṛmattvataḥ /
anapāyitvataś cāsāv ātmety api nigadyate //89//

| dṅos po rnams ni ma skyes ñid |
| raṅ bźin bcos ma med pa’i phyir |
| ’di la ñams pa med pas na |
| bdag ces kyaṅ ni brjod pa yin |

eko ’sāv ekarūpatvād bhāvabhede ’py abhedataḥ /
sarvagaḥ sarvadharmatvān nityaś cāpy avināśataḥ //90// 21a[3]

| tha dad dṅos kyaṅ dbyer med phyir |
| ṅo bo gcig phyir gcig ñid yin |
| kun khyab chos rnams thams cad phyir |
| rtag pa’aṅ de yin mi ñams phyir |

89b ’kartṛmattvataḥ: kartṛmatvataḥ *Ms*: ’kṛtrimatvataḥ (*ex con T.* bcos ma med pa’i phyir) L, H
89c anapāyitvataś *ex con T.* ñams pa med pas na: anayāyitvataś *Ms*
90a dbyer: dbye PK
90c sarvagaḥ *ex con T.* kun khyab: sarva[ ] *Ms*; °tvān *ex con T.*: phyir: °tvā *Ms*
90d pa’aṅ: pa P

ajātatvād ajāto ’yam ata evājarāmaraḥ /
acyutaś cyutyabhāvāc ca prakarṣatvāt paraṃ matam //91//

| ma skyes phyir na skye med ñid |
| de ñid phyir na rga śi med |
| ’pho ba med phyir ’di ’pho med |
| rab mthar thug phyir mchog ñid yin |

na rūpaśabdagandhādir na bhūmyagnijalānilāḥ /
nākāśaśaśisūryādir na manojñānalakṣaṇaḥ //92//

| gzugs daṅ sgra daṅ dri sogs min |
| sa daṅ me daṅ chu rluṅ min |
| nam mkha’ zla ba ñi ma min |
| yid daṅ śes pa’i mtshan ñid min |

sarvaś cāsau svabhāvatvān na sarvaṃ cāvināśataḥ /
tatra kleśādyanutpatteḥ śuddho ’sau śānta eva ca //93//

| thams cad ’di yin raṅ bźin phyir |
| ñams pa med phyir thams cad min |
| de la ñon moṅs skye med phyir |
| dag pa ’di yin źi ñid yin |

91a ajāto ’yam *ex con T.* skye med ñid de ñid: ajātaś cāyam *Ms*
91b °ajarāmaraḥ *ex con T.* rga śi med: °jarāmaraḥ *Ms*
91d ñid yin: yin ñid PK, DK
92b bhūmy *ex con T.* sa: bhūpy *Ms*; °anilāḥ: °anilaḥ *Ms*
93a sarvaś cāsau *ex con T.* thams cad ’di: sarvasyāsau *Ms*
93b cāvināśataḥ: cādināmataḥ *Ms*
93d yin: ’di PK, P, DK, D

sa kalpanāsamāropād vācyo ’vācyas tu tattvataḥ / 21a[4]
sarvathā cāpy avācyatvād ukta eṣa nirañjanaḥ //94//

| de ni brtags pas sgro btags nas |
| brjod bya yaṅ dag brjod bya min |
| ye nas brjod bya ma yin phyir |
| ’di ni dri ma med ces bstan |

īdṛśo yady abhipreta ātmā hi bhavatām api /
nāmādibahusādharmyān nirdoṣaḥ sopapattikaḥ //95//

| gaṅ źig ’di ltar mṅon ’dod pa |
| khyod kyis bdag kyaṅ yin na ni |
| miṅ sogs chos maṅ ’dra ba la |
| skyon med rigs pa daṅ bcas yin |

nairātmyād eva bhītānāṃ bhītyā tatraiva ca sthitiḥ /
ākāśād iva bhītasya kva cānyatra sthitir bhavet //96//

| bdag med ñid kyis ’jigs pa rnams |
| ’jigs kyaṅ de ñid la gnas te |
| nam mkha’ ’jigs par gyur pa dag|
| gźan pa’i gnas ’ga’ med pa bźin |

94a °samāropād *ex con T.* sgro btags nas: °samāropa[ ] *Ms*
94a brtags: btags P, D
94b vācyo *ex con T.* brjod bya: [ ]cyo *Ms*; ’vācyas *ex con T.* brjod bya min: vācyas *Ms*
95b bhavatām *ex con T.* khyod kyis: tavatām *Ms*
95d rigs: rig PK
96b bhītyā *ex con T.* ’jigs: dṛṣṭyā *Ms*; ca: va *Ms*
96d ’ga’: ’ga’ aṅ DK

svāgataṃ kriyatāṃ tṛptir nātra kaścin nivāryate /
buddhānāṃ lokabandhūnāṃ tattvāmṛtam idaṃ param //97// 21a[5]

| saṅs rgyas 'jig rten gñen rnams kyi |
| de ñid bdud rtsi mchog 'di ni |
| 'di la 'ga' yaṅ bkag med pas |
| legs par 'oṅs so ñoms par gyis |

api tv ātmatvakartṛtvabhoktṛtvādir nirāspadaḥ /
saṃtyajyatām asadgrāho bhūtadṛkpratibandhakaḥ //98//

| yaṅ dag lta la sgrib med pa'i |
| bdag ni byed po za po sogs |
| rten med brdzun pa'i 'dzin pa ni |
| des na spaṅ ba kho nar gyis |

97a kyi: kyis P, D
97b nivāryate *ex con T.* bkag pa: na vāryate *Ms*
97d tattvāmṛtam *ex con T.* de ñid bdud rtsi: ta[ ]m *Ms*; paraṃ *ex con T.* mchog: padaṃ *Ms*
98b °tvādir: °tvādi *Ms*
98c °grāho: °graho *Ms*
98d bhūtadṛk°: bhūtadrik° *Ms*

svabhāvājātito 'jātir bhāvānāṃ tattvato matā /
svabhāvato hy ajātatvād uktaiṣā niḥsvabhāvatā //99//

| dṅos rnams raṅ bźin skye med phyir |
| de ñid du na skye med 'dod |
| ṅo bo ñid kyis skye med ñid |
| 'di yi ṅo bo ñid du bstan |

naiḥsvābhāvyaṃ ca nairātmyaṃ na tad ātmā virodhataḥ /
anātmā ced bhaved ātmā gorabhāvo 'pi gaur bhavet //100//

| dṅos med ñid ni bdag med pa |
| de ni bdag min 'gal ba ñid |
| bdag med bdag tu 'gyur źe na |
| ba [g]laṅ min pa'aṅ ba [g]laṅ 'gyur |

99a 'jātir *ex con T.* skye med: jāti *Ms*
99c kyis: kyi P
100a naiḥ°: nai° *Ms*
100b tad ātmā: tadātmā H

yuktaḥ svabhāvābhāvo 'sau kathaṃ kartṛtvabhoktṛte / 21a[6]
dṛṣṭe vandhyāsutasyeha nākasmāt kartṛbhoktṛte //101//

| dṅos po'i ṅo bo med 'di ni |
| ji ltar byed po za por rigs |
| gaṅ phyir mo gśam dag gi bu |
| byed po za por ma yin bźin |

itthaṃbhūtāt kathaṃ janma pralayas tatra vā katham /
na vyomakusume yuktā pralayotpādakalpanā //102//

| de ltar gyur las skye ji ltar |
| de la ñams par 'gyur ji ltar |
| mkha' la me tog med pa la |
| ji ltar skye 'jig brtags pa bźin |

101a yuktaḥ *ex con T.* rigs: yataḥ *Ms*
101b kartṛtvabhoktṛte *ex con T.* byed po za por: kartṛ ...(illeg.)[ ] ktṛte *Ms:* syāt: kartṛtābhoktṛte H: kartṛbhoktṛte L
101b ji: 'di PK, DK
101c °sutasyeha: sutasyeva L

svabhāvābhāvaviṣayā yāvad buddhiḥ pravartate /
dhīkalpanāsamāropās tāvad ekādikā matāḥ //103//

| dṅos po med pa'i yul dag la |
| ji srid blo ni 'jug gyur pa |
| blo yis brtags pas sgro btags phyir |
| de srid gcig la sogs par 'dod |

savikalpāvikalpā ca yadā buddhir nivartate /
dhiyām aviṣaye tasmin prapañcopaśamaḥ śivaḥ //104// 21b[1]

| rtog bcas rtog pa med pa las |
| gaṅ tshe blo ni log gyur pa |
| de tshe blo ni yul med phyir |
| spros pa ñer źi źi ba ñid |

vedāntatattvaviniścayo 'ṣṭamaḥ paricchedaḥ //

103c dhī°: dhīḥ° *Ms*; °samāropās: °samāropā *Ms*

103c brtags: btags PK, P, DK

103d ekādikā *ex con T.* gcig la sogs par: ekāntikā *Ms*; matāḥ: matā *Ms*

104a °vikalpā: °vikalpāś *Ms*

104a las: la PK

104c dhiyām *ex con T.* blo ni: viyām *Ms*

104d °śamaḥ: °śama[ ] *Ms*; śivaḥ *ex con T.* źi ba ñid (*śivatā or śamatā): [ ] ... (illeg.) *Ms*

TRANSLATION

[The Definitive Conclusion of Reality According to Sāṃkhya]

[Sāṃkhya Philosophy According to Bhāviveka]

[This sixth chapter introduces Sāṃkhya's definitive conclusion regarding the nature of ultimate reality. From the perspective of ultimate reality (*paramārtha*), Kapila[134] has taught that:]

[Primordial Matter and Self]

VI.1 [Primordial] Matter ([*mūla*]*prakṛti*) is unconscious, with three constituents (*guṇa*), of the nature of procreation (*prasavātmikā*). The Self (*puṃs*) is the opposite of this. Thus [Primordial Matter and Self should] incessantly [be meditated upon] by the [Sāṃkhya] practitioner (*abhyāsavat*).[135]

[Primordial Matter is unborn (*ajāta*), eternal (*nitya*), that which is enjoyed by an enjoyer (*bhoktṛ*), single (*ekākin*) and all-pervading (*vyāpin*).[136] It is unmanifest (*avyakta*), and thus is directly perceivable neither by the gods, the demons nor the humans,[137] being devoid of distinguishing features such as colour, size and form.

---

[134] On Kapila in Sāṃkhya and Sāṃkhya-Yoga, see Jacobsen 2008:31-56.

[135] The content of the *Sāṃkhyakārikā* 64 indicates that MHK-TJ VI.1-3 can be viewed as a syntactical and doctrinal unit. This notwithstanding, I have chosen to emendate VI.2b (°*anukāriṇaḥ* to °*anukāritā*) in accordance with the Tibetan translations and thus treat this apparent unit as three separate verses.

[136] For a comprehensive study of the concept of *prakṛti* in Sāṃkhya-Yoga, see Jacobsen 2002.

[137] Cf. *Sāṃkhyakārikā* 8.

> Primordial Matter is ungenerated (*avikṛti*); the great one (*mahat*), etc., are the seven aspects (*ākāra*) [or transformations of Matter]; these seven are both generative (*prakṛti*) and generated (*vikṛti*); the sixteen aspects are (derived) transformations (*vikāra*) [of Matter]; the Self (*puruṣa*) is neither generative nor generated.[138]

From Primordial Matter, the "great one" (*mahat*) – i.e., the intellect (*buddhi*) – emerges; and from the intellect comes egoity (*ahaṃkāra*).[139] Out of egoity emerge the five subtle elements (*tanmātra*): sound (*śabda*), contact (*sparśa*), form (*rūpa*), taste (*rasa*) and smell (*gandha*). These seven modifications (*vikṛti*) are both generated and generative, and constitute the seven aspects (*ākāra*) of the transformation of Matter, which constitutes the eighth generative principle. Out of the five subtle elements, the sixteen derived products (*vikāra*) are generated: the five gross elements (*mahābhūta*), the five senses of knowing (*buddhīndriya*), the five senses of action (*karmendriya*) and the mind (*manas*).[140] The five gross elements[141] have specific properties (*viśeṣa*), since they have

[138] On this almost verbatim quotation of *Sāṃkhyakārikā* 3, see Introduction. The seven aspects or transformations (*vikṛti*) of Matter (*prakṛti*) are basic principles (*tattva*) that are both produced and productive of other products. They include the intellect (*buddhi*) or the great one (*mahat*), egoity (*ahaṃkāra*) and the five subtle elements (*tanmātra*). The sixteen transformations of Matter, however, are principles that are produced but do not in turn produce other products. They include the mind (*manas*), the five 5 senses of knowing (*buddhīndriya*), the five senses of action (*karmendriya*), and the five gross elements (*mahābhūta*).

[139] On the emergence and functions of the principles (*tattva*), see *Sāṃkhyakārikā* 22-38.

[140] *Sāṃkhyakārikā* 22-38.

[141] The five gross elements are space or ether (*akāśa*), wind (*vāyu*), fire (*tejas*), water (*āpas*), and earth (*pṛthivī*).

become different from the subtle elements by way of their nature of being tranquil (*śānta*), turbulent (*ghora*), etc.[142] The five sense-capacities (*buddhīndriya*) are eyes (*cakṣus*), ears (*śrotra*), nose (*ghrāṇa*), tongue (*rasana*) and skin (*tvac*).[143] They are called senses of knowing because they either comprehend their own objects (*viṣaya*) or anticipate the operations of the intellect (*buddhivṛtti*).[144] The Self perceives the object by means of these "doors" (*dvāra*).[145] The five senses of action (*karmendriya*) are speech (*vāc*), hands (*pāṇi*), feet (*pāda*), rectum (*pāyu*) and genitals (*upastha*). They are called senses of action because they precede activity and are in proximity to the Self. The sixteen derived products are transformed through desire (*tṛṣṇā*). That which is characterized by equilibrium (*sāmyāvasthā*) of the three constituents (*guṇa*) is the unmanifest (*avyakta*) Matter.[146] The intellect is characterized by ascertainment (*adhyavasāya*) of objects.[147] Egoity is characterized by self-conceit (*abhimāna*).[148] Mind has a double nature. When it is similar to the intellect, it is a sense of knowing, and when it is similar to action, it is a sense of action.[149] Intellect, mind and egoity constitute the so-called internal organ

---

[142] *Sāṃkhyakārikā* 38.

[143] *Sāmkhyakārikā* 26.

[144] *Sāṃkhyakārikā* 34, 35.

[145] The Self perceives the object by means of these sense capacities ("doors") together with the three "door-keepers" (*dvārin*): the intellect, egoity and the mind. See *Sāṃkhyakārikā* 35.

[146] The occurrence of the term **sāmyāvasthā*/**avaiṣamya* (*cha mnyam*) in TJ VI.1 and VI.25-26 is of significance because previous researchers (Larson and Bhattacharya 1987:37) have regarded this as an innovation that first appeared in the 16th century with Vijñānabhikṣu. Jens W. Borgland's (Oslo University) recent studies indicate that this term also appears three times in the *Sāṃkhyaśāsanaparīkṣā* of the *Satyaśāsanaparīkṣā* (30, 3-4; 30, 6-8; 30, 12) by Vidyānandin, the 8th-century Jain philosopher.

[147] Cf. *Sāṃkhyakārikā* 23, 27.

[148] *Sāṃkhyakārikā* 24.

[149] *Sāṃkhyakārikā* 27.

(*antaḥkaraṇa*).[150] The subtle element of sound (*śabdatanmātra*), etc., is the generic essence of sound (*śabdasāmānya*), etc., and is thus devoid of the characteristics of specific sounds,[151] such as soft (*śānta*), violent (*ghora*), indistinct (*mūḍha*) and so forth.[152] Out of the five subtle elements emerge the five gross elements: from sound comes space, from touch comes wind, from form comes fire, from taste comes water and from smell comes earth. The fifty categories (*padārtha*) of the phenomenal creation include the nine contentments (*tuṣṭi*), the eight spiritual attainments (*siddhi*), the twenty-eight dysfunctions (*aśakti*) and the five misconceptions (*viparyaya*).[153] All things that emerge from the transformation of Matter are known as "the field" (*kṣetra*), and the Self is understood to be the knower of the field (*kṣetrajña*).[154] The Self is neither generative nor generated; it is of the nature of consciousness (*caitanya*). It is unborn, eternal, unmade, the enjoyer (*bhoktṛ*), the most essential thing (*pradhāna*), all-pervasive and uncaused. It is contrary to the three constituents and is not characterized by

---

[150] *Sāṃkhyakārikā* 33.

[151] Larson 1979:188; *Sāṃkhyakārikā* 38.

[152] *Sāṃkhyakārikā* 38.

[153] See *Sāṃkhyakārikā* 46-51 regarding traditional and scholarly interpretations of the Sāṃkhya notion of the phenomenal creation (*pratyayasarga*) and its fifty categories (*padārtha*), divided into the nine contentments (*tuṣṭi*), the eight perfections (*siddhi*), the 28 dysfunctions (*aśakti*), and the five fundamental misconceptions (*viparyaya*). Technical terms such as *ambhas/salila* and *tāra/sutāra* seem to have presented an almost incomprehensible problem not only for contemporary reseachers, but also for Bhāviveka himself, and most certainly for the Tibetan translator of TJ. Apart from this, TJ seems to present alternate explanations to those presented in the various *Sāṃkhyakārikā* commentaries (see Larson and Bhattacharya 1987:56-59, 631-34, n.20).

[154] The term *kṣetrajña* is not found in *Sāṃkhyakārikā*. According to Johnston (1937:55, 83), after classical Sāṃkhya formally adopted *puruṣa* as the technical term for the Self all earlier terms gradually fell into disuse. However, apart from *puruṣa*, MHK-TJ VI also employs *ātman* and *kṣetrajña*.

production. It generates knowledge by means of the intellect (*pratyaya*). It is unborn, and because it is capable of enjoying, it is the subject (*viṣayin*). It is eternal, because it is without dissolution and creation; it has no distinguishing feature since it is neither generative nor generated and it is devoid of parts because it is a single entity. It is endless (*ananta*) because it without beginning and end. These are the defining characteristics of the Self.[155] The definition of perception is as follows: "Perception is the activity of the ear, etc." (*śrotrādivṛtti pratyakṣam*).[156] The sense-organ (*indriya*) is that which receives the object of perception, perception (*dṛṣṭa*)[157] is that which has an object (*viṣayin*), and the Self (*puruṣa*) is the perceiver (*draṣṭṛ*) of the object. Form (*rūpa*) and so forth are not different from substance (*dravya*). Parts and their possessor, cause and effect, defining characteristics and their possessor are all one.]

[The Imitation of the Operations of the Intellect through Reflection or Transformation]

VI.2 When the mind is dominated by [the constituent of] *sattva*, the Self imitates the operations of the intellect (*buddhivṛtti*)[158] either

---

155 Cf. *Sāṃkhyakārikā* 17, 19.

156 According to Frauwallner (1958), this definition of perception derives from a revised version of the *Ṣaṣṭitantra,* composed in the 4th century CE by Vārṣagaṇya (see *Yuktidīpikā* p. 76, l. 21; p. 5, l. 11; Larson and Bhattacharya 1975:10). In the *Sāṃkhyadvātriṃśikā* (see above), Siddhasena Divākara's doxographical account of Sāṃkhya philosophy, perception is similarly defined. See *Pramāṇasamuccaya* (Hattori 1968:52f.) with regard to Dignāga's critique of *pratyakṣa* as the functioning of the auditory and other organs. On *Sāṃkhya* epistemology according to the *Yuktidīpikā*, see Harzer 2006.

157 Cf. *Sāṃkhyakārikā* 4, 5.

158 Cf. *Yogasūtrabhāṣya* IV.22.

through the arising of a reflection (*pratibimba*) or by means of a transformation (*pariṇāma*).[159]

[When there is a cognition (*avabodha*) of an object (*artha*) by the mind (*manas*), a reflection (*pratibimba*) of this cognition arises in the Self (*puruṣa*) like the reflection of the moon in still water; however, no transformation (*pariṇāma*) of the Self occurs. Then again, despite the fact that no real transformation occurs, a reflection of the object, which is first fully comprehended (*parijñāta*) by the intellect (*buddhi*), nonetheless arises in that Self. Alternatively, because the Self imitates the intellect's comprehension of the object, there is a transformation (*pariṇāma*) that is similar to a reflection in a mirror, although no factual change (*vikṛti*) occurs.]

[Liberation of Self from Matter]

VI.3 "I am one, and Matter is another"; by realizing this truth (*tattva*), the Self, having turned away from cause and effect, is said to be liberated.

[There are three kinds of liberation (*mokṣa*) of the Self which correspond to the three kinds of bondage (*bandha*):[160] (i) bondage

---

[159] Cf. *Yogasūtrabhāṣya* I.2.

[160] In contrast to *Sāṃkhyakārikā*, which only refers to one type of bondage and one type of release, the commentaries on *Sāṃkhyakārikā* (*Gauḍapādabhāṣya* 44, 62; *Yuktidīpikā* 45; *Māṭharavṛtti* 44, 45), refer to three forms of bondage (*bandha*) and three forms of liberation (*mokṣa*). According to Larson (1987:34-35), this indicates these to be old formulations that were simplified or eliminated in later accounts of Sāṃkhya. For information regarding the historical background of this theory in Sāṃkhya, see Frauwallner 1973:266. TJ deviates from the explanations given in these texts, especially concerning the third form of bondage, but agrees that ignorance, desire and activity are the root causes of bondage and that knowledge, the cessation of desire and activity liberate one from these three forms of

through Matter (*prākṛtikabandha*); (ii) bondage through modification (*vaikārikabandha*); and, (iii) bondage through material possession (*dhanabandha*). *Prākṛtikabandha* manifests as transformation into numerous bodies, such as those of the gods, the demons, the human beings, the animals, the hellish beings, the spirits and so forth. And since this bondage through Matter is comprised of pleasure, pain and delusion and characterized by egoity, subtle elements, the senses, etc., it is known as bondage through Matter. *Vaikārikabandha* consists of a modification of the senses by way of objects such as sound, touch, taste, form and smell. *Dhanabandha* refers to the bondage by material possession (*dhana*) of householders (*gṛhasta*), forest dwellers (*vanaprastha*), students (*brahmacārin*), etc. Merely through the desire (*tṛṣṇā*) for an object in cyclical existence one is deluded into identifying Self with Matter, believing them to be one and the same thing. Having developed supreme knowledge (*abhijñāna*) and full satisfaction through realization of the truth (*tattvadarśana*) that "I am one, and Matter is another", all cause and

---

bondage respectively. This threefold understanding of bondage and liberation is also found in other Sāṃkhya texts (e.g., the *Tattvasamāsa*). Here it is most interesting to note that in his *Lokatattvanirṇaya* (73) Haribhadrasūri quotes the *Tattvasamāsasūtra* (43), a text that according to Oberhammer (1960:87) is identical to the *Sāṃkhyakramadīpikā*. Prajñākaramati quotes this same verse in his commentary (*Pañjikā*) on Śāntideva's *Bodhicaryāvatāra* (La Vallée Poussin 1901-1914:455), and it is also quoted in the *Tattvasamāsasūtravṛtti* (Dvivedī 1969:79). If the latter is a commentary on the *Tattvasamāsasūtra* (see Garbe 1917:95) then, as suggested by Max Müller, the *Tattvasamāsasūtra* is an old text rather than a late one, as has been suggested by Keith (1975:103-4) and Larson (1987:318). Here it should be noted that, for his part, Larson does admit that some of the *sūtras* could indeed be rather old. Cf. Chakravarti (1975:168-170), who refers to the *Bhagavadajjukīyam* as an old Jain text (perhaps from the 8th or 9th century CE) that quotes the *Tattvasamāsasūtra*. With regard to the threefold understanding of bondage, see *Yogasūtrabhāṣya* I.24 and Jacobsen 2002:289f.

effect withdraws. In this way, according to some followers of Sāṃkhya, the Self becomes liberated from the bondage of Matter.]

[Liberation of Matter from Self]

VI.4 Alternatively (*vā*), [other] followers of Sāṃkhya declare the doctrine that Matter, having fulfilled its purpose [as expressed] by the understanding "I am not [it; it is not] mine",[161] is liberated as a result of compliance (*anugraha*) [to the Self].[162]

[At the beginning of creation, the manifold but fundamentally non-different objects of enjoyment emerge out of the one material substance. At the point of liberation (*muktikāla*), when one realizes that "I am not [it; it is not] mine", the purpose of egoity, in providing the Self with the objects of enjoyment, has been accomplished. As a result, Matter then becomes liberated, having made everything available to the Self. They are called Sāṃkhyas because they maintain that liberation is achieved when one completely understands the enumeration (*sāṃkhyā*) of the twenty-five principles.]

[Bhāviveka's Refutation of Sāṃkhya Philosophy]

[Critique of Consciousness as Intrinsic Nature or Self]

VI.5 Thus primordial materiality (*pradhāna*) and the Self (*puruṣa*) have been explained as employed [by the Sāṃkhyas]; but now they are [to be] scrutinized. Consciousness is claimed [by us] not to be the Self (*ātman*).

---

[161] *Sāṃkhyakārikā* 64.

[162] Cf. *Sāṃkhyakārikā* 59-61.

[In the *Tattvajñānaiṣaṇā*, the incompatibility of Matter and Self is briefly established in light of the negation of a supreme god (*īśvara*).[163] In this chapter their incompatibility will be scrutinized in greater detail. According to Sāṃkhya doctrine, consciousness is the intrinsic nature (*svabhāva*) of the Self, just as heat is intrinsic to fire. In our opinion, however, consciousness is the cognition (*avabodha*) of an object and the claim that it is a cognition of the Self is illogical.]

[Consciousness as the Cognition of an Object]

VI.6 Consciousness is the cognition of an object; in the absence of an object [it has] no existence. What, now, may this Self be – conscious or unconscious?

[Since a direct cognition of the object is based on the operations of the intellect (*buddhivṛtti*), which are, in turn, conditioned by cause and effect, the implication is that at the moment of liberation, when all cause and effect ceases, the operations of the intellect also cease since no object of cognition and hence no consciousness remains existent.[164] Thus, if it is said that at the moment of liberation the Self is endowed with consciousness, how can there be no cognition of an object (*jñeyāvabodha*)? And if the Self is said to be devoid of consciousness (*acaitanya*), this changes your doctrine since the intrinsic nature of the Self would then have to be abandoned. Objection: even after burning wood has been extinguished and transformed into charcoal, its intrinsic nature yet obtains. Similarly, although in the state of liberation all cause and effect ceases and no object of cognition exists, the intrinsic nature of the Self or

---

[163] MHK-TJ III.214-222.

[164] Cf. *Yogasūtrabhāṣya* I.3: *tadavasthe cetasi viṣayābhāvād buddhibodhātmā puruṣaḥ kiṃ svabhāva iti* /.

consciousness would still not have been abandoned. Answer: this is not a good comparison.]

VI.7 By the reasoning "The unburnt does not burn", due to the absence of burnables, it is as [we said] before [regarding the non-existence of consciousness in the absence of an object of knowledge (*jñeya*)]. Therefore, by the example of burning, [an intrinsically] conscious Self cannot be established.[165]

[Although burning wood that has reached a charcoal state does still burn to some degree, when the charcoal finally turns to ash, the word "burning" is no longer applicable. Similarly, as long as the cognition of an object exists, it is logical to claim that the Self is endowed with consciousness. However, in the state of liberation, where it is said that all cause and effect ceases and no object of cognition exists, it cannot be endowed with consciousness, just as ash cannot be endowed with fire. Hence, you have not established your point by way of the example (*dṛṣṭānta*). At the moment of liberation, then, the Self is not endowed with consciousness and its intrinsic nature has indeed been abandoned.]

VI.8 [In transmigratory existence (*saṃsāra*)] the cognition of the intellect (*buddhibodha*) is claimed [by Sāṃkhya] to assume the image of the object (*bodhyākāra*); and because a condition (*bhāva*) is dependent on a substance (*dravya*), that [cognition of the intellect] is dependent on the Self.[166]

[The senses (*indriya*) apprehend a given object (*artha*) by coming into conformity with it, after which it is apprehended by the mind

---

[165] Cf. MHK-TJ VIII.46.

[166] Cf. *Yogasūtrabhāṣya* II.20 (=IV.22).

(*manas*). Then the object is ascertained and fully comprehended by the intellect (*buddhi*), which grasps its image (*ākāra*). Just as a cloth's colouring depends upon the cloth, so does a substance's attribute (*bhāva*) depend upon the substance (*dravya*). Similarly, the intellect's apprehending capacity depends upon the Self, which benefits from that capacity merely by being in its proximity. If this is your proposal, then my response is as follows:]

VI.9 If the Self is [said to be] unchanged and self-sufficient (*svārtha*), this is a defective statement. Consciousness is nothing but the cognition [of an object]: what else could it be supposed to be?

[It is logical to define cognition (*bodha*) as the imitation (*anukāra*) of an image (*ākāra*) of something else that manifests the property (*dharma*) of change. However, since the Self is eternal and non-changing, it cannot take on the changing feature of that "something else". As such, a "consciousness of the Self" (*puruṣacaitanya*) that is distinct from that which is called *bodha* cannot possibly exist.]

[Critique of Consciousness as Distinct from the Intellect]

VI.10 It is not logical that the intellect (*mati*) is [identical to] consciousness, as it has a cause, just like a pot. Therefore, consciousness is not [identical to] the intellect. If it would be [identical to] the intellect, [we say the following:]

[It is reasonable to say that the Self is an exceptional (*asāmānya*) form of consciousness, being unborn and uncaused, and that the intellect is not exceptional, having been caused or generated. The conclusion is that the intellect cannot be the same as consciousness, since that would imply that a pot, which has a cause, can be consciousness. If this is indeed your position, then my response is as follows:]

VI.11 If [you say that] the intellect should be established as something other than consciousness, [we reply that] there is no evidence [for that claim]. And if [you say that there may be] an absence of it [(i.e., consciousness)] in the intellect, you are undone by agreement [with our position].

[You claim that consciousness – defined as the intrinsic nature of the Self – is different from the intellect since it is unmanifest and has no cause. Within the framework of this conception, however, it is impossible to find an example that proves your claim. And without an example, your claimed distinction cannot be established. Moreover, your contention that there is an absence of consciousness in the intellect is in opposition to your own conclusion, since this would imply that that there is an absence of consciousness in the Self as well – the intellect being dependent on the Self, according to your own doctrine.]

VI.12 [The idea of] an unborn [Self] having consciousness [as its intrinsic nature] is not reasonable, since it is unborn. If it (i.e. consciousness) belongs to the non-existent [Self], it is considered [by us] to be only the intellect.

[Just as a horn cannot be intrinsic to the nature of a hare, consciousness cannot be intrinsic to the nature of the unborn Self. Moreover, in order for the Self to possess consciousness it would have to be a manifest or apparent entity. It is therefore logical to conclude that consciousness, which arises in conformity with its object, is nothing more than the intellect. If you maintain that consciousness exists independently of the intellect, while at the same time postulating that there is no distinction between the operations of the knower (*abhijñavṛtti*) and the operations of the intellect (*buddhivṛtti*), which imitates the image of the object,[167] then we reply:]

VI.13 As an activity in the knower (*abhijñavṛtti*), not distinct from the activity in the intellect (*buddhivṛtti*), is claimed [by you], [we reply:] [even] if a difference (*bheda*) should exist [between the Self and the intellect], it is without distinction (*viśeṣa*); [therefore], if one does not exist, the other, too, is non-existent.[168]

[While it is possible to establish that separate substances are distinct based on their specific characteristics, the intellect and the Self are not separate substances, but rather one substance (intellect) and one metaphorical entity (the Self). As such, there can be no distinction between them in relation to any given act of cognition.][169]

VI.14 Whatever conception of a Self there may be, then, it is considered [by us] to be correct from one point of view (*kvacid*), but the opposite from another point of view (*kvacid*), like the view of a cairn (*sthāṇu*) as a cairn.

[Just as one can erroneously hold the notion that a pile of stones is a cairn, one can erroneously hold the false conception that an

---

[167] The introduction to MHK VI.13 in TJ VI.12 seems to be a corrupt rendering of MHK VI.13.

[168] See Introduction; *Yogasūtrabhāṣya* I.4, II.20, IV.22

[169] If there is a difference, which Sāṃkhya would argue, then they co-vary; *bheda* denotes an ontological difference, *viśeṣa* a functional difference, i.e., in both cases - whether different or not – there does not exist a consciousness that is independent of an object.

intrinsic Self exists. When the error (*bhrānti*) is removed, however, and one perceives things as they are, one realizes that there is no Self, but only the appearance of a Self, just as one realizes that there is no cairn, but only the appearance of cairnness (*sthāṇutva*). Objection: you yourself have erred by concluding that the notion of a Self is erroneous. However, when you have an insight into reality, you will know that the Self or consciousness exists in fact. Answer: to this argument I respond as follows:]

VI.15 In the perspective from which [the conception of a Self] is correct, [namely], by convention (*saṃvṛti*), it is [merely] proving what is [already] proved. Since [that conception], when correct, [only] denotes the mental faculties (*citta*),[170] it is not considered a Self by us.

[From the point of view of conventional truth (*vyavahārasatyanaya*), we also accept the conception of a Self (*ātmadhī*) that has the intellect (*citta*) as its object; this is merely stating the obvious. However, one cannot establish the reality (*yathārthatā*) of the Self on the basis of a vague understanding (*dhī*).]

VI.16 As for the truth of the conception of attributes such as omnipresence [ascribed to the Self], there is no evidence [for it] either in reality (*tattvatas*) or conventionally (*saṃvṛtyā*).

[Neither from the conventional nor from the absolute perspective can one find evidence establishing an omnipresent, etc., Self that is different from the intellect. Therefore your position has been refuted. To your statement that liberation consists of perceiving Matter (*prakṛti*) and Self (*puruṣa*) as ontologically distinct, I say:]

---

[170] The term *citta* is, in MHK-TJ VI, used synonymously with *buddhi*.

[Critique of Liberation of Self or Matter]

VI.17 [You say that] there is no consciousness in the unconscious [Matter (*prakṛti*)], nor any modification in the conscious [Self (*puruṣa*)]; for whom, [then], does the knowledge of reality dawn, so that he may attain liberation?

[Neither Matter, since it is without consciousness, nor the Self, since it has the characteristic of non-transformation (*apariṇāma*), is by itself capable of comprehending something outside itself (*anyadarśana*). After having identified itself with Matter, should the Self perceive that it is different, it must have then undergone a modification, and this is a contradiction in terms since a different cognition (*dhī*) cannot exist. And if knowledge of reality is defined as being different from the Self, how can this form of liberation exist. Since the Self is of the nature of (unchanging) consciousness, it cannot have a genuine cognition of something outside itself, and if Matter is devoid of consciousness, it is fundamentally incapable of even having a cognition.]

VI.18 Even if [it is said that] she [i.e., Matter] conforms (*anugraha*) to consciousness, the conviction 'I am not [that]' and so forth [ascribed to her] would be illogical as [she has] no consciousness; how much more [illogical this would be] in the absence of that [conformity]![171]

[Matter and Self are perceived as one (*ekatva*), being both the enjoyed and the enjoyer, respectively. Thus it is contraditory to say that at some point there arises the understanding, 'I am not that', since Matter is utterly unconscious. Similarly, the perception at the time of liberation that Matter and Self are separate contradicts the

[171] Critique of MHK VI.4.

notion that Matter conforms to consciousness. 'I am not [it; it is not] mine':[172] how can one consider such an understanding to be logical? All of this is entirely unreasonable.]

VI.19 Nor is her turning away logical, as she is common to many: it is claimed [by us] to be like [the turning away] of a common harlot one of whose lovers has died.

[Matter, as an object of enjoyment, is said to have been enjoyed by innumerable Selves in beginningless time, thus fulfilling its purpose through egoity. It is not reasonable, then, to say that at the point of liberation, Matter withdraws from a single Self, since this would logically imply that it has withdrawn from all Selves, all Selves being bound by one and the same material substance. One person's liberation from material attachment at the time of death cannot logically imply that all those that remain alive are automatically liberated from worldly existence as well. With regard to the liberation of the Self, there is the following error:]

[Critique of an Omnipresent Self]

VI.20 When the mind is dominated by [the constituent of] *sattva*, how is the realization of the truth (*tattva*) thought to be restricted [to one individual], when the Self is not separated in space from other Selves, nor covered?

[According to you, an individual Self dwells in each and every living body, such as that of a god, demigod, human being or animal, and all these Selves are omnipresent. When one such Self has become free from the covering of the mind – at the stage in which *sattva* has

---

172 MHK VI.4a.

become the mind's primary constituent – it is said to have achieved liberation. But how can such liberation occur in one space only (*ekadeśamātra*)? How can there be liberation of a single Self, while others remain in bondage, since all Selves are resting in the same space (*deśābheda*)? The liberation of one Self would thus logically imply the liberation of all others.]

VI.21 In the perception of sounds and so forth, too, and likewise [in qualities] such as virtue and vice, as it is equally questionable, a restriction [which is] not demonstrated is [deemed by us to be] non-existent.

[If the Self is omnipresent, and neither separated in space from other Selves nor covered by the mind, etc. (*āvṛti*), the activity (*vṛtti*) of the ear, etc., in relation to sound, etc., would be received in the same way by all Selves. Furthermore, one Self's engagement in virtuous behaviour (*dharma*) would imply that all Selves are also devoted to the same, as it would be with unrighteous behaviour as well. Nothing, in fact, could be logically confined to a single Self, since all Selves are considered to abide in the same space. This is as unreasonable as suggesting the dual appearance of light and darkness, rain and drought – all at the same time, all in the same space! If the Self is said to be omnipresent, it would have to exist as the intrinsic nature of everything. But then all the Selves would have to be merged into one and the same Self, and all the innumerable senses, intellects and bodies would have to be commonly shared (*sādhāraṇa*). Furthermore, the actions performed by one would automatically be performed by all, and those renounced by one, would be automatically renounced by all. Similarly, statements that delineate the separate duties of the priestly caste, the warrior caste and the servant caste would become meaningless. Not only would the system of *varṇas* be destroyed, but distinct categories like father, son, enemy, parent and so forth would be destroyed as well. Morever, the doctrine that the Self imitates the operation of the intellect via a transformation cannot be established.]

[Critique of the Self Imitating the Operation of the Intellect by Means of Transformation]

VI.22 If [you say that] the Self transforms,[173] [then] due to transforming just like sour milk, the Self is unconscious, nor is it causeless, nor omnipresent.

[And to those who maintain that liberation consists of the Self imitating the operation of the intellect via a reflection,[174] I reply:]

[Critique of the Self Imitating the Operation of the Intellect by Means of Reflection]

VI.23 The defects just stated likewise apply to the unchangeable consciousness, just as to an original image, on account of the reflection. [Objection: even though the close proximity of an original image causes the occurrence of a reflection in the water, no fundamental change of the water has occurred. Similarly, even though the close proximity of the object cognized by the intellect causes the occurrence of a reflection in the consciousness, no fundamental change of the consciousness has occurred. Answer: since the Self is said to contain the reflection of the object cognized by the intellect, it must be caused, non-omniscient and devoid of

---

[173] MHK-TJ VI.2.

[174] MHK-TJ VI.2.

unchangeable consciousness. Thus, as defined, it runs counter to its own intrinsic nature.]

[Liberation as Metaphorical]

VI.24 And because the Self does not conceptualize, [the statement] "I am another" is not logical. If [you say that it] is not a defect, being employed as a metaphor, [then perhaps] liberation [itself] may be metaphorical?

[Since cause and effect are said to cease at the time of liberation, and there is no object in proximity to the Self, what then remains to be conceptualized? How can the Self, which does not conceptualize, generate the conceptual construction, "I am another"? If we assume that the Self is free from conceptual construction, then a metaphoral Self must be concocted via the intellect. This would imply the existence of a metaphorical Self and its creator, a construction that would also subsist in the liberated state. If this is indeed the case, the very state of liberation would have to be regarded as a mere metaphor as opposed to something that is real. And because it is ultimately related to neither Primordial Matter nor the Self, the creation of a metaphor of liberation is unfortunate (*abhadra*). Beyond this, I reject the existence of Matter (*prakṛti*) as well. And if Matter is also a metaphor (*upacāra*), how can bondage and liberation exist? If you nonetheless maintain that Matter exists, you must present proof in support of your claim.]

[The Five Proofs for the Existence of Primordial Matter]

VI.25-26 [You say that undifferentiated] Matter (*pradhāna*) exists (i) because the separate evolutes (*bheda*) have a logical connection (*anvaya*) and (ii) because [they are] transformations (*pariṇāma*) [of

Matter (*prakṛti*)];[175] (iii) because of the relation of cause and effect; (iv) because [it is the locus] of causal capacity (*śakti*); and (v) because [there is no division] of manifoldness (*vaiśvarūpya*). What has been described in any way, [let it be] described like that. Just like the shards of pots, so, too, the separate evolutes [arise] from that which possesses them; therefore, the separate parts have a [common] cause.[176]

[When there is equilibrium (**sāmyāvasthā*)[177] between *sattva, rajas* and *tamas,* Matter is unmanifest (*avyakta*). There are five logical reasons (*hetu*), known as exclusionary inferences (*avīta*),[178] that prove the existence of Primordial Matter: 1) since all evolutes consist of pleasure, pain and delusion, they are connected (*anvaya*) to Matter; 2) even though Matter is unchangeable, all evolutes are transformations of Matter – i.e, the intellect emerges from Matter, egoity from the intellect, the subtle elements from egoity, the senses of knowing and action from the subtle elements and the gross elements from the senses of knowing and action;[179] 3)

---

[175] The second of the five classical arguments for the existence of *prakṛti* (found in *Sāṃkhyakārikā* 15) states that *prakṛti* exists because the separate evolutes have [limited] dimensions (*parimāṇa*), not because they are transformations (*pariṇāma*) of Matter! This "mistake" might be explained away as a typographical error (*pariṇāma* for *parimāṇa*) were it not for the fact that the commentary on this verse assumes that the verse reads *pariṇāma*! However, no known *Sāṃkhyakārikā* commentary has this reading and it is highly unlikely that the the learned Bhāviveka could have commited such an error. As such, it appears that this section of the TJ could not have come from his pen! One plausible explanation, according to Helmut Krasser (see Introduction), is that this and other interpolations were written by students on the basis of the teacher's oral instructions.

[176] Cf. *Sāṃkhyakārikā* 15-16.

[177] See MHK VI.1 n.

[178] Larson 1986:96ff.

[179] The order of the different evolutes deviates from that given in TJ VI.2. As

Primordial Matter (*pradhāna*) is the root cause of the intellect, egoity and so forth,[180] which are capable of transformation and are thus both cause and effect; 4) Matter possesses causal capacity (*śakti*) through which it generates all evolutes and the evolutes possess causal capacity through which they generate the different effects; and, 5) manifoldness consist of the intellect, egoity and the subtle and gross elements. Just as from the seed emerge the sprouts, trunk, branches, leaves and flowers of a tree, there emerge innumerable evolutes from the one Primordial Matter. In this way, the existence of a single omnipresent agent (*kartṛ*) can be ascertained. Everything that is endowed with *anvaya, pariṇāma, kāryakaraṇa, śakti* and *vaiśvarūpya* is generated from one and the same cause. The shards of a broken pot are connected to the earth and the fragrance of sandalwood is connected to the tree. Transformation indicates that the whole of a broken pot has changed into splinters. The shards come from the pot and the sandalwood splinters come from the tree, indicating the relation of effect to cause. The pot generates the shards as the sandalwood tree generates the splinters, indicating causal capacity. The existence of the numerous parts of a single sandalwood tree indicates the quality of manifoldness. In this way the evolutes are derived from the one Primordial cause; and this is our conclusion. Objection: I will now disprove each of your five proofs for the existence of Matter:]

Honda (1967:438-439) has pointed out, the enumeration placing the five gross elements (*mahābhūta*) last appears only in the *T'i-p'o-p'ou-sa-che-leng-k'ie-king-tchong-wai-tao-siao-tch'eng-nie-p'an-louen: prakṛti-buddhi-manas-ahaṃkāra-pañcamātra-pañcabuddhīndriya-pañcakarmendriya-pañcamahābhūta.*

[180] On the seven modifications of Matter (*prakṛtivikṛti*), see TJ VI.1.

[Refutation of the Five Proofs for the Existence of Primordial Matter]

VI.27 If it is [to be] proved [by this] that the evolutes have causes, that is [merely] proving what is [already] proved. And by failing to prove both the ordered connection (*samanvaya*) and [the nature of] the [single] cause, you have failed [to prove your position].

[If you maintain that evolutes such as the intellect are caused, this is merely establishing what has been already established. Even we maintain that all things emerge from causes and conditions, while rejecting the proposition that there is one uncaused substance from which everything comes. As such, your various proofs for the existence of Matter – e.g., the existence of a logical connection between evolutes – do not apply to a Buddhist. Should it be established that there is one material substance that is the cause of everything, then all that emerges from that substance would also have to be comprised of that same substance. From our perspective, however, Primordial Matter is considered to be non-existent because it is unmanifest, exactly like the horn of a hare. Thus the statement that the evolutes are constituted of material substance in no way proves that Primordial Matter exists. Moreover, the arguments concerning transformation, etc., contain the same defective logic.[181] And if you maintain that the separate things possess a common origin because they possess common properties,[182] to this I reply:]

[181] See MHK-TJ VI.26.

[182] The introduction to MHK VI.28 in TJ 27 is a corrupt rendering of MHK VI.28.

[Critique of a Logical Connection between Evolutes and Primordial Matter]

VI.28 If it is claimed that [the evolutes] having a common origin [can be proved] by [their] having common properties, [then] just as before, there is no evidence either of commonality or of particularity.

[Because you can provide no example that establishes a logical connection between the evolutes (e.g., happiness) and some other thing that exists as the nature of everything (i.e., Primordial Matter), your argument has not been proved. Hence, with respect to your commonality argument, the same deficiency exists as with the others: you have not proved that because the evolutes have common properties they have a common origin, nor have you proved that they have a logical connection to Primordial Matter, nor that Primordial Matter exists. Since you say that all the evolutes originate from of Primordial Matter, just like the shards of a broken pot, they would all have to possess common, as opposed to distinctive, properties (e.g., pleasure, etc.). Objection: we can establish that the evolutes have both a common origin and distinctive properties by equating them with your concept of the aggregate of sensation.[183] Answer:]

VI.29 Nor [do we] consider the [presumed] quality of having pleasure and so on for their inherent nature to be comparable to the aggregate of sensation (*vedanāskandha*), as aggregates alternate individually between pleasure, pain, and so on.

[183] The introduction in TJ VI.28 to MHK-TJ VI.29 seems to be corrupt and confuse among other things *bheda* and *skandha*!

[If you say that the evolutes possess pleasure, pain and delusion as their intrinsic nature, then they are not comparable to our conception of the aggregate of sensation, in which these three characteristics are not intrinsic but alternate between one or the other individually. Thus while the aggregate contains pleasure, or alternatively pain, it possesses neither the nature of pleasure nor the nature of pain. And with regard to the idea that delusion is of the nature of sensation, I answer as follow:]

VI.30 Furthermore you are lacking examples [to prove] that delusion (*moha*) [too] is of the nature of sensation (*vedanā*); and because it proceeds from a cause, it cannot be established, just like pleasure and pain.

[If delusion is caused, how can it be an intrinsic feature of sensation? Moreover, being caused, like a pot, delusion is alterable and can be replaced by pleasure, etc. The fact that within the aggregate of sensation delusion can be replaced by alternate characteristics indicates that it cannot be of an intrinsic nature. Thus comparing it (to Primordial Matter and its qualities) is not valid:[184]]

VI.31-32ab Even disregarding the alternation [between pleasure, pain and so on], [your conclusion] is still unsupported, owing to the defect accruing to [your] thesis (*pratijñā*) from the argument (*anumāna*) of a logical connection (*anvaya*), etc., as the particular qualities of being unborn, endless and so on are contradicted.

---

[184] TJ VI.31ab contains a paraphrase of MHK VI.30.

[The thesis that Primordial Matter exists[185] is not upheld by your five proofs – i.e., that there is a logical connection between the evolutes and Primordial Matter and so forth. This is because these proofs lead to the conclusion that Primordial Matter is neither eternal nor omnipresent. And if you declare that Primordial Matter is neither eternal nor omnipresent, you must also declare that it has no intrinsic nature. In other words, the logical proofs you used to establish the existence of Primordial Matter can be used to establish that it has a beginning and an end as well, leading to a logical contradition. The nature of Primordial Matter is pure potentiality, and its constituents are *sattva, rajas* and *tamas*. And since you deem these agents to be causeless constituents of Primordial Matter, they would be agents in name only, unable to generate the evolutes or anything else.]

VI.32cd-33 The [individual] causes which [you] postulate alternate with respect to the [three] constituents of Primordial Matter. If [they are] preceded by a single cause, there will be inconsistency among them. Similarly, if [they have] different causes, there is no evidence [for the existence of Primordial Matter].

[The general proposition that your five proofs are applicable to the evolutes must be scrutinized. With respect to the idea of a logical connection, either this means that the evolutes are caused, like the shards of a broken pot, or it means that are uncaused like the constituents of Primordial Matter. And with regard to the other four proofs, the same exact reasoning can be applied. Furthermore, either one must say that the single Primordial Matter is the cause of all evolutes, such as the intellect, etc., or one must say that it is the cause of the intellect and that the intellect is the cause of egoity and

[185] MHK VI.25a.

that egoity is the cause of the different subtle elements. This, however, would mean that there are different causes. In the phenomenal world things are seen to have different causes. The earth, for example, is the cause of the pot and the pot of the shards and so forth. Similarly, the sandalwood tree is the cause of the trunk and the trunk of the splinters and so forth. As such, it cannot be established on the basis of what we perceive that the evolutes have an intrinsic nature that comes from a single cause. And when this is the conclusion, the non-existence of Primordial Matter has been established, as have your contradictions. The example of the shards of a broken pot pertains to non-eternal existences in the phenomenal world, but Primordial Matter is eternal. Therefore this analogy is not applicable to Primordial Matter, and thus does not establish its existence. Other followers of Sāṃkhya attempt to substantiate the eternality of Primordial Matter by means of the following argument:]

VI.34 It is understood that [the intrinsic nature of a] sandalwood tree is not lost in the production of splinters, [and] by analogy (*pratyāsatti*) with respect to [healing] power, colour, [aggregate] dimension and so on, [the sandalwood tree] has the same intrinsic nature [as the splinters.]

[The fundamental substance of a sandalwood tree permanently persists (or has not perished) even when it is cut into pieces known as splinters and the sandalwood tree has disappeared from view. Because the sandalwood tree and the sandalwood splinters contain the same substantial qualities – e.g., healing power, colour and cumulative measure – the intrinsic nature of the tree that caused the splinters has not been lost in the process. By analogy, the tree's capacity to heal is contained within the splinters. An analogy with respect to colour and cumulative measure indicates the same.

[Critique of Causal Capacity]

VI.35 If [you say that] there is therefore no lack of an established example [supporting the doctrine] of different causes, as they exist potentially [in Primordial Matter], [then] like before, there is no evidence.

[Objection: if it is found to be true that Primordial Matter's quality of causal capacity (*śakti*) permanently persists within the evolutes such as the intellect, etc., this would indeed indicate that your proofs for the existence of Primordial Matter are valid. However, because you can find no concrete example, and it is impossible to compare this to some other unmanifest, no such logical connection between Primordial Matter and the evolutes can be proved.]

VI.36 [But] if [you claim that] they exist manifestly, you will have forfeited your position in establishing the identity of cause and effect, as with the doctrine above.

[If you persist in claiming that a logical connection between Primordial Matter and the evolutes nonetheless exists manifestly, you are in conflict with your own scriptural doctrine, which states that Primordial Matter is unmanifest. And if you refer to the example of the sandalwood tree and its sameness with the splinters, claiming that this establishes that cause and effect are one, I reply as follows:]

[Critique of the Identity of Cause and Effect]

VI.37 In establishing identity [between cause and effect by] the doctrine of a single origin [you are merely] proving what is [already] proved; and in imagining them to be different, like before, [there will be] a deluge of defects.

[It is self-evident that since the evolutes have the same origin, there is oneness of cause and effect, just as it is self-evident that the sprout, trunk, branches, leaves, etc. originate from the same seed, are thus fundamentally non-different. This is confirmed in the *Tattvajñānaiṣaṇā,* which notes that if there is oneness of cause and effect, all distinctions – such as those between father and son or agent and action – are rendered non-existent.[186] Some followers of Sāṃkhya even claim that previous thoughts somehow exist in the present; this claim will be systematically evaluated below.]

VI.38 By this [reasoning], making inferences from preceding thoughts is ruled out, [and] causes always alternate between pleasure, pain, and so on.

[You maintain that the permanent existence of a single origin has been firmly established and that this proves the present existence of preceding thoughts. However, this oneness of cause and effect would make it impossible for a new object to occur, since its occurrence would negate the identity between cause and effect. You also maintain that on the basis of the logical connection between the evolutes and Matter, you have established that all things are one and are of the nature of pleasure, pain or delusion. But how can something with the intrinsic nature of pleasure turn into pain and how can something with the intrinsic nature of pain turn into pleasure. In the phenomenal world we see that the sensations of pleasure, pain and delusion are not simultaneously present but rather alternate from one to the other. In conclusion, because you

[186] MHK-TJ III.214-222.

cannot point to one acceptable example of a concrete perceivable entity that has an intrinsic nature, we cannot accept your arguments in favor of the existence of Primordial Matter.]

VI.39 If in truth there is no difference ... as was said, because of the lack of division of time in the state of non-difference, [your position] will conflict with common knowledge.

[Your claim that there is no difference between cause and effect (or agent and effect) cannot be accepted. Curd is different from milk, being the indirect result of its fermentation. At the same time, it is non-different from milk because it retains milk's intrinsic nature. The example of curd thus disproves your idea that cause and effect are one, because curd is both different and non-different from the subtance that is its cause – namely milk. Moreover, if you assume that cause and effect are non-different because cause and effect are proximate, or occurring at the same time, you are in conflict with the established principles of this world. Within this world, the time at which the seed is planted and the time at which it sprouts are different. Similarly, the time at which the foetus resides within the womb differs from the time at which it takes its birth. This is commonly accepted. Objection: even though the sandalwood tree disappears from view after having been splintered, it nonetheless exists because it can be shown that according to its intrinsic nature the sandalwood tree has six stages of temporal transformation.[187] Answer: even if you establish the temporal existence of a past, is this not defeated by your own doctrine of the present moment?]

---

[187] Cf. Yāska's *Nirukta* I.2: *ṣaḍbhāvavikārā bhavantīti vārṣyāyaṇir jāyate asti vipariṇamate vardhate apakṣīyate vinaśyatīti /.../ vinaśyatīty aparabhāvasya ādim ācaṣṭe na pūrvabhāvam ācaṣṭe na pratiṣedhati.*

VI.40-41 If [you say that] in the disappearance (*tirobhāva*) of the sandal-wood tree [and the emergence of splinters, the sandalwood tree does] not cease to exist, that [non-existence] is [nevertheless] proved. And even if [you] refer to the sixth [period of] time, [it still does] not [exist], just like the present moment [ceases to exist immediately]. But is not this [just so much] exertion to cover the holes in your doctrine? Does not the defect stated [by us] follow [it], as the utterance of 'Utkaca' [follows that of] 'Ghaṭa'?

[On three separate occasions Karṇa fought against and was defeated by Ghaṭotkaca, the son of Bhīmasena and the forest demoness [Hidimbā]. Then, taking up the secret javelin that Indra had awarded him to kill his enemies, he hurdled it at Ghaṭotkaca. [To avoid the deadly javelin], Ghaṭotkaca transformed into a serpent, whereupon the javelin transformed into an eagle; Ghaṭotkaca then transformed into a mouse, whereupon the javelin transformed into an owl; finally, when Ghaṭotkaca transformed into fire, the javelin transformed into water. Every time Ghaṭotkaca transformed, the weapon continued to pursue him. No matter what form he assumed, the javelin transformed into a form that could defeat him until he was finally killed. In the same way, regardless of how many attempts you followers of Sāṃkhya may make to modify the tenets of your system, you will not be able to escape the errors we have charged you with; they will hound you forever! Just as Karṇa's javelin was ever on the heals of Ghaṭotkaca, you will be ever dogged by error so long as you continue to propagate such fallacious doctrines.[188] What, for example, is the meaning of "similarity"

---

[188] The detailed story of the duel between Karṇa and Ghaṭotkaca is found in *Mahābhārata* 7.150-154 (Poona Edition), 7.176-179 (Bombay Ed.). However, the details in MHK-TJ VI.40-41 do not match with those in the *Mahābhārata*. Thus Bhāviveka either knew a different version of this episode, and presumably of the *Mahābhārata*, or the theme of this fight might have been elaborated in a work of

(*tādrūpya*)? Does it mean that something is similar in nature to something else or does it mean that something is identical in nature to something else? And what is changed into what?]

VI.42 If similarity (*tādrūpya*) is imagined to be the meaning of 'cause' (*hetu*), there is ambiguity [as to which is the cause and which the effect]; and if [it is imagined to be] non-difference (*abhedarūpatā*), no cause can be established.

[Does similarity of nature (*tādrūpya*) refer to the fact that cause and effect are one, like the intrinsic nature of wood, or does it refer to the fact that they are in some way different, like the difference between the splinters and the wood? This is ambiguous. And if cause and effect are said to be non-different then what has has changed into what? The statement that this very man is non-different from that very man is unreasonable, and thus a primordial cause has not been established.]

[Critique of the Existence of an Experiencer]

VI.43-44 And if it is claimed that the ear and other [sense organs] must have a subject (*bhoktṛ*), as they [themselves] have no consciousness, then, if [you mean] an experiencer without the specified attributes (*viśeṣa*), [you are merely] proving what is [already] proved. But how does [the function of an experiencer] agree with the attributes of [being] indifferent, eternal, and so on? The state of experiencing [sense objects] is not claimed [to arise] from indifference even when consciousness is present.

---

kāvya, a genre the subjects of which are frequently inspired by the epics. Bhāviveka may also have mixed the Karṇa-Ghaṭotkaca battle with other *rākṣasa*-contests, thus creating a garbled version of several *Mahābhārata* stories.

[You claim that the ear and other sense organs are objects of experience and that the Self is the experiencer. To this I reply as follows: if you posit that there is an experiencer that is experiencing the objects of enjoyment, it is not acceptable then to claim that this experiencer is endowed with definable attributes such as eternality and omnipresence. I also accept an experiencer of the objects of enjoyment, but this I identify as the mind, which has emerged out of the combination of the senses and their objects. Further, you consider the Self to be detached, eternal, omnipresent *and* an enjoyer. But how can you claim that the Self is an enjoyer when you cannot establish a logical connection between it and the objects of enjoyment, which are not of the same nature (*ekajāti*)? Even assuming that the Self is endowed with consciousness, you still cannot claim that it is an enjoyer since you have already claimed that it is inactive – like a person who is sleeping, insane or bound hand and foot. Moreover, your premise that the constituent of passion (*rajoguṇa*) produces the experience of enjoyment and that this quality manifests both within and outside of all existences, endowing them with activity, leads to the contradictory conclusion that the Self is also active, benefitting as it does from its proximity to objects. To this the follower of Sāṃkhya objects as follows:]

VI.45-46 What has been said – that the inactivity of things is proved by [their] being objects of knowledge (*prameya*) – is recognized [by us]. Like pleasure and delusion, pain, too, should be understood to be inactive on account of being caused, unconscious, an object of speech or measurable, like delusion.

[To be an object of knowledge means to be devoid of activity. Objection: if you say that objects of knowledge such as pain are devoid of activity and at the same time you say that all objects are comprised of the constituent of passion (*rajas*) (which causes activity) is this not a contradiction? Answer: it should be understood that pain, like delusion, is characterized by inactivity even though its intrinsic nature is constituted of the quality of passion (*rajas*). All that is caused is unconscious, measurable, inactive and an object of speech. Objection: earlier you mentioned that the constituents of *sattva, rajas* and *tamas* alternate as a result of the connection between the evolutes and Primordial Matter. This, however, is not logical.[189] Answer: this is not illogical because the connection between the evolutes and Primordial Matter enables these constituents to express the particularity of the evolutes. As such, the qualities of goodness, passion and ignorance continue to be differentiated even while resting in nondifferentiated Primordial Matter. Reply:]

VI.47-48 If you claim that the ordered connection (*anvaya*) and so forth are causes of the existence of the separate parts, [then] truly, those [causes could] not alternate with respect to the constituents of Matter (*pradhāna*). Thus, [while the relation of] cause and effect and so forth is proved by the reason of [things] having causes, there is inconsistency in your [position] with regard to the [specified] attributes of the causes [proposed by you].

[According to you, the argument that the evolutes have a logical connection with Primordial Matter, that they are transformations of Primordial Matter, that they originate from Primordial Matter and that they have their own causal capacity and manifoldness proves that Primordial Matter exists. However, for that which is fundamentally non-differentiated, such a logical connection, etc., can be neither rationally nor empirically established. Thus you have not established the existence of Primordial Matter on the basis of

[189] Cf. MHK VI.32.

this argument, which could just as easily be used to establish its non-existence. Furthermore, even if you were to maintain that, like the evolutes, Primordial Matter contains differentiation and that the five arguments proving its existence thus apply, this would mean that, like the evolutes, Primordial Matter would be manifest, have a cause, function as an agent and also be an effect. The problem is that such a conclusion is self-contradictory since it is the complete opposite of your original definition of Primordial Matter as being non-differentiated, unmanifest, etc. You cannot argue that "when the sandalwood tree becomes unmanifest (through splintering) it continues to exist,"[190] since this would imply that there is no difference between the sandalwood tree and the splinters.][191]

VI.49 The nature of the splinters cannot be comprehended without taking into account their form (*rūpa*), etc. Thus, although in one sense the splinters and their form, etc., are connected to the sandalwood tree, the sandalwood tree and the splinters are fundamentally different, since they constitute different entities (*vastu*). Why? Because the sandalwood tree has one form, whereas the splinters can have many, in the same way that there is one perceiver, but can be many objects of perception. Thus there is a difference between the splinters and the sandalwood tree.[192]

VI.50ab As such, concerning that which appears manifest or visible, there is not even the necessity of positing the existence of an effect. The unmanifest sandalwood tree cannot be considered to have *created* the splinters any more than the splinters can be considered to contain the intrinsic nature of the whole sandalwood tree (trunk

---

[190] MHK VI.40ab.

[191] On verses 49-64, see "Text and Translation".

[192] Cf. TJ VI.39, MHK VI.40.

and all). As such, the splinters cannot be accepted as the effect of an unmanifest cause.[193]

VI.50cd Madhyamaka adherents do not commonly accept the notion that the present moment exists.[194] Even if one maintains that the present moment does exist in order to prove the identity of cause and effect, we reject this proof since the beginning segment of a moment of time (*ekakṣaṇa*) can be differentiated from the middle segment, which in turn can be differentiated from both the beginning and the final segment, which in turn can be differentiated from the first two segments. Thus, since the present moment is in this way a composite construction, it cannnot be said to exist.[195]

VI.51a-c The object of enjoyment requires an enjoyer precisely because it is an *object of enjoyment*. It is like a seat that is precisely designed to accommodate a sitter. Thus the comprehender of the object holds the status of being the enjoyer of the object of comprehension.[196]

VI.51d [Objection:] From the Madhyamaka perspective, it is *the enjoyer* (the sitter) that is a composite construction, the nature of which is reliant upon the object of enjoyment (the *seat*). Thus consciousness has been shown to be a composite construction, and thus you are attempting inconsistently to establish the opposite of that which characterizes the enjoyer.

---

[193] Cf. TJ VI-39, MHK VI.40.

[194] VI.40.

[195] Cf. TJ VI.39, MHK VI.41.

[196] Cf. MHK-TJ VI.51a-c.

VI.52 Consciousness, being the cognition of an object, is an attribute (*bhāva*); as such, it must be dependent upon an underlying substance. The relationship can be compared to the relationship between the dyeing of a cloth (the cognition of an object) and the cloth itself (the object), or that between the cooking of rice (the cognition) and the rice itself (the object). Accordingly, so-called *caitanya* is nothing more than *buddhi*.[197]

VI.53 Regardless of whether or not the Self is transformed in the process of acquiring knowledge, perceiving sound and so forth, how does that acquisition take place?[198] According to you, the Self is not transformed in the process of imitating that which has been ascertained by the *buddhi* because it is intrinsically non-transformable. How then can the Self *become* a knower? If one accepts that the acquisition of knowledge involves some sort of transformation, then one would also have to accept that the Self is transformed by that acquisition, which undermines your position. If the Self is considered to be inactive, how can it become an agent or exhibit agency? If, on the other hand, the Self is said to be an agent, since it imitates that which has been already ascertained by the *buddhi*, then I say:

VI.54 If one characterizes the Self as being unborn and inactive, how then can one regard the Self as an agent? To ascribe agency to that which is intrinsically unborn is to superimpose something extraneous upon the Self.[199] Postulating that an unborn Self can have agency is illogical, like postulating that a hare can have a horn. Agency can only be ascribed to a Self that is born. To state that the

---

[197] VI.8, 9.

[198] Cf. MHK-TJ VI.21.

[199] Cf. MHK-TJ VI.24.

thief has burnt down the house is wrongly to ascribe the burning to the thief when it should be ascribed to the fire. Similarly, to state that the Self possesses knowledge is wrongly to ascribe the knowing to the Self when is should be ascribed to the *buddhi*.] [Objection:] despite the fact that the Self is inactive, it can still be conceived as an agent, just as the thief can be conceived as the agent of burning.

VI.55 [Answer:] since the word "agent" (*kartṛśabda*) is an object of speech, the Self as you conceive it must be a caused, active and activating object of experience [like fire]. Even in conventional speech, the designation "agent" is superimposed upon the Self.[200]

VI.56 The Self is neither all-pervading nor different from Matter, nor is it ultimately a Self. Accordingly, the notion that it possesses an intrinsic nature should be rejected.[201] The Self, like fire, is located in one place, and thus it cannot be all-pervading. Moreover, like fire, it is non-different from Matter, and thus must be a transformation of the same. Finally, it cannot even be considered a "Self," since, like fire, it is endowed with a characteristic that differs from consciousness. Thus, the intrinsic nature of the Self has been disproved.

VI.57ab Thus your claims have been negated and your thesis contains various errors.

VI.57cd Like those who say that the Lord is the cause (*īśvara-hetuvādin*), one has to give up the notion of consciousness as a cause. The *īśvarahetuvādins* maintain that the Lord is the one unborn eternal cause of the world. However, from the Buddhist perspective,

---

[200] Cf. MHK-TJ VI. 46.

[201] Cf. MHK-TJ VI. 20.

being unborn logically infers being non-existent, just as there is no logical meaning to the notion of a son of a barren woman.

VI.58 According to you, the understanding that the Self which imitates that which has been ascertained by the *buddhi* is neither "I" nor "mine" represents the realization of the truth or liberation. However, our system regards this as a false view that is not representative of reality as it is.[202]

VI.59 Matter is the object of enjoyment and the Self is the enjoyer. The perception that the Self is different from Matter, like the perception that a woman (the enjoyed) is different from a man (the enjoyer), does not constitute the liberated state, since the *buddhi* (that is having the perception) is different (from the Self.)

VI.60 The Self is perceived as being distinct from Matter because of the conditioned constitution of the mind, just as a man is perceived as being distinct from a woman. As such, this sort of perception cannot be described as liberation. How can it be logical to see the Self and Matter as being different since, according to you, this Self is wholly inactive?

VI.61 In conclusion, it must be said that the entire Sāṃkhya system is from beginning to end highly inconsistent and illogical, and those that are intelligent would do well to reject it.

VI.62-63 Neither the potential tree within the seed, nor the potential child within the womb, nor the potential sound of the drum, nor the potential pearl of the oyster, nor the potential fire

---

[202] Cf. MHK VI.4a.

within wood can be directly perceived. How then can the Sāṃkhya philosopher speak the truth?

VI.64 Even if such potentialities do exist, they are not manifest and because of this cannot be directly perceived as active realities. In the end, alas, you have not established your claim that all things are the transformation of unmanifest Matter, making our system the superior and more logical of the two.

[The Determination of Reality According to Vedānta]

[Vedānta Philosophy according to Bhāviveka]

VIII.1 The adherents of Vedānta[203] state[204]: Outside [our own school] one who [really] knows the Self (*ātman*) is extremely difficult to find. How could those who hate [the notion of] a Self, maintaining that all conditioned entities (*saṃskāra*) are empty (*śūnya*), [bereft of intrinsic nature (*svabhāvarahita*) and momentary (*kṣaṇavinaṣṭa*)] possibly obtain liberation (*mokṣa*)?[205]

[The Characteristics of the Self]

VIII.2 An intelligent man conquers death when, [through his divine eye (*divyacakṣus*)], he perceives the transcendent Person (*puruṣa*)[206]

---

[203] On Bhāviveka's definition of *vedānta* and *vedāntavādin*, see Introduction.

[204] Cf. MHK IV.1: *durvigāhām imāṃ nītiṃ boddhuṃ durbalaśaktayaḥ / asthānatrāsasaṃrabdhāḥ prāhur hīnādhimuktayaḥ //* "Those attached to the lesser [vehicle], weak in ability to understand this [Madhyamaka] system [presented in the *Tattvajñānaiṣaṇā* chapter of MHK-TJ] which is difficult to fathom, speak out in agitation for fear of losing their foothold." For a translation of TJ IV.1, see Eckel 2008:103f.

[205] Cf. the discussion on *nirvāṇa* in Bhāviveka's *Prajñāpradīpa* XXV.1-21. Here a statement with a similar impact to that of TJ VIII.1 is set forth by an opponent: "For those who hold the doctrine of no intrinsic nature (*niḥsvabhāvavādin*), the *nirvāṇa* of something with no intrinsic nature cannot be attained, because [something with no intrinsic nature] is neither produced nor destroyed, like the son of a barren woman." (Eckel 1980:302.)

[206] In the *pūrvapakṣa* (vv. 1-17), the Self is variously termed *puruṣa, ātman, īśvara, maheśvara, brahman,* etc. Since the Self is the all-pervading nature of the three-realm universe (*traidhātuka*), it is viewed, e.g. in TJ VIII.3, as a Person (*puruṣa*) comprising both the three-realm universe and the Self. This notion is said in TJ VIII.1 to be derived from the Vedas, i.e. probably from the *Puruṣasūkta* of the *Ṛgveda* (X.90), see n. *ad* VIII.4. In the *pūrvapakṣa,* the notion of a Person is therefore

who is on the other side of darkness (*tamaḥparastāt*), radiant like the sun (*sūryavarcas*),[207] [and who is] the Self (*ātman*) [and] the great Lord (*maheśvara*).[208]

VIII.3 When the seer perceives the golden-coloured (*rukmavarṇa*) Lord [through the eye of meditation (*dhyānacakṣus*)] as the agent (*kartṛ*), then, having abandoned demerit (*pāpa*) and merit (*puṇya*), he will attain the [non-active, non-conceptual (*nirvikalpa*)] supreme unity (*sāmya*) [with that golden-coloured Person (*puruṣa*). Question: if He is beyond the three spheres of existence (*traidhātuka*), how could He be the agent? And if He is so distant, whose Lord is He? Answer: in spite of his distant abode, He is all-pervading:]

VIII.4 Whatever is past, present and future is all regarded as the Person. He is within and without, distant and nearby, and He is the agent of actions (*karmakṛt*).[209] [Question: if the Person is one (*eka*),

---

integrated with the notion of an all-pervading (*sarvatraga*), eternal (*nitya*) and singular (*eka*) Self. The *uttarapakṣa* (vv. 18-104) consistently uses the concept of *puruṣa* as identical to that of a Self (*ātman*).

[207] TJ VIII.2 and VIII.17 contain the following quotation from the *Śvetāśvatara Upaniṣad* III.8: "I have known that great Seer, radiant like the sun and living beyond darkness. Having known Him, one surpasses death. There is no other way leading to the place of non-birth." (quoted from Gokhale 1958:168 with n. 9, 177-78.) Cf. TJ III. 288ab. In the *Dāśabhūmikāvibhāṣa* (vol. 16, *Taisho* vol. 26, p. 74b), we find a passage with a similar doctrinal content: "Before the creation of the world, there was nothing but darkness. In the beginning the Great Man came into existence, like the sun. Those who saw him were saved from death, etc." (Nakamura 1981, n. 8.)

[208] On early Buddhist refutations of *īśvara*, see Chemparathy 1968/1969. See also the **Dvādaśadvāraka* (ch. 10, tr. by Hsueh-li Chen 1982:93-100), incorrectly ascribed to Nāgārjuna (Lindtner 1982b:11 with n. 13, 11-12), and the **Skhalitapramathanayuktihetusiddhi* of Āryadeva (Clark/Jamspal 1979:33-34).

[209] Cf. *Prajñāpradīpa* ch. 1: "Die Weltseele ist dies alles, was da war und was sein wird, usw. Ferner: Sie regt sich und regt sich nicht; sie ist fern und sie ist nah. Sie

why is He able to under take a variety of activities and yet remain unimpaired? This is shown by the following example:]

VIII.5 All entities are born out of that [Person], like threads coming out of a spider[210] [which at the same time remains unimpaired]. Wise men, absorbed (*pralīna*)[211] in Him [through the practice of meditation (*dhyāna*), perceiving Him with the eye of wisdom (*prajñānetra*)], do not come to [be reborn into] another existence. [Why does the *yogin*[212] not attain immortality (*amṛtatva*) if he has not perceived the Person?]

VIII.6 [The whole world (*sarvaloka*) which is] mortal [by nature] cannot be immortal (*amṛtatva*), just as fire [cannot] be cold. Therefore it is inconsistent that immortality [could be obtained] if one has not awakened [to become absorbed] into the immortal

---

ist innerhalb, sie ist beides und sie ist auß erhalb aller Dinge, usw." (Kajiyama 1963:58). *Prajñāpradīpa* states furthermore: "Again, those who regard *puruṣa* as the cause of origination say, 'Because all beings have *puruṣa* as their cause.' What does it mean? Just as threads are woven into a net, just as water comes out of a moonstone and just as trees sprout their branches and leaves, so do all beings have Him as their cause. What are called past and future, movable and immovable, far and near, inside and outside, are all caused by *puruṣa*." (Quoted from Nakamura 1983:218.) Cf. also *Īśā Upaniṣad* I.5: *tad ejati tan naijati tad dūre tad v antike / tad antar asya sarvasya tad u sarvasyāsya bahiḥ //*; *Ṛgveda* X.90.2 (*Puruṣasūkta* = *Śvetāśvatāra Upaniśad* III.15): *puruṣa evedaṃ sarvaṃ yad bhūtaṃ yac ca bhavyam.*

[210] Cf. *Tattvasaṃgrahapañjikā*: *ūrṇanābha ivāṃśūnāṃ candrakānta ivāṃbhaṣām / prarohāṇām iva plakṣaḥ sa hetuḥ sarvajanminām //* (quoted from Kajiyama *ibid.*).

[211] Cf. *Gauḍapādīyakārikā* III.4 (see n. *ad* VIII.11); TJ III.288ab.

[212] *rnal 'byor pa* (*yogin*) in TJ VIII.5 (cf. MHK III.28) seems synonymous with *vidvas* (MHK VIII.5) and *matimat* in MHK VIII.2 (cf. MHK III.2). The latter term is not found in the Vedic Upaniṣads or in the *Bhagavadgītā*. First in the late *Yogaśikhā Upaniṣad* 4, we find *matimat.* It may therefore be a specifically Buddhist term (cf. *Lalitavistara* 299.7) used by Bhāviveka in VTV and by Nāgārjuna, etc. Cf. Lindtner 1985b:121, n. 3.

Person. [The following serves the purpose of eulogizing His great prowess (*mahānubhāva*):]

VIII.7 This entire [world][213] is pervaded by Him than whom nothing superior exists, and than whom nothing greater or more subtle is found.[214]

VIII.8 He is endowed with the power to attenuate himself (*aṇiman*), the power to extend himself (*mahiman*), the power to levitate himself (*laghiman*), supremacy (*īśitā*) [over the elements, etc.], the power to control (*vaśitā*), the power to reach (*prāpti*), the irresistability of will (*prākāmya*) and the power to proceed at will (*yatrakāmāvasāyitā*).[215] [Although He is one, He has the nature which epitomizes the manifoldness of the three-realm universe. Therefore:]

VIII.9 To him who sees [truly], all beings become [his] very Self in that [Person], and ignorant and learned, outcast and brahmin, etc., are equal.[216] [If someone were to raise the question: Regarding this Person (*puruṣa*) who is said to be all-pervading (*sarvavyāpin*) and from whom, although He is One, the bodies of all kinds of living beings (*gati*) such as gods and men are said to be born, how is it that He does not become a nature which is non-eternal (*anitya*) and non-

---

[213] Cf. *Śvetāśvatāra Upaniśad* III.9.

[214] Cf. Gokhale 1958:172-173.

[215] MHK-TJ seems to draw some information regarding "supernormal powers" (*siddhi*) from the *Yogasūtra*(*bhāṣya*) III.44-45; Gokhale 1958:172, n. 27.

[216] Cf. *Bhagavadgītā* V.18: *vidyāvinayasaṃpanne brāhmaṇe gavi hastini / śuni caiva śvapāke ca paṇḍitāḥ samadarśinaḥ //* "The wise see the same in a brahmin endowed with knowledge and proper conduct, in a cow, in an elephant and in a dog, and even in an outcaste." See also *Bhagavadgītā* VI.29 and *Aṣṭāvakragītā* VI.4.

omnipresent (*asarvatraga*), like all embodied beings? The following is said as a rejoinder:]

VIII.10 When a pot (*ghaṭa*) is produced or destroyed, the space (*ākāśa*) [in it] does not have the same nature [of being produced or destroyed]. When bodies, etc. (*dehādi*), are born or die, they cannot be considered to have the same nature as the Self.[217]

VIII.11 If [the objection is raised that] the one [Self (*ātman*)] is many, like space in pots, [we reply that space] is one, because it is not differentiated through the breaking of pots [and] because it is considered the same for all [pots. The Self therefore does not exist separately in all embodied beings. In spite of the multiplicity of bodies, the Self is the same in all of them].[218] [Now to prove the oneness of the Self by a different approach (*naya*):]

---

[217] Cf. *Gauḍapādīyakārikā* III.3: *ātmā hy ākāśavaj jīvair ghaṭākāśair iveditaḥ / ghaṭādivac ca saṅghātair jātāv etan nidarśanam* / "The Self, which can be compared to space, has arisen in the form of individual selves, which can be compared to the space in pots, and in the form of conglomerations, which can be compared to pots, etc." Cf. also Ādiśeṣa's *Paramārthasāra* 51. On the historical background of this passage, see Vetter 1978:117f.

[218] The Vedāntavādin's reply takes the form of an actual syllogism (*prayogavākya*); see MHK VIII.68 and MHK-TJ VIII.68. Cf. *Gauḍapādīyakārikā* III.6cd, and III.4: *ghaṭādiṣu pralīneṣu ghaṭākāśādayo yathā / ākāśe sampralīyante tadvaj jīvā ihātmani* // "Just as space in pots, etc., are merged into Space, when pots, etc. [are broken], so are the individual selves completely merged into the Self [when the conglomerations are broken]." The *Prajñāpradīpa* states: "There is the following opinion: what is to be asserted by me is only this one *ātman*, which is comparable to space. Discrimination into pots and the like is all provisional [not really true]. Since they are provisional, the *ātman* cannot be measured. Therefore the *ātman* cannot be compared. It is impossible to refute it by any evidence, for the theory is without defect." (Quoted from Nakamura 1983:218.)

VIII.12 Though, the pots, etc., may be different, there is no difference in the clay. In the same way there is difference between bodies, [but] the Self is not differentiated.[219]

VIII.13 [Objection: Since your Self is omnipresent, if one person is happy, everybody else should also be happy. Answer:] Just as when space in a pot, which is one, becomes covered by such [things] as dust and smoke, the same is certainly not the case (*na hi*) for all [pots], so [when] the Self [of a person, being one], possesses pleasure, etc. (*sukhādi*), it is not the case [that the Self of all other persons also comes to possess pleasure, etc.].[220] [Question: how do happiness and suffering arise at all in each of these individual continua (*saṃtāna*)? The answer is:]

VIII.14 It is because one is unawakened (*aprabodha*) [to absorption into the immortal *puruṣa*] that one who does not know the Self collects *karma* and experiences its result which is good or bad (*śubhāśubha*), just as one who dreams imagines himself to have [real] experiences.[221] [Since the Person (*puruṣa*) is the agent (*kartṛ*) and the

---

[219] Cf. *Gauḍapādīyakārikā* III.6, 13.

[220] Cf. *Gauḍapādīyakārikā* III.5: *yathaikasmin ghaṭākāśe rajodhūmādibhir yute / na sarve saṃprayujyante tadvaj jīvāḥ sukhādibhiḥ //*. On the relationship between VTV and the *Gauḍapādīyakārikā*, see Introduction.

[221] On *abhimāna*, cf. MHK V.1: *anye pracakṣate dhīrāḥ svanītāv abhimāninaḥ /*. Kambala's *Ālokamālā* 184-185 (Lindtner 1985b:182-183) states: *svapnanivartitānāṃ tu karmaṇām kiṃ śubhāśubham / na prabuddhaḥ phalaṃ bhuṅkte svapna evākhilo naraḥ // prabodhe 'sad iti jñānāt svapne vṛtter asat phalam / tenaivāsty udite jñāne sarvasyānte vṛthā phalam //* "How can any of the actions performed in a dream [really] have a good or bad [result]? When he wakes up nobody enjoys the fruit [experienced] only in dream. When one is awake and understands that it is unreal the fruit due to activity in a dream [proves to be] unreal. Therefore, the fruit of every [action] is false once understanding has finally arisen." Apparently, Kambala (Yogācāra) is quite close to Vedānta on this point.

enjoyer (*bhoktṛ*), it may be objected that, inasmuch as He accumulates and enjoys evil deeds as well as merits, He is himself an evil-doer, etc.,[222] but we say:]

VIII.15 Although He resides in the body, He is not defiled when He enjoys [objects], since He is not attached; just like a king who behaves according to his pleasure, that [*puruṣa*] remains innocent of transgressions. [Thus, to follow up the above line of argument:]

VIII.16 When a *yogin* practising [meditation (*dhyāna*)] comes to know the one, all-pervasive, eternal, supreme Brahman, the immortal state, then he is not born into another existence. [The characteristics of that Self, which is removed from all enjoyment of wholesome and unwholesome actions, are extolled in the following:]

VIII.17 That [Self] is eternal [because it is capable of being objectified by the Yogin at all times]. It is non-conceptual (*avikalpa*) [because it is something different from senses and mind], and it is beyond the realm of speech (*vācām agocara*) [because it is not within the reach of the mind]. [Various] words, [like *brahman, ātman, puruṣa, īśvara, sarvatraga, nitya,* etc.] are, [however], applied to it by those whose minds are led astray by difference. [The meaning of other such terms is to be understood just like the meaning of the term Self.]

---

[222] See MHK-TJ VIII.72.

[Bhāviveka's Critical Examination of Vedānta Philosophy]

VIII.18 As far as this [teaching in the *pūrvapakṣa* and the meaning which has been stated previously in the work (*prakaraṇa*)] is concerned, it is [to be] critically investigated by persons who do not take up a dogmatic position (*pakṣa*) [and who are free from attachment (*anurāga*) and anger (*krodha*)]. Because a person whose mind is clouded by attachment to a position (*pakṣarāgāvṛtamati*)[223] does not even understand the truth.[224]

[Refutation of Liberation as a Result of the Perception of the Self]

VIII.19 The existence of the Self has [already] been refuted [by me in the *Tattvajñānaiṣaṇā,* the *Sāṃkhyatattvanirṇayāvatāra* and the *Vaiśeṣikatattvaviniścaya* chapters of MHK-TJ][225] and so has (*tathā*) its status as cause of the world (*jagatkāraṇatā*). Therefore, liberation (*mukti*) that results from seeing (*darśana*) that [Self] is entirely false (*abhūtaiva*), [since it is only] mentally fabricated (*prakalpitā*). [There is also the following great fault in the view of a *puruṣa*:]

---

[223] I.e. he is "biased". Cf. MHK III.23: *pakṣapātasaṃ taptaḥ.*

[224] In the *Catuḥśataka* VIII.10, Āryadeva states that *nirvāṇa* is not attained if one has attachment to one's own position (*svapakṣa*). See Lang 1986:81 with n. 10. Cf. also *Catuḥśataka* XII.1, Lang *ibid.*, pp. 110-111 with n. 1, p. 111. According to Bhāviveka, not only humans are obstructed from true comprehension of reality due to attachment, but also gods are! TJ IV.68 states: "/... / Brahmā is habitually attached to the view of his own excellence and thinks: 'I create living beings.' He does not understand reality (*tattva*). /... /." (quoted from Eckel 2008:208).

[225] TJ VIII.18.

VIII.20 The innate (*sahaja*)[226] belief in an existing individuality (*satkāyadṛṣṭi*),[227] [i.e. the attachment (*abhiniveśa*) to a personal identity (*satkāya*), which is to hold that the five aggregates of attachment (*upādānaskandha*) are the Self (*ātman*) and what belongs to the Self (*ātmīya*)],[228] leads to non-tranquility (*aśānti*) even [for the minds] of animals (*paśu*).[229] [Therefore, this is not the right way to liberation], since it is the root of all afflictions (*saṃkleśa*), [like pride in a Self (*ātmamāna*), delusion regarding a Self (*ātmamoha*), belief in a Self (*ātmadṛṣṭi*), love of a Self (*ātmasneha*), etc.]. This [belief in a personal identity is in even greater degree] promoted by you [in the Vedāntadarśana.]

VIII.21 For those people who cherish a belief in "I" and "mine" (*mamāhaṃkāra*), full of belief in a personal identity as they are, liberation also arises out of that from which *saṃsāra* arises[230] [i.e.

---

[226] The *Abhidharmakośa* V.41 refers to the following Sautrāntika position: "La *satkāyadṛṣṭi* naturelle (*sahaja*), qui se trouve chez les bêtes sauvages et chez les oiseaux, est non-défine. La *satkāyadṛṣṭi* méditée (*vikalpitā*) est mauvaise." On the concept of *sahaja* in Indian Buddhist tantric literature, see Kværne 1975.

[227] *Satkāyadṛṣṭi* is in TJ VIII.19 translated with *'jig tshogs la lta ba* "the [wrong] view that the aggregates, [wrongly subsumed to exit, in the end will] perish". Cf. the following Sautrāntika position, referred to by Vasubandhu in the *Abhidharmakośabhāṣya* V.7: "Croire au moi et au mien (*ātmātmīya grāha*), c'est la *satkāyadṛṣṭi; sat,* parce que périssant; *kāya,* parce que accumulation multiplicité. *Satkāya,* c'est-à-dire les cinq *upādānaskandhas*".

[228] The *Prajñāpradīpa* XVIII.1.2 states: "/... / As the Lord said, 'A monk or brahman who correctly sees the Self, also correctly sees the aggregates of attachment (*upādānaskandha*)' " (tr. by Eckel 1980:192). Regarding the impossibility of the Self to be either identical with, or different from, the *skandhas,* see Nāgārjuna's *Mūlamadhyamakakārikā* XVIII.1 and Buddhapālita's *Mūlamadhyamakavṛtti* XVIII.1.

[229] Cf. TJ III.297-300.

[230] All Tibetan recensions translate Skt. *uditā* in MHK VIII.21d with *yin par smra[s]*, i.e. as a slightly incorrect rendering of the perfect passive participle of Skt. *vad.* TJ VIII.24, together with the parallelism in MHK VIII.21cd between *bhāvitaḥ* and

from the belief in a personal identity, etc. The Omniscient One has said that having destroyed the twenty high mountain peaks of *satkāyadṛṣṭi,* such as thinking that form (*rūpa*) is the Self (*ātman*), there is form in the Self, the Self possesses form, the Self is inside form, etc.,[231] one will see Reality (*tattva*). But you say that the very thing which increases *saṃsāra* is the cause of liberation, but this is like someone who tries to put out fire by heaping fuel on it. Objection: that which is not the cause of peace can, however, become the cause of peace by some method (*upāya*), just as one who is intoxicated becomes free from intoxication due to more liquor. For one who does not know the right method, if he relies on the view of a Self, defilements (*saṃkleśa*) will arise. But for the *yogin* meditating on that very same view of a Self, defilements will be pacified. Answer:]

VIII.22 If cessation [of *saṃsāra*] (*śānti*) could arise on the basis of seeing that [Self], then someone suffering from indigestion (*ajīrṇa*) would recover by eating, just like a person recovering from intoxication (*madātyaya*)[232] through [more intoxicating] liquor.

VIII.23 The adherents of Vedānta (*vedāntavādin*) postulate that this Self appears in two forms: the Self that is bound up with the so-

---

uditā, corroborate our construal Skt. *ud* + √*i* of the perfect passive participle *uditā* (**byuṅ bar gyur*).

[231] In TJ VIII.21 Bhāviveka elaborates upon the various forms of *satkāyadṛṣṭi* with regard to the 5 *skandhas*: (1-5) form (*rūpa*), feeling (*vedanā*), discernment (*saṃjñā*), disposition (*saṃskāra*) and consciousness (*vijñāna*) are the Self (*ātman*), (6-10) there is form, feeling, etc. in the Self, (11-15) the Self possesses form, feeling, etc., (16-20) the Self is inside form, feeling, etc. On the twenty "peaks" (*koṭi*) of the mountain of *satkāyadṛṣṭi,* see Yaśomitra's *Spuṭārthavyākhyā*: *viṃśatikoṭikā hi satkāyadṛṣṭiḥ paṭhyate rūpam ātmeti samanupaśyati rūpavantam ātmānam ātmīyaṃ rūpam rūpe ātmeti evaṃ yāvad vijñānaṃ vaktavyam.* See also Lamotte 1949-1980:37.

[232] On *mada* (intoxication), see Jolly 1977:146; *Yogaśataka,* v.48; *Siddhasāra,* ch. 22.

called body and the liberated (*mukta*) Self that rests in the supreme (*parameṣṭhātman*).

VIII.24 (p)[233] The cognition (*dhī*) that has as its object (*viṣaya*) the Self which rests in the supreme (*pareṣṭhātman*)[234] is not considered true (*yathārtha*), (h) because in this way there is attachment (*parāmarśa*) to the Self [as an object, and therefore movement (*pracāra*) in relation to that Self will occur], (d) like the idea of the Self [occuring] in regard to the body, etc.[235] [Objection: This supreme Self

---

[233] p: *pratijñā* (thesis); h: *hetu* (reason); d: *dṛṣṭānta* (example). Bhāviveka's usage of syllogisms shows, *inter alia*, his dependence on Dignāga. See Introduction.

[234] Bhāviveka seems to have coined (*metri causa?*) the term *pareṣṭhātman* (*mchog na gnas pa grol pa'i bdag*, P. *fol. Dza*: 289a4-289a5; D. *fol. Dza*: 256b1), which is short for *parameṣṭhātman.*

[235] TJ VIII.24 states: "Why is the idea that the [individual mortal] Self has as its object the supreme Self not correct? Because movement (*rgyu ba/pracāra*) in relation to that occurs, as in saying, the Self is like this. Like what? Like the idea of the Self occuring in regard to the body and sense-organs and objects. The idea of the body and the objects is correct in conventional reality, because it is apprehended by perception (*pratyakṣa*), but the idea of resting in the supreme is not correct conventionally, because it is not apprehended." MHK III.11 refers to a *prajñā* which has a movement which is non-moving (*/.../ apracārapracāra /.../*). Cf. TJ I.2: */.../apracārayogena pracāragocaratvāt /.../* (see Gokhale 1985:83 with n. 14, 84), and the *Akṣayamatinirdeśasūtra*: */.../paramārthasatyaṃ katamat? yatra jñānasyāpy apracāraḥ kaḥ punar vādo 'kṣarāṇām /.../* (quoted from Lindtner 1986:80, n. 30). The latter passage is alluded to in Candrakīrti's *Prasannapadā* (La Vallée Poussin ed., p. 374.1): *paramārthasatyaṃ katamat? yatra jñānasyāpy apracāraḥ* "What is ultimate truth? That toward which even cognition does not move." In TJ III.284, Bhāviveka states: "If we thought he [i.e. Buddha, defined as a single moment's cognition of the sameness of all *dharmas* (TJ III.273)] had intrinsic nature, he could be grasped like things that are active /.../ But something that is empty of intrinsic nature has no action". "/.../ Since no *dharmas* are established, the moment of cognition that does not arise is called 'Buddha'" (tr. by Eckel). Cf. also TJ III.276; *Gauḍapādīyakārikā* III.34, and IV.80: *nivṛttasyāpravṛttasya niścalā hi tadā sthitiḥ / viṣayaḥ sa hi buddhānāṃ tat sāmyam ajam advayam //* "Der Stand [des

is imagined (*parikalpita*) to be a "Self" by the power of the residues (*vāsanā*) of attachment (*abhiniveśa*) to the Self. Answer: Nothing at all is established by imagination (*parikalpa*):]

[Refutation of the Self as Agent]

VIII.25. Even if the Self is by nature imagined (*parikalpitasattva*), what does it make in your [opinion]? If [you say that it makes] a cognition (*buddhi*) that has form (*rūpa*), speech (*śabda*), etc., as its object, that is not logical. [I prove this as follows:]

VIII.26. (p) Cognitions (*dhī*), which have form, etc., as an object, do not arise having the Self as agent (*kartṛ*), (h) because [their] origination (*janma*) is dependent on conditions (*pratyaya*), [such as the group of sense-object (*jñeya*), sense-organ (*āśraya*), consciousness (*vijñāna*) and attention (*manasikāra*)], (d) just as fire (*anala*) [depends] on a magnifying glass (*sūryakānta*). [So if one performs such actions as seeing and hearing, what is the use of imagining a Self which is different from the object, sense-organ and cognition (*vijñāna*). Moreover:]

VIII.27. (p) Nor can sound (*dhvani*), which has the nature of syllables (*varṇa*), be regarded as having the Self as agent, (h) because it is audible (*śrāvaṇatva*), or because it is a sound, (d) just like an echo (*pratiśabdaka*).

Citta], das nun aufgehört hat [unruhig zu sein] und sich nicht mehr [auf Ähnliches] richtet ist dann nämlich unbewegt. Dies ist nämlich der Bereich der Buddhas. Das ist die Gleichheit, die nichtentstanden und ohne Zweiheit ist" (tr. by Vetter 1978:100). The above quoted passages display the "non-dynamic" character of the Absolute in Mahāyāna Buddhism and in the *Gauḍapādīyakārikā*.

VIII.28. By virtue of these [arguments], the remaining physical activities, such as going and coming, characterized by motion (*vispanda*) of hands and feet, etc., have [implicitly] been negated [as having the Self as agent. Therefore a Self does not exist apart from the body and sense-organs.][236]

VIII.29 The act of discernment (*saṃjñāna*) [arises] when one has understood by discrimination (*vyavaccheda*) [that which originates from the assembled causal conditions (*pratyaya*) of object (*viṣaya*), organ (*āśraya*), consciousness (*vijñāna*) and attention (*manasikāra*)]. The act of recollection (*smaraṇa*) [arises] due to remembrance (*smṛti*) [of the object experienced by the sixfold group of cognitions].[237] The act of insight (*prajñāna*) [arises] by virtue of an insight (*prajñā*)[238] of a specific nature (*prakāra*), [discriminating the individual (*sva°*) and general characteristics (*sāmānyalakṣaṇa*) of *dharmas*]. The act of feeling (*vedanā*) [arises out of] the experience (*vid*) [of the object. Not even the slightest action of a Self is apprehended apart from the mind (*citta*), which has the characteristic of cognizing the nature of an object, and the mental factors (*caitta*), such as feeling (*vedanā*), desire (*chanda*), contact (*sparśa*), absorption (*samādhi*), etc., which have the characteristic of cognizing individually the particularities (*viśeṣa*) of an object.]

---

[236] Cf. *Mūlamadhyamakakārikā* ch. II.

[237] According to *Abhidharmakośabhāṣya* I.30-31, the *vijñānaskandha* consists of six classes of cognition: visual (*cākṣus-*), auditive (*śrotra-*), olfactive (*ghrāṇa-*), gustual (*jihvā-*), tactile (*kāya-*) and mental cognition (*manovijñāna-*).

[238] In *Abhidharmakośa* I.3, II.24, *prajñā* is defined as "the distinguishing of *dharmas*" (*dharmānāṃ pravicaya*). For references to Madhyamaka definitions of *prajñā*, see Lindtner 1981:188, 205, n. 84. See also MHK-TJ III.6, 7, 9-11 (tr. by Heitmann 2004:85-101). On *vedanā, saññā*, and *paññā* in the Pāli canon, see Johansson 1979:87-91, 92-95, 197-216.

VIII.30 No other function of the Self can be ascertained, nor any intrinsic nature;[239] hence, not even its existence can be ascertained, like that of a flower in the sky. [Objection: The Self (*puruṣa*) does indeed see, hear, smell, taste, think, remember, etc.,[240] because the Self is the agent, whereas the eye, and so forth, are its instruments. For example, one says that the sickle cuts, although the sickle itself does not cut, but Devadatta cuts by means of the instrument, i.e. the sickle. Likewise one says that the eye, etc., see, but the eye and the other sense-organs themselves do not see, etc.; rather by means of that instrument the Self sees, etc. Thus, according to this method, action is established as follows: Because one sees by means of this, it is the eye, etc. Answer:]

VIII.31 If instrumental status (*karaṇatva*) is attributed [to such sense-organs as the eye] because it is said that knowledge, etc. (*jñānādi*), [presupposes] an [intermediary] instrument, or [if] agent status (*kartṛtva*) different from that [instrumentality is attributed to the Self], like a cutter (*dātṛ*), this [assertion is not logical:

VIII.32 Since these [sense-organs] do not have instrumental status because the agent [presupposes] the arising of causal conditions, the logical reason (*hetu*) therefore has an unestablished meaning (*asiddhārthatā*) or it is inconclusive (*anekāntikatā*).[241] [The eye sees by

---

[239] According to TJ VIII.30, one cannot precisely determine the intrinsic nature of the Self as a function different from perception, memory, insight, feeling, etc. For a discussion of Bhāviveka's notion of intrinsic nature (*svabhāva*), see Introduction; MHK III.29cd; *Mūlamadhyamakakārikā* XV.1, 2, 8; VII.30; *Gauḍapādīyakārikā* IV.9, 29.

[240] In MHK-TJ III.95, Bhāviveka denies that the existence of the Self can be established on the basis of the notion that the Self remembers, recollects, produces knowledge, etc. (See Iida 1980:177-178.)

[241] On Bhāviveka's usage of *asiddhārthatā* and *anekāntikatā*, see Lindtner 1986:63.

itself, but it is not the agent of another. Because it hears, it is the ear; because it smells, it is the nose; because it tastes, it is the tongue; because it feels, it is touch (*sparśa*); because it thinks, it is the mind (*manas*); because it remembers, it is memory, and so on. The eye itself sees, but the Self does not see. Therefore:]

VIII.33 Knowledge, etc., as an agent, naturally presuppose a word designating the agent, just as agent status is seen here in the expression: "Devadatta cuts". [Objection: Devadatta does not cut, but rather, the sword cuts. Answer: this is not correct, because the action will be accomplished here by means of the assemblage (*sāmagrī*) of the agent and the object of action. Regarding this, one sometimes emphasizes the agent as the chief thing, for example when saying: "Devadatta cuts". Sometimes one emphasizes the instrument as the chief thing (*pradhāna*), for example when saying: "The sword cuts". The act of cutting depends on both. The instrument does not act without an agent, and the agent too cannot act without an instrument. Without both of these, it is not possible to conceive of an agent and an instrument acting independently of each other. Things are brought about due to the assembled conditions, not due to a principal (*pradhāna*) condition. If not so, it is just a metaphor (*upacāra*).]

VIII.34 One may [assume the existence of] an agent, but it must be said [that such an agent exists] only [on the basis of] the group (*rāśi*) of completely motionless (*nirīha*)[242] conditioned entities (*saṃskāra*), just as when you say: "The lamp sheds light", although the lamp is [only] a means [whereby you shed light, since the light is brought about dependent on the causal conditions of oil, a wick, a vessel and

[242] On *nirīha*, see Nāgārjuna's *Lokātītastava* 24 (Lindtner 1982b:136 with n. 24, 137).

fire.[243] Objection: the Self is supreme, because dependent on that chief agent all actions proceed. But the lamp, etc., are just designations, just as the potter himself is the agent although many conditions such as clay, etc., are present. Answer:]

VIII.35 In reality (*tattvatas*), there is no fundamental (*mukhya*) agent, since a man cannot make a pot alone. Therefore, it is not accepted that a lamp, etc., [are merely regarded] as the agent in a [transferred or] figurative sense. [The Self alone is not the cause of all actions, because those actions are dependent on a complex of [causes and] conditions (*pratyayasāmagrī*). The eye, etc., and the lamp, etc., are therefore chief (*pradhāna*) agents, not just metaphorical agents, because a chief agent ruling out those is not established. Conventionally (*saṃvṛtyā*), the collection of causal conditions (*pratyaya*) is shown to be the agent, but in ultimate reality, it is not established that there is any chief agent. Objection: since Reality (*tattva*) is under consideration, by the power of past

---

[243] From a relative perspective (*saṃvṛtitas*), Bhāviveka maintains that an "agent" (*kartṛ*), a "cutter" (*dātṛ*) (MHK-TJ VIII.31), and a "sentient being" (*sattva*) (MHK-TJ VIII.37) only designate a collection of causal conditions (*pratyaya*). Cf. *Abhidharmakośabhāṣya* IX.245-246: "Les quatre derniers termes, *vijñāna, vedanā, saṃjñā, cetanā,* sont les éléments (*skandhas*) immatériels (*arūpin*); l'oeil et la couleur-figure sont l'élément *rūpa*. Voilà tout ce dont on parle quand on dit «homme» . Pour exprimer diverses nuances, on se sert de divers vocables, tels que *sattva*, être, *nara*, homme, *manuja*, né de Manu, *mānava*, jeune homme, *poṣa*, qui se nourrit, *jīva*, principe vital, *jantu*, qui nâit, *pudgala*, personne./... / Bhikṣus, sachez que ce sont là seulement des manières de dire, des paroles, des expressions conformes à l'usage du monde." According to the *Mahāvyutpatti* (§CCVIII, 4668-4683, pp. 309-310) the following terms are used by the heterodox sectarians (*tīrthika*) as synonyms (*paryāya*) of the Self: *ātman, sattva , jīva , jantu, poṣa, puruṣa, pudgala, manuja, mānava, kāraka, kārāpaka, vedaka, jānaka, paśyaka, utthāpaka,* and *samutthāpaka.* See also the *Śatasāhasrikāprajñāpāramitā* 472, 522 (referred to by Dayal 1978:341, n. 186). In the *Saṃyuttanikāya* V.10, for instance, it is said that conventionally we speak of a "being" when the *skandhas* are present.

acts, the stream (*saṃtāna*) of momentary *dharmas* cannot be bound or liberated, since what ceases at each instant is without activity. Therefore, one should understand that only the Self is the basis of bondage, liberation and continuance. Answer: although the mind ceases to exist at each instant and is without independent power and intrinsic nature, it continues like the stream of a river:]

[Refutation of the Self as Bound or Liberated]

VIII.36 The mind (*citta*) which is subjected to such [things] as desire (*rāgādi*) [and] attached (*sakta*) to the sphere of form, etc. (*rūpādigocara*), [is therefore said to be] obstructed from liberation and bound in the prison of *saṃsāra,* [since it is without independence and lacks the light of insight (*prajñā*).][244]

VIII.37 When this aggregate of hands and the like (*pāṇyādisamudāya*) is associated with a mind, it is designated "[sentient] being" (*sattva*). Because the volition of giving, etc. (*tyāgādicetanā*) arises, it is said to be a "giver" (*dātṛ*), etc.

VIII.38 When knowledge arises due to the bonds of ignorance (*avidyā*) and the rest being removed, [then the continuum (*saṃtāna*) of the aggregates (*skandha*) itself is] freed from the bondage of desire, etc.,[245] [having accomplished the path of liberation by the

---

[244] On *prajñā,* see n. *ad* MHK-TJ VIII.24.

[245] In the *Prajñāpradīpa,* ch. XXV ("The Investigation of *Nirvāṇa*"), vv. 1cd, 3, Bhāviveka distinguishes between two kinds of *nirvāṇa*: one with residual aggregates (*skandha*), and one without residual aggregates. *Nirvāṇa* is thus considered as either the removal (*prahāṇa*) of defilements (*kleśa*) or the cessation (*nirodha*) of aggregates (*skandha*) (see Eckel 1980:301f, 305). Candrakīrti makes a similar distinction in ch. XIX of his *Prasannapadā.* Here *nirvāṇa* with a residual base (*sopadhiśeṣa*), i.e. with residual aggregates, is said to result from the removal

illumination of insight (*prajñā*) consisting of hearing (*śrutamayī*), reflecting (*cintāmayī*) and meditating (*bhāvanāmayī*)], it is designated "liberated" (*mukta*). [It is therefore acceptable (*yukta*) to say that liberation (*mokṣa*) is the last moment of mind which has arisen and which is superior to the former moment of the complex of mind (*citta*) and mental factors (*caitta*) that have the property of ceasing and arising.][246]

VIII.39 But since the Self is like the sky (*vyoman*), then all this [namely, the Self being the basis of bondage and liberation] is very difficult to talk about, [since even if the sky is full of snow, hail, wind, etc., defilements (*saṃkleśa*) are not produced for the sky. Likewise, even if desire (*kāma*), anger (*krodha*) and pride (*abhimāna*) have arisen, there is no change in the very Self, and therefore it cannot be said to be bound or liberated even with great exertion]. If

---

(*prahāṇa*) of the basic afflictions, such as ignorance, desire, etc., and to consist of the mere aggregates (*skandhamātra*). *Nirvaṇa* without a residual base (*nirupadhiśeṣa*) or aggregates results from the cessation (*nirodha*) of the aggregates, and consists not even of the mere aggregates. (See La Vallée Poussin's ed. of the *Prasannapadā*, p. 519.) Bhāviveka seems in MHK VIII.38 to refer to the first kind of *nirvāṇa*. On *skandhamātra*, cf. the notion of pure *skandhas*: *dharmaskandhas*, *lokottaraskandhas*, *anāsravaskandhas*, stated in *Vibhāṣā*, *Abhidharmakośa*, etc. (See Lamotte 1980:129.)

[246] Bhāviveka describes the state of liberation in TJ I.3 as "a single moment of self-originating knowledge (*ekakṣaṇasvayambhūjñāna*) (Gokhale 1985:83 with n. 14). TJ III.268 (cf. TJ III.273) states also: "/... / He understands the similarity of all *dharmas* in a single moment of self-generated knowledge /... /." Cf. the following passages from the *Mahāvastu* and the *Lalitavistara*, quoted by Lamotte 1980:124: "Through a wisdom associated with a single moment of thought, I acquired supreme and perfect enlightenment (*ekacittakṣaṇasamāyuktayā prajñayā anuttarāṃ samyaksaṃbodhim abhisaṃbuddhe*) /.../." "When the Buddha had reached supreme and perfect enlightenment through a wisdom associated with a single moment of thought (*ekacittakṣaṇasamāyuktayā prajñayā*), the three knowledges (*traividyā*) were acquired."

you still greatly cherish your Self [due to your attachment to the Self by the power of the residues (*vāsanāsāmarthyāt) of grasping a Self from beginningless time, [then why not] consider the Self as a skyflower, [which also has the same characteristic and which therefore also would be a "Self".]

[Refutation of Cognition as the Intrinsic Nature of the Self]

VIII.40 If one maintains that "the intrinsic nature of the Self is cognition (*jñāna*)", then its oneness (*ekatā*) is not logical, since [cognition] is dependent on instruments (*karaṇa*) [such as the eye,] etc., [and besides, if this Self already has the nature of cognition, why does it depend on instruments such as the eye, etc.? If you say that without the eye and the other organs, the fact that this is a cognition is not apprehended, then since something other than the instruments is not apprehended, its oneness would be lost, which is contrary to your own doctrine.]

VIII.41 Furthermore, if the Self, etc., were an existing object of knowledge (*jñeya*), [then] that cognition [of the Self] would not cease [since, even if you say that having accomplished the object to be accomplished, cognition does not act on the object, as in the case with a lamp which, having illuminated its object, does not act on that object. We answer that] it is [nevertheless] seen that even if a lamp has accomplished its function, it comes into being by virtue of its own causes (*svakāraṇa*), [such as a wick, oil, etc. Therefore the Self, like a lamp, will not, even at the time when it has accomplished its object, be without activity (*pravṛtti*). Consequently, even when one has seen the Self (*puruṣa*) with the eye of cognition, liberation will not be produced:]

VIII.42 As long as there arises a cognition which has an existing [object], so long will [a new] seed (*bīja*)[247] be accumulated [in the consciousness], just as, as long as there arises a sound (*ārāva*), so long [will] the echo (*pratirava*) [continue, but when the activity of sound ceases and does not exist, the echo will not arise. Likewise, if the object of knowledge does not exist, cognition also will not arise.]

VIII.43 How can *saṃsāra* [arise] for the knower, and how can knowledge [arise] without an [intermediary] instrument [of knowledge]? And how and whence can bondage and liberation [arise] when [the Self] is always without distinctions?

VIII.44 Moreover, [the Self] cannot be free from suffering (*duḥkha*) even in [the state of] liberation if one maintains that there is only the Self, because that [suffering] cannot be different from the Self, just as fire (*vibhāvasu*) [cannot be different] from the heat (*uṣṇa*) [of the fire.]

VIII.45 How can someone whose intellect is latent (*līna*) or unoriginated be a knower without an [intermediary] instrument [of knowledge]? It would be as inconsistent as the woodpecker (*pūrṇaka*) [being able to peck] without a beak (*paraśu*). [Objection: Just as even if fire burns, it is indicated that the person burns by means of fire; likewise, even when cognition knows, it is said that

---

[247] The term *bīja* in MHK VIII.42 seems to have a connotation identical to that of the term *vāsanā* (residue/impression) in, e.g., TJ VIII.24. It is therefore not related to the Yogācāra concept of "seeds" (*bīja*) residing in the store-house consciousness (*ālayavijñāna*). The VTV-MHK does not give any information as to whether Bhāviveka follows the Sautrāntika theory of *bīja* or not. On the Sautrāntika theory of *bīja*, see Jaini 1959. Cf. May 1959:273, n. 1002 (*vijñānabīja*).

the person knows but not the cognition. Answer: that is not correct:]

VIII.46 When it is said: "He burns by means of fire", it is the fire that burns, not the one who achieves it, just as when it is said: "One knows by means of the mind", it is the cognition that knows, not [that] Self (*puṃs*) of yours. [In the statement "fire burns" either fire itself burns or else Devadatta does. As to that, the so-called burning exists in fire, not in the one who makes something burn, i.e. the agent of the burning. Likewise, when it is said that the mind here knows, the mind itself knows, not the Self. Objection: just as a potter is called a potter even at the time when he is not making pots, and fire is called "burner" (*dāhaka*) even at the time when it is not burning wood, just so the Self, too, has the nature of cognition, even though it is not related to any instrument.]

VIII.47 That [Self which, even though it does not depend on any instrument, has the nature of cognition] could not be established in analogy with a pot-maker (*kulāla*), since he has not [the function of being a pot-maker] as his intrinsic nature (*svabhāva*). The establishment [of the Self] in analogy with something that burns is not acceptable [either], since without something to be burned (*dāhya*), fire (*agni*) does not exist. [When the Self is active or proceeds by means of instruments, then it is correct that it has the intrinsic nature of cognition, but apart from that, the intrinsic nature of cognition is just a designation in relation to the intrinsic nature of non-cognition (*ajñāna*). Cognition is, however, not established by merely stating it in regard to non-cognition.[248]]

---

[248] According to Bhāviveka, space is established on a conventional level in relation to a substance, just as unorigination (*ajāti*) is established in relation to origination (*jāti*). Cognition (*jñāna*) as the intrinsic nature of the Self cannot, therefore, be ultimately established, since, like space and unorigination, it is only possible to

VIII.48 Nor [can] the non-knowing [become] a knower. How can that [Self] of yours become an agent (*kartṛ*) or experiencer (*bhoktṛ*)? And how can [the Self], which is devoid of conceptual construction like the sky, be conceived on the basis of mere scriptures (*āgama*), [which are no means of valid knowledge (*pramāṇa*)]? Objection: even though the Self has the nature of non-cognition, it will have the nature of cognition when the instruments are present. Answer: nevertheless, prior to the first existence of cognition, because the instruments had not arisen, the Self had the nature of non-cognition. It could therefore not be an agent or an experiencer.][249]

VIII.49 Furthermore, [if you say that] the intrinsic nature [of the Self] is neither cognition nor non-cognition, [then] this [Self] would be without intrinsic nature. But the Self could not be without intrinsic nature, [since then] it would be [as non-existent] as a son of a barren woman. [Moreover, you have stated that because the Self pervades all bodies, it is the single Self of all:]

[Refutation of an Individual Mortal Self and an Immortal Self which Rests in the Supreme]

VIII.50 That for which pain or pleasure does not arise when someone is tormented or pleased is not fit [to be called] his Self, just as the sky cannot [belong] to [an individual such as] Devaśarman.

VIII.51 If [you] maintain that meditative cognition (*dhyānajñāna*), etc., lead to liberation of the individual [mortal] Self (*antarātman*),[250]

---

conceive of cognition in relation to non-cognition (*ajñāna*). Something which is dependent on something else for its existence cannot ultimately be self-existent or intrinsic.

[249] On *āgama* and *yukti* in the works of Bhāviveka, see Iida 1966.

[250] Bhāviveka uses the term *antarātman* connotating an "individual [mortal] Self".

then [this] must [imply] an effort (*prayatna*) to negate the Self, [since in reality there is no deviation from a certain intrinsic nature]: How would the mortal (*martya*) [Self] become immortal (*amṛta*) [without being impermanent, etc.]?[251]

VIII.52 [If it is said that the individual Self and the supreme Self are both different and non-different, this should be examined in the following way:] If the individual [mortal] Self (*antarātman*) is different from the Self [which rests in the supreme (*parameṣṭha*)], your assertion ["All is the Person (*puruṣa*)"][252] is abandoned, [because the individual mortal Self is different from the Self which rests in the supreme. And:]

VIII.53 If the individual [mortal] Self is non-different from the Self [which rests in the supreme], [then] your thesis is [once again] abandoned, [because the supreme Self does not at all experi-ence pleasure and pain, etc. It (i.e. the mortal individual Self) could therefore not be identical with the supreme Self.][253]

This rare usage of the term *antarātman* is also found, e.g., in the *Manusmṛti* VI.73, XII.13, and in Āryadeva's *Catuḥśataka* X.1 (see Lang 1986:95 with n. 1). The Upaniṣads use it consistently for an "inner/internal Self".

[251] Cf. *Mūlamadhyamakakārikā* XV.1-2, 8; the *Triśaraṇasaptati* 12-13 (see Sørensen 1986a:21-22, 65-66, n. 12-13); *Gauḍapādīyakārikā* III.21-22, 4.7-8, 29.

[252] Cf. MHK VIII.4ab.

[253] Cf. *Brahmasūtra* I.2.8 (translated with Śaṅkara's commentary): *saṃbhogaprāptir iti cen na vaiśeṣyāt* "If it is said: [Because the individual Self and the supreme Self are identical], there is arising of experience [of pleasure and pain also for the supreme Self], it is not so because of difference [with respect to their respective nature]."

[Refutation of the One Self as having a Manifold Nature]

VIII.54 If it [i.e. the Self] is subtle (*sūkṣma*), this [Self] cannot [at the same time] be large (*mahat*). If it is large its subtleness does not exist, and it is not one [either]. How could the formless Self have the property of form [without the occurence of the mental constructions (*vikalpa*), "subtle" and "great", "one" and "many", etc.? Objection: those who do not see Reality see it in many forms: some say that it is all-pervasive (*sarvatraga*), some say that it is just the extent of the body (*deha*), others again think that it just has the nature of an atom (*paramāṇu*). Like the elephant's intrinsic nature (*svabhāva*), it is just one (*eka*), but like the major and minor limbs (*aṅga/pratyaṅga*) of the elephant (*hastin*), it is also many. Answer:]

VIII.55 On the basis of the example of the elephant, it is not logical that one [thing] has a manifold nature, since [the part, i.e.] the trunk (*kara*) is not considered to be [the whole, i.e.] the elephant (*karin*). Furthermore, oneness does not [apply] to the trunk, etc. [The trunk of the elephant is just the trunk. The foot is just the foot, and the ear is just the ear. The elephant itself does not exist. Therefore, there is no single nature and the trunk, etc.][254]

VIII.56 If the Self has the colour of the sun, etc. (*sūryādivarṇa*) [as you maintain],[255] how could it [also] be without colour? [Objection: like the *palāśa*-tree, one thing pervades all, and as the *palāśa*-tree exists in its own parts, such as the root, the trunk, the branches, the twigs, etc., that has also a manifold nature. Answer:] a manifold

---

[254] I.e. none of the single parts is identical with the whole – neither alone nor collectively.

[255] See MHK VIII.2 (*sūryavarcas*), VIII.3 (*rukmavarṇa*). Cf., however, *Abhidharmakośa* IX.301: *tathāgatāditya*.

nature of the Self is not [to be] accepted on the basis of the example of the *palāśa*[-tree].

VIII.57 Since a *palāśa*[-tree] is not one [in as much as] it always changes its nature [into the states of youth, middle-age and its end], and moreover, since the roots, etc., are not one [in as much as] they are differentiated by causal conditions (*pratyaya*) [such as fire, wind, an axe, etc., the example of the *palāśa*-tree is not able to establish the meaning which is the purpose of the example, i.e., a non-changing and non-differentiated Self.]

VIII.58 [Concepts like] "being greater" (*jyāyastā*) and "superior" (*paratva*) are meaningful [only] in relation to [something] other than that [which is said to be so]. How can the existence of [such] a notion be accepted when there is identity [between the Self and all entities?[256] Furthermore, how could it be right that the Self is a substance and also all-pervasive?]

[Refutation of the Self as a Substance and a Support]

VIII.59 If the Self were a substance (*dravya*),[257] it could not be all-pervasive (*sarvaga*) because of its substantiality (*dravyatva*), as is the case with a pot, nor could it be eternal. How, [then], could the whole world be full of it? [With regard to your statement that all that has arisen, is arising and will arise is the Person (*puruṣa*),[258] we reply:]

VIII.60 To have the status of being a support (*ādhāratā*) is possible [only] for a substance, but the Self cannot logically be a substance.

---

[256] This is a criticism of MHK VIII.7.

[257] For a discussion of "substance" (*dravya*) designating the ultimate reality in Vedānta and Madhyamaka, see Introduction; Qvarnström 1988, 1989:96-130.

[258] MHK-TJ VIII.4.

Therefore, since [the Self] is unoriginated, like a skyflower, it does not have the status of being a support. [Furthermore, since the Self is not established as a substance:]

VIII.61 Where do all beings become the very Self of the one who experiences [the Self]?[259] Status of Self should not be ascribed to non-Self, just as status of being [should not be ascribed] to non-being.

VIII.62 Therefore, [since the supreme Self is not established], the non-difference between the ignorant [and the learned], etc., does not exist, [being] without support [or] illustration. From [the assumption of] the oneness of the Self, a deluge of manifold errors occur:

VIII.63 Let the Self of Maitra be perceived by the senses of Caitra, just like the Self of Caitra himself, if the nature [of Maitra] is non-different from [that of] Caitra, or there is no difference in the space [they occupy]. [Such a perception does not exist. The Self of Maitra and the Self of Caitra are, therefore, not one.]

VIII.64 [Let him then] experience [the other's] pleasure and pain, be liberated when he is liberated, be in bondage when he is in bondage, and suffer when he is suffering.[260] [Objection: although I have determined the support of the elements, etc., and the oneness without distinction of fools, etc., what harm is done? For I show as an example the "pot-space" simile, which is accepted by both sides.[261] Answer:]

[259] Cf. MHK VIII.9.

[260] A similar objection is found in MHK-TJ VIII.11.

[261] In TJ VIII.64, the Vedāntavādin maintains that the "pot-space" simile is accepted even by the Madhyamakas. The *Prasannapadā ad* XVIII.9 quotes an early

[Refutation of the Oneness and Existence of Space and Self]

VIII.65 [The oneness] of all [beings] cannot [be proved] by the pot-space simile.[262] It is impossible because the oneness of space, and its very existence (*bhāvatā*), is not proved.

VIII.66 [In the view of the Sautrāntikas, we accept on the conventional level that] that object (*bhāva*) which is empty of substance is, as is known (*hi*), the relative space, [since it is the mere absence of a resistant substance (*sapratighadravyābhāvamātra*)]. There is movement for those who move; there is room for those demanding room.[263] [Space exists, therefore, only as a designation. And since space was given as an example of a permanent (*nitya*), all-pervasive (*sarvatraga*) and singular (*eka*) Self, it is in fact dissimilar to that. Therefore, the Vedāntavādins have not established the Self.][264]

Mahāyāna sūtra, the *Āryasatyadvayāvatārasūtra,* which, apparently, already knows this simile. This is historically significant. See Introduction.

[262] See MHK VIII.10, 11, 13.

[263] TJ VIII.66 states (P. 299a[2]-299b[6]): "In the view of the Sautrāntikas, we accept on the conventional level (*saṃvṛtyā*) that space is the mere absence of a resistant substance (*sapratighadravyābhāvamātra*). Because that [space] is neither a substance (*dravya*) nor permanent (*nitya*), entities (*bhāva*) that are mobile move and perform actions of going and coming, etc., in it, and in that same space those who desire room (*avakāśa*) acquire room. Therefore, that is designated 'space' (*ākāśa*). /.../ Therefore there is not any substance (*dravya*) called space (*ākāśa*), and since space was given as an example of a Self (*ātman*) which is said to be permanent (*nitya*), all-pervasive (*sarvatraga*) and single (*eka*), it is in fact dissimilar to that, and thus it is not established for the other (i.e. for the Vedāntavādin)." On "space" as the mere absence of a substance, cf. *Abhidharmakośabhāṣya* II.55d; Nāgārjuna's *Ratnāvalī* I.99ab; Āryadeva's *Śataka* IX.3; Lang 1986:89, n. 5.

[264] In TJ VIII.66, the Vedāntavādins object to Bhāviveka's denial of the existence of space by quoting an interesting *sūtra*passage. See Introduction.

VIII.67 Space therefore is not an unimpeded (*anāvṛti*) [substance] and it is not an [active] provider (*dātṛ*) of room.[265] When this reason is given [by the opponent and incidentally by the Vaibhāṣikas] regarding its [i.e. space's] existence, it should not be accepted as a valid reason (*hetu*),[266] [since space is not an existing substance (*dravyasat*).][267]

VIII.68 [As to the statement that the Self is a permanent entity, all-pervasive, and the support of all entities, like space:] Again, (p) space cannot be regarded as an entity (*bhāva*), (h) since it does not stand in relation to a cause. (d) It is, therefore, not one [but inexisting], just as [the unreal] son of a barren woman [is not one.][268]

---

[265] According to Bhāviveka, space is conventionally the absence of substance, and as such is not unblocked. An all-pervading (i.e. an unblocked) Self could therefore not be likened to space. Furthermore, since space is not an active provider of room, because it *is* room, the Self as an agent cannot be likened to space either.

[266] On the usage of a simile (*dṛṣṭānta*) as a logical reason (*hetu*), see *Gauḍapādīya-kārikā* IV.20; *Nyāyasūtra* I.1.34-37, V.1.11.

[267] TJ VIII.67 states (P. 299b⁷-300a⁴): The Vaibhāṣikas maintain that space (*ākāśa*) has the characteristic of non-obstruction (*anāvṛti*) and has the result that it provides room (*avakāśa*), but that does not exist for me because space is not a substance possessing existence (*dravyasat*). Objection: space indeed exists, because it has the characteristic of non-obstruction (*anāvṛti*) and because it has the result of making room (*avakāśa*). /.../ [Answer:] These reasons mentioned here are unestablished for others. We maintain that space (*ākāśa*) is just devoid of the nature of a substance (*dravya*). Moreover, as to the statement [of the opponent] that the Self (*ātman*) is a permanent (*nitya*) entity (*bhāva*) and is all-pervasive (*sarvatraga*) and is the support (*ādhāra*) of all entities (*bhāva*) like space, in order to adduce a disproof differently from that, the *ācārya*[5] [i.e. Bhāviveka] says the following: [MHK VIII.68]. (Bhāviveka here refers to himself as *ācārya*, see Introduction.)

[268] TJ VIII.68 (P. 299b⁷-300a⁴) explains: "The subject (*dharmin*) is 'space', the property [which is to be proved] (*sādhyadharma*) of [the subject in the thesis] is 'that is not an entity'. The logical reason (*hetu*) is 'because it is not originated (*anupapannāt*) from a cause (*hetu*)'. A synonymous way of expressing this is that it

VIII.69 [Even though] clay (*mṛd*) in the shape of pots, etc., is one [and the same thing] in the sense that it belongs to the category clay (*mṛjjātīya*), in [each individual] pot, etc., there is always a different and new [portion of clay]. Therefore the Self is not one.[269] [You have said that, because one has not awakened to absorption into the Self and has not known the Self, one's experiences are like the enjoyments in a dream.[270] In that case, will one be conceited because one knows or because one does not know?]

VIII.70 When one knows, [like one who has a visual organ through which he gets his knowledge conforming to reality (*yathārtha*)], one cannot regard it as a state of imagination of the knower because there is no error. And again, when one does not know, [like one who is blind from birth], one cannot regard it as a state of imagination of the non-knower because there is no error [here either].[271] [As to

---

originates having been produced from causes and conditions (*hetupratyaya*). Space has not originated from a productive cause (*janakahetu*). How can that which has no cause (*hetu*) be an entity (*bhāva*)? [It is, therefore, unreal] like the son of a barren woman (*vandhyātanaya*)."

[269] This is a criticism of MHK VIII.12.

[270] MHK VIII.14.

[271] The notion of dependent origination (*pratītyasamutpāda*), the middle way (*madhyamā pratipad*) or emptiness (*śūnyatā*), which underlies Bhāviveka's argumentation in VTV, see Introduction, is here instrumental in criticizing the Vedāntavādin's claim that the non-knower of the Self is conceited. According to Bhāviveka, everything is to be understood complementarily, i.e., in relation to its opposite: knowledge (*jñāna*) presupposes non-knowledge (*ajñāna*); space (*ākāśa*), substance (*dravya*); origination (*jāti*), non-origination (*ajāti*); etc., and vice versa. Ignorance therefore cannot have a characteristic of its own (*svalakṣaṇa*), since it does not exist in or by itself (*niḥsvabhāva*). Consequently the ignorance of the non-knower of the Self cannot be characterized as erroneous or imaginary. Ultimately, knowledge and non-knowledge, etc., are purely abstractions, designations (*nāma*) or metaphors (*upacāra*). Bhāviveka seems furthermore to maintain that one cannot be a part of the Self and yet be ignorant of it, as the

your statement that though the "Person" exists in the body, He is not attached, and though He enjoys objects, He is not stained by them,[272] we answer:]

[Refutation of the Self as Agent and Enjoyer]

VIII.71 Because [the Self] does not change (*avikāritva*) and is not attached (*asaṅgatva*),[273] like space (*vyoman*), it is not logical that the Self is the agent (*kartṛ*), and it is not logical that it is the enjoyer (*bhoktṛ*) either. [Something which always remains the same, not engaged in its own activity and not attached to objects, could not be an agent or an enjoyer.][274]

Vedāntavādins maintain. If one does not know the Self, it cannot exist. Either one knows the Self, or one does not. See also MHK VIII.47 with n.

[272] MHK-TJ VIII.15.

[273] This is a criticism of MHK VIII.15ab.

[274] A fundamental (*pradhāna*), independent agent does not exist apart from causes and conditions, according to Bhāviveka. It is only if something has the property of change that it is true to say that it is an agent (*kartṛ*) or experiencer (*bhoktṛ*). In TJ VIII.30, Bhāviveka refers to the science of grammar (*śabdaśāstra*), according to which an action must have an independent agent. On *svatantraḥ kartā* (independent agent), see the *Aṣṭādhyāyī* (I.4.54) of Pāṇini. In ch. XXV of Bhāviveka's *Prajñāpradīpa*, it is said, however, that the *nirmāṇakāya* acts without disturbing the non-activity of the *dharma-* or *tathāgatakāya*. Bhāviveka's position in PP regarding agenthood seems, therefore, to contradict that of VTV. The *Mahāyānottaratantra* or *Ratnagotravibhāga* takes a similar stand as that of PP: *mahākaruṇayā kṛtsnaṃ lokam ālokya lokavit / dharmakāyād aviralaṃ nirmāṇaiś citrarūpibhiḥ* // (II.53) *jātakāny upapattiṃ ca tuṣiteṣu cyutiṃ tataḥ* / (II.54ab) *kṣetreṣv apariśuddheṣu darśayatyā bhavasthiteḥ* // (II.56cd) "Having surveyed the entire world with His Great Compassion the Knower of the World (*Buddha*) without locomoting from his Absolute Medium (*Dharmakāya*) by way of His Transformation [Medium] (*Nirmāna*[*kāya*]) in protean garbs [He] displays origination in *Vita* [of any individual] in impure Realms [such as our World] as long as the World is durating." (Sørensen 1986b:172-173).

VIII.72 [The characteristic mark of an agent, when he is an agent, is that he is stained by the results (*phala*) of beneficial (*kuśala*) and non-beneficial (*akuśala*) actions. Therefore:] If the agent, which is the Self, is not defiled [by the result of action (*karma*)], how can the agent [produce] the result (*phala*) wished for? [If there is no later enjoyment (*anubhoga*) of the results, all the actions of the agent will be pointless. Therefore, because the agent will not possess the quality of enjoying the results, agenthood is very difficult to establish.] The example of the king is [therefore] not logical, because the king partakes of evil.[275] [As to the statement of yours that the Self is one (*eka*), all-pervasive (*sarvatraga*) and eternal (*nitya*):][276]

[Refutation of the Self as One, All-pervasive, Permanent, Inexpressible and Inconceivable]

VIII.73 It is not logical that [the Self, which is] without a second (*advitīya*), is one, since it is independent of anything external (*bāhya*). If it is one from its connection to oneness, [then] the relation (*yoga*) is only to itself; there is no other [relation. Since the Self exists as everything internal and external, in relation to what will it be one? And if the Self is said to be one by being related to the number one, then how will the Self relate to itself since there does not exist anything different from the Self? This is impossible, just like it is impossible that a finger itself can touch the tip of that very same finger. If you say that the Self is imagined to have many ways of manifesting itself as subject (*viṣayin*) and object (*viṣaya*), and that

---

[275] This is a criticism of MHK-TJ VIII.15. In TJ VIII.72, Bhāviveka states furthermore that, because the king would have the fear of falling into hell, etc., it is taught that he should perform actions in accordance with *dharma*. But if he were not stained by sin, etc., this would not be taught.

[276] See, e.g., MHK-TJ VIII.16.

by means of excluding that manifoldness, the Self should be said to be just one, we say:]

VIII.74 If, although conceptualized [to be] many, [the Self] is one due to the rejection (*apoha*) of that [manifoldness], oneness would not exist in reality (*tattvatas*), since the conception (*kalpanā*) [of oneness, etc.,] is relative (*sāṃvṛtī*):

VIII.75 If this [Self] existed in reality with the nature of permanency, oneness, etc., [then] the function of words and cognitions of "the one", etc. (*ekādiśabdadhīvṛtti*), [would be] infallible (*niratyayā*), if [its] referent (*artha*)[277] existed. [But since there is nothing but the Self, the Self and the cognition of which it is an object are not different. Therefore, this method has a fault:]

VIII.76 Since one conceptualizes [the Self] to be one, etc., how can this Self be devoid of conceptual construction? [This is impossible, since there does not exist any difference between the cognition and the Self.] The usage of words in relation to a referent (*artha*) which is the object of conceptual construction (*vikalpaviṣaya*) meets no obstacle.

VIII.77 How can [you] therefore [maintain that the Self] is neither an object of cognition (*dhī*) nor an object of speech (*gir*)? In accordance with the previous argument (*nīti*), it is false (*vitatha*) that

[277] The reason why Bhāviveka in MHK VIII.76 does not distinguish between the fact that the Self has a conceptual construction (*vikalpa*) and that we have a *vikalpa* of the Self is due to the fact that he maintains that for the Vedāntavādins, there does not exist any difference between the Self (*ātman*) and the cognition (*jñāna*).

[such a Self] is inexpressible (*avācya*) [and] without conceptual construction (*nirvikalpa*).[278]

[Refutation of Liberation or Enlightenment as a State of Self-identity of Non-origination Resulting from the Cognition of the Self]

VIII.78 If liberation (*mukti*) comes from seeing (*darśana*)[279] [that Self] by means of cognition (*buddhi*), how can oneness exist? [There cannot be oneness] because they [i.e. the cognition and the Self] are different. Furthermore, this [liberation] would also be false in analogy with the previous [argument],[280] because it [i.e. the Self] would be grasped [as an object], like the cognition of multiplicity (*nānātvadhī*).[281]

VIII.79 If there is a cognition (*jñāna*) which knows the self-identity of non-origination (*ajātisamatā*),[282] [then], because there is no

---

[278] MHK-TJ VIII.73-77 seems to be Bhāviveka's critique of MHK-TJ VIII.17.

[279] As mentioned in n. *ad* VIII.24, Bhāviveka expresses the cognition of the enlightened in terms of a cognition which "moves without moving". Cf. MHK V.106: *akalajñeyayāthātmyam ākāśasamacetasaḥ / jñānena nirvikalpena buddhāḥ paśyanty adarśanāt //* "Then, without seeing, they see all objects of knowledge just as they are, with non-conceptual knowledge and with minds like space." (Eckel 2008:295, 442.) The *Dharmasaṃgītisūtra* states also: *adarśanaṃ bhagavan sarvadharmāṇāṃ darśanaṃ samyagdarśanam*, "O Lord, not to see is to see all *dharmas*: this is true seeing" (Eckel 1987:115, n. 15). See also Gokhale 1963. Expressions like "to see without seeing" or "to move without moving" I take as metaphorical, referring to a cognition which is of a non-grasping nature. See the interesting information on *a-dassana* ("not seeing" and "not being seen"!) in *A Critical Pāli Dictionary*, p. 118.

[280] See MHK VIII.24.

[281] Cf. *Gauḍapādīyakārikā* III.13, IV.91.

[282] On *ajātisamatā*, see *Gauḍapādīyakārikā* III.2b, III.38d. Cf. *Gauḍapādīyakārikā* IV.93d (*ajaṃ sāmyam*), IV.95a (*aje sāmye*), IV.100b (*ajaṃ sāmyam*) (see Lindtner 1985a:275-276). The *Āryasatyadvayāvatārasūtra* quoted in the *Madhyamakavṛtti* (La Vallée

difference [between the cognition and the state of self-identity of non-origination], how could seeing exist? Liberation would [then] result from "non-seeing", otherwise there would not be liberation (*mukti*) for anyone.

VIII.80 If enlightenment (*bodha*) results from the arising of that [seeing], how could non-origination be self-identical? If it (i.e. seeing) does not arise because it is not an existing entity, it would be the same as a conceptual construction of that [self-identity of non-origination.]

VIII.81 Non-origination (*ajāti*) is a phenomenon (*dharma*) which resembles origination (*jāti*), but it exists [only] as the non-existence [of origination]. It is [therefore] not at all (*nāpi na*)[283] logical that [this phenomenon of non-origination] is identical with the Self or abiding in it (*tatsthatā*).[284]

Poussin ed., p. 374) states: *paramārthataḥ sarvadharmānutpādasamatayā paramārthataḥ sarvadharmatyantājātisamatayā paramārthataḥ samāḥ sarvadharmāḥ* /.../. This passage should have been mentioned by Lindtner 1985a. It proves, however, that Lindtner was right in taking *ajāti* and *samatā* in the *Gauḍapādīyakārikā* III.38 as a compound. On *anutpādasamatā,* see Conze 1973:32 (*°samatā, °sama, °jñāna*), and *Mūlamadhyamakakārikā* XVIII.12 (*saṃbuddhānām anutpāde* /.../).

[283] The expression *nāpi na* ("not at all") is of rare occurrence.

[284] MHK VIII.81cd seems to be Bhāviveka's answer to the *Gauḍapādīyakārikā* III.38cd (*ātmasaṃsthaṃ tadā jñānam* /.../) (see Lindtner 1985a:276). Non-origination (*ājati*) is then the absence of origination (*jāti*), just as space (*ākāśa*) is the absence of a resistant substance (*sapratighadravyābhāvamātra,* MHK-TJ VIII.66). The Self could therefore not be likened to either *ajāti* or *ākāśa,* which consequently do not possess intrinsic nature (*svabhāva*).

VIII.82 In the non-originated, no difference is allowed to exist by which potentiality (*samarthana*),[285] [could exist], since in reality unbornness (*ajatva*) is not accepted either for the born or the unborn.

VIII.83 If [you claim] that [Self] is non-different from a skyflower (*khapuṣpa*), [then you are] holding on to an unreal position (*asatpakṣa*). If [you alternately say that] there is differentiation (*bheda*) in the absolute (*pariniṣpatti*), [then] non-duality (*advaita*)[286] cannot be established.

VIII.84 The Self is neither being nor non-being,[287] neither separate (*pṛthak*) nor non-separate, neither eternal nor non-eternal, nor an object of cognition or speech (*buddhidhvanigocara*).[288]

VIII.85 [If you say: do not also the Buddhists maintain that which transcends the sphere of speech and cognition to be ultimately real?" we answer: that is true. Nevertheless this is the reasoning (*yukti*):][289] since no object of knowledge can be established in any

---

[285] Cf. *Gauḍapādīyakārikā* IV.19: *aśaktir aparijñānaṃ kramakopo 'tha vā punaḥ / evaṃ hi sarvathā buddhair ajātiḥ paridīpitā* // "As there is absence of capability, or complete ignorance, or, again, incompatibility of orders, the Buddhas elucidated [the theory of] absolute non-origination (*ajāti*)." (ed. and tr. by Bhattacharya 1940:121). See also Bhattacharya *ibid.*, pp. 121-123. Cf. also Lindtner's (1984b:152-153, n. 9) discussion of the objection stated in *Pramāṇavārttika* III.4a (*aśaktaṃ sarvam iti ced* /... /), where, according to Lindtner, Dharmakīrti is compelled to admit that *śakti* is only real from a relative perspective (*saṃvṛtyā*). We are consequently dealing here with a tradition which is far from considering the absolute as "dynamic" – it holds just the contrary.

[286] On *advaita*, see Vetter 1979:31-34.

[287] Cf. MHK III.287; TJ III.111; *Ratnāvalī* I.72.

[288] Cf. *Gauḍapādīyakārikā* II.34; *Mūlamadhyamakakārikā* X.16.

[289] Cf. TJ VIII.77.

respect,[290] there is logically no domain of operation for cognition (*buddhi*). When the realm of cognition [therefore] has ceased, the domain of speech could not exist [either.[291] Conventionally, the object of knowledge, which is the object of the six forms of cognition (*vijñāna*), is imagined (*parikalpita*), but in reality (*tattvatas*), what is imagined or conceptually constructed is completely unestablished. Therefore, since cognition does not arise in regard to that non-existing object, that is not an object of cognition, and because the object of cognition has ceased, speech also does not function, since its basis does not exist.]

[The Vedāntadarśana - A Completely Heterogeneous System]

VIII.86 Being convinced that this infallible system of the Tathāgata is a good one (*śubha*), here [in the Vedānta system] the heterodox sectarians (*tīrthya*), being desirous (*spṛhā*) of [that doctrine], have therefore [even] made it their own,[292] [saying: "This is our system". But that is eclecticism, endowed with the fault which consists in the contradiction of former and latter parts, and it is therefore to be classified as a mental construction (*vikalpa*). Therefore:]

VIII.87 Who would have faith in this [Vedānta philosophy], the former and latter [parts] of which are incompatible (*atyantātulya-jātīya*), and which consists of [elements] as utterly disparate as a jewel and [a piece of] iron?[293] [If you Vedāntavādins say that

---

[290] MHK VIII.85ab=III.266ab. See n. *ad* VIII.24.

[291] MHK-TJ III.285-286 states that Reality could not be reached by logic (cf. MHK-TJ V.104; *Laṅkāvatārasūtra* II.122) or by conceptual or non-conceptual cognition.

[292] On Bhāviveka's attitude towards the Vedāntadarśana, see Introduction.

[293] Bhāviveka is clearly reflecting Mātṛceṭa: The *Varṇārhavarṇastotra* VII.19 states: *ito bāhyeṣu yat sūktaṃ ghuṇākṣaravad īk[ṣy]ate / tat tatrātulyajātīyaṃ jātarūpam ivāyasi //* "Was bei denen, die auß erhalb [dieser Lehre stehen], an Wohl-

contradictions also occur for the Madhyamakas who say that there is something which possesses a Self and something which does not possess a Self, and that there is emptiness (*śūnyatā*) and external emptiness (*bāhyaśūnyatā*), origination and non-origination, existence and non-existence, then we answer:]

VIII.88 Due to the manifoldness (*vaicitrya*) of the [Buddhist] teaching (*deśanā*), let this principle (*naya*) [of Self and non-Self etc., which is in accordance with relative (*saṃvṛti*) and absolute truth (*paramārtha-satya*)] be like this here, for the sake of attracting some and [for the sake of] turning the rest away from grasping (*grāha*). [In order to divert those who grasp and advocate non-existence, and whose minds are impaired by the view (*dṛṣṭi*) which negates (*apavāda*) causality (*hetuphala*), the existence of the Self is taught. And in order to stop attachment to, or grasping at a Self (*ātmagraha*) by the adherents of a Self (*ātmavādin*), the non-existence of the Self is taught. To those endowed with receptivity (*kṣānti*) for the vast and profound doctrine (*dharma*), it is ultimately taught that neither the Self nor the non-Self exists. Therefore, there is no contradiction. If you ask: how is that? we answer:][294]

---

gesprochenem – gleichsam wie ein von einem Holzwurm [hervorgebrachter] Buchstabe – gefunden wird, das ist dort von so ungleicher Natur wie Gold zwischen Eisen" (Hartmann 1987:228). *Varṇārhavarṇastotra* VII.20ab: *kaḥ śraddhāsyati tat tasmin pūrvāparaparāhatam* / (Hartmann 1987:229) has clearly inspired Bhāviveka in MHK VIII.87ab: *kaḥ śraddhāsyati tāṃ tatra pūrvāpara-virodhinīm* /.

[294] TJ VIII.88 states: The Blessed One (*bhagavat*) has taught the very existence of the Self (*ātman*) in order to divert those who grasp non-existence and advocate non-existence, [and] whose minds are impaired by the view (*dṛṣṭi*) which negates (*apavāda*) causality (*hetuphala*). He attracts those and in order to stop attachment to the grasping of a Self (*ātmagraha*) among the adherents of a Self (*ātmavādin*), he teaches: "The Self does not exist" (*ātmā nāsti*). Conventionally (*saṃvṛtitas*), he teaches the abandonment of the Self, and to those who are endowed with

[Unoriginatedness and Lack of Intrinsic Nature as the "Intrinsic Nature" or "Self" of All Entities]

VIII.89 For the intrinsic nature of [all] entities is non-originatedness, because they have no creator (*kartṛ*), [existent and non-existent entities not having originated (*utpanna*) from themselves (*svatas*), from another (*paratas*), from both (*dvābhyām*), or from no cause (*ahetutas*)]. And because it does not cease, this [intrinsic nature] is also called the Self.

VIII.90 That [nature] is one (*eka*) by virtue of its single nature (*ekarūpatva*), [and] because it is undifferentiated (*abheda*) even when there is differentiation of entities. It is all-pervasive (*sarvaga*), because [it possesses the property of grasping the own-characteristic of no-characteristic (*alakṣaṇasvalakṣaṇa*)] of all *dharmas* (*sarvadharma*). Furthermore, it is also eternal (*nitya*) because it does not disappear (*avināśa*). [That nature is also the Self, because it is unoriginated intrinsic nature.]

VIII.91 That [nature] is unoriginated (*ajāta*), since it is not originated (*ajātatva*). Precisely for that reason, it is not subject to old age and death (*ajarāmara*). It is imperishable (*acyuta*) because it is free from extinction. It is considered supreme (*para*) because of excellence (*prakarṣa*) [with regard to its nature.]

---

receptivity (*kṣānti*) for the vast and profound doctrine (*dharma*), he teaches that in ultimate reality (*paramārthatas*) there is neither Self (*ātman*) nor non-Self (*anātman*). Thus the very teachings in the many preachings (*pravacana*) of the Blessed One are taught in accordance with relative (*saṃvṛti*) and absolute (*paramārtha*) [truth (*satya*)], so there is no contradiction. On references to the pedagogical attitude in various Buddhist texts, see the *Prajñāpradīpa* XVIII.5d, 6 (Eckel 1980:217-220); Introduction.

VIII.92 It is not form, sound, smell, etc. It is not earth, fire, water [or] air. It is not space, the moon, the sun, etc. It does not have the defining characteristic of mind (*manas*) [which is to think] or of knowledge (*jñāna*)[295] [which is to know.]

VIII.93 That [nature] is everything, because it is the intrinsic nature [of all entities], but it is not every particular [entity], since it is without destruction. Because defilements (*kleśa*), etc., do not arise there [in that unoriginatedness or Self], that is pure and tranquil (*śānta*), [because it has completely transcended all actions.]

VIII.94 It is expressible by virtue of the imposition of conceptual constructions (*kalpanāsamāropa*), but it is inexpressible (*avācya*) in reality, and furthermore because it is in every respect in expressible (*avācyatva*), it is said to be unmanifest (*nirañjana*).[296]

VIII.95 Obviously, if such a Self [or intrinsic nature described above] is accepted even by you, [then] that [Self or intrinsic nature, which is the general characteristic (*sāmānyalakṣaṇa*) of non-origination], is faultless and completely proper because of extensive conceptual correspondences (*sādharmya*) with regard to name, etc.: [you say "supreme Self" (*paramātman*) and we say "non-origination" (*ajātitva*). Therefore:]

VIII.96 Those who are afraid of the absence of a Self (*nairātmya*), remain in fear only there [in that very absence, because there is no support apart from that], just as one who is afraid of space [remains

---

[295] Cf. the characteristics of a person (*skyes bu/puruṣa*) in the *Ratnāvalī* (I.80) and the description of *nirvāṇa* given in the *Suhṛllekha* 105.

[296] On *nirañjana,* cf. MHK III.274cd; *Ālokamālā* 53, 194 (Lindtner 1985b:138-139, 186-187).

exactly there in that space, because there is no other place than space]. Where else could he remain?[297]

VIII.97 Welcome [you Vedāntavādins]! Quench your thirst![298] Here [in this preaching (*pravacana*)] no one is turned away. The Buddhas, the friends of the world (*lokabandhu*),[299] [offer] this very exquisite nectar of reality (*tattvāmṛta*).

VIII.98 But abandon this false notion (*asadgrāha*) to there being a Self, an agent, an enjoyer, etc. It is groundless (*nirāspada*), [and] it prevents one from seeing the real (*bhūtadṛś*).

VIII.99 [Objection: if our Self (*ātman*) and your non-Self (*anātman*) are similar, then our systems (*siddhānta*) would be equal. Answer:] in reality, one has to accept that entities are unoriginated, because they do not arise by their own nature. [When] they are said to be without intrinsic nature (*niḥsvabhāvatā*), it is because they do not arise by virtue of [their] own nature.

VIII.100 Lack of intrinsic nature and lack of Self, that is not [the same as] Self, because that would be contradictory. If lack of Self would be the same as Self, [then] the absence of a cow would be the same as [the presence] of a cow.

VIII.101 This absence of intrinsic nature is logical. How, [then, can there be] the condition of agent or enjoyer? Is not the status of a barren woman's son as agent or enjoyer seen here to be without cause?

---

[297] Cf. MHK III.278 (*apratiṣṭha*), III.294; TJ I.21 (*apratiṣṭhita*), TJ I.16 (*apratiṣṭhita-nirvāṇa*). On "fear of emptiness", see *Ratnāvalī* ch. I, etc.

[298] *Svāgataṃ*! *kriyatāṃ tṛptir*! = "Welcome!" "Cheers!"

[299] *lokabandhu*, cf. MHK III.315.

VIII.102 How can [all worlds and beings] originate from such a [fictitious Self], and how can they dissolve into it?[300] It is impossible to imagine anything arising from or being dissolved into a skyflower.

VIII.103 As long as a cognition occurs which has as its object the absence of intrinsic nature, so long will we think of the existence of "one", etc., by the imposition of conceptual construction of the mind. [The intrinsic nature of oneness, etc., does not, however, exist in reality.][301]

VIII.104 When conceptual and [finally] non-conceptual cognition[302] [which apprehends non-Self (*anātman*) without conceiving it as either having or not having an intrinsic nature] cease, [then] the peaceful, [completely inexpressible] cessation of diversity [occurs] when it is not an object of the mind.[303] [That nature in which all entities are completely unestablished (*aparinispanna*) and which is beyond speech and cognition is, therefore, Reality.[304] The view of a Self which is conceptually constructed by you is, however, not Reality.]

---

[300] Cf. MHK-TJ III.288; MHK-TJ VIII.5; *Madhyamakavṛtti Prasannapadā* by Candrakīrti (pp. 533.9, 194.14, 195.2, La Vallée Poussin's ed.)

[301] Cf. MHK VIII.74.

[302] Cf. MHK III.265: *nirvikalpārthaviṣayā nirvikalpāpi dhīr mṛṣā / anātmādisvabhāvatvāt tadyathā savikalpadhīḥ* // "A cognition that has 'no concept' as an object is false, even though it is non-conceptual, because it is [a cognition of] no-self and so forth, like a conceptual cognition" (tr. by Malcolm D. Eckel).

[303] Cf. MHK III.284d: *'yaṃ prapañcopaśamaḥ śivaḥ* / "This is the peaceful cessation of conceptual diversity", a clear echo of Nāgārjuna's *Mūlamadhyamakakārikā* XXV.24, etc.

[304] Cf. Bhāviveka's description of reality (*tattva*) in MHK-TJ I.1-3 (See Gokhale/ Bahulkar 1985:82-83).

Bibliography

Primary Sources

Abhidharmakośa of Vasubandhu

Edited and translated into French by Louis de La Vallée Poussin as *L'Abhidharmakośa de Vasubandhu. Nouvelle Édition. Présentée par Étienne Lamotte.* Mélanges Chinois et Bouddhiques XVI, Tome 1-6. Bruxelles 1923-31.

Index to the Abhidharmakośabhāṣya. Akira Hirakawa, in collaboration with Shunei Hirai ... [et al.]. Pts. 1-3. Tokyo: Daizō Shuppan, 1973-1978.

Acintyastava of Nāgārjuna

See Lindtner 1982b.

Aṣṭādhyāyī of Pāṇini

La grammaire de Pāṇini. Texte sanskrit, traduction française avec extraits des commentaires par Louis Renou. 2 vols. Paris: École française d'extrême-orient, 1966.

Aṣṭāvakragītā

Edited and translated into German by R. Hauschild as *Die Aṣṭāvakragītā.* Abhandlungen der Sächsischen Akademie der Wissenschaften zu Leipzig. Philologisch-Historische Klasse. Band 58, Heft 2. Berlin 1967.

Bhagavadgītā

Edited with Śaṅkara's commentary, *Śrīmadbhagavadgītā[bhāṣya].* Ānandāśrama Sanskrit Series 34. Poona 1896.

Bodhicaryāvatārapañjikā
Commentary to the *Bodhicaryāvatāra* of Śāntideva. Edited by Louis de la Vallée Poussin. Calcutta 1901-1914.

Bodhicittavivaraṇa of Nāgārjuna
See Lindtner 1982b.

Bodhicaryāvatārapañjikā of Prajñākaramatī
Commentary to the *Bodhicaryāvatāra* of Śāntideva. Edited by Louis de la Vallée Poussin. Calcutta 1901-1914.

Brahmasūtrabhāṣya of Śaṅkara
Edited by A. Śāstri as *The Brahmasūtra Śaṅkara Bhāṣya.* Bombay: Nirṇaya Sagar Press, 1938.

Catuḥśataka of Āryadeva
See Lang 1986.

Dvātriṃśikā ascribed to Siddhasena Divākara
See Qvarnström 2003, 2014.

**Dvādaśadvāraka*
See Cheng 1982.

Gauḍapādīyakārikā of *Gauḍapāda*
See Bhattacharya 1943.

Lalitavistara of Nāgārjuna
Edited by P.L. Vaidya. Darbhanga: Mithila Institute of Post-Graduate Studies and Research in Sanskrit Learning, 1958.

Lokatattvanirṇaya of Haribhadrasūri

Sanskrit text edited and translated into Italian by L. Suali as "Il «Lokatattvanirṇaya» di Haribhadra. *Giornale della Societa Asiatica Italiana* 10:263-319, 1905.

Madhyamakahṛdayakārikā and *Tarkajvālā* of Bhāviveka

Bahulkar, Shrikant S. 1994. *The Madhyamaka-hṛdaya-kārikā of Bhāvaviveka. A Photographic Reproduction of Prof. V.V. Gokhale's Copy.* Nagoya Studies in Indian Culture and Buddhism. Saṃbhāṣā 15. University of Nagoya, i-iv, 1-49.

Lindtner, Christian. 2001. *Madhyamakahṛdayam of Bhavya.* Adyar: The Adyar Library and Research Centre. [Edition of MHK based on Ms.]

He, Huānhuān. 2013. *A Study of the Madhyamakahṛdayakārikā and the Tarkajvālā.* Vols. I-II. Beijing. [Edition and Chinese translation of MHK-TJ VI-VIII based on Ms.]

Tattvajñāneṣanā

Ed. and tr. by Annette Heltmann as *Nektar der Erkenntnis. Buddhistische Philosophie des 6.Jh.: Bhavya's Tarkajvālā I-III.* Aachen: Shaker Verlag, 2004.

Sāṃkhyatattvanirṇayāvatāra

Nakada, Naomichi. 1972. "The Sanskrit Text of the *Madhyamaka-hṛdaya-kārikā (dBu-ma'i snying-po'i tshig-le'ur byas-pa)* and the Tibetan text of the *Madhymaka-hṛdaya-vṛtti-Tarkajvālā (dBu-ma'i snying-po'i 'grel-pa rtog-ge 'bar-ba)*, ṣaṣṭhaḥ paricchedaḥ/ Sāṃkhyatattvāvatāraḥ // (Part 1. Pūrvapakṣa, vv. 1-4)." *Tsurumi Jyosi Daigaku Tankidaigaku bu Kiyo* 6:145-155.

Nakada, Naomichi. 1983. "The Sanskrit Text of the *Madhyamakahṛdaya-kārikā (dBu-ma'i snying-po'i tshig-le'ur byas-pa)* and the Tibetan text of the *Madhymakahṛdaya-vṛtti-Tarkajvālā (dBu-ma'i snying-po'i 'grel-pa rtog-ge 'bar-ba)*, ṣaṣṭhaḥ paricchedaḥ/ Sāṃkhyatattvāvatāraḥ // (Part 2. Uttarapakṣa, vv.5-7)."*Tsurumi Daigaku Kiyo* 20-4:1-3.

Vedāntatattvaviniścaya
Gokhale, V.V. 1958. "The Vedānta Philosophy Described by Bhavya in his Madhyamakahṛdaya." *Indo-Iranian Journal* 2/3:165-180. [Edition of MHK VIII.1-17 (*pūrvapakṣa*) based on Msc.]

Nakamura, Hajime. 1958. "The Tibetan Text of the Madhyamaka-hṛdaya-vṛtti Tarkajvālā (dBu-ma'i snying-po'i 'grel-pa rtog-ge 'bar-ba)." *Indo-Iranian Journal* 2/3:181-190. [Edition of TJ VIII.1-17.]

Nakamura, Hajime. 1975. "The Vedāntic Chapter of Bhavya's Madhyamakahṛdaya." *Adyar Library Bulletin* XXXIX:300-329. [Edition of MHK VIII based on Msc.]

Nakamura, Hajime. 1981. *Shoki no Vedānta Tetsugaku.* Vol. 1. Tokyo. [Edition of MHK VIII based on Msc.]

Walleser 1910.
[German translation of MHK VIII.1-3, 5, 11-14.]

Qvarnström, O. 1989. *Hindu Philosophy in Buddhist Perspective. The Vedāntatattvaviniścaya Chapter of Bhavya's Madhyamaka-hṛdayakārikā.* Lund: Almqvist Wiksell International. [Edition of MHK VIII based on Ms.]

Qvarnström, Olle. 1990. "The Vedāntatattvaviniścaya Chapter of Bhavya's Madhyamakahṛdayakārikā." *Wiener Zeitschrift für die Kunde Südasiens* XXXIV:181-198. [Edition of MHK VIII based on Ms.]

Mahābhārata

Critical Edition of the Mahābhārata. Pune: Bhandarkar Oriental Research Institute, 1919-1966.

Majjhima Nikāya

Edited by V. Treckner (Vol. I) and R. Chalmers (Vols. II-III). London: Pali Text Society, 1888, 1896, 1899.

Mahāvyutpatti

Edited by R. Sakaki. 2 vols. Kyoto 1916-1925 (Repr: 1962, 1965). Tibetan index by Nishio, K. Kyoto 1936 (Repr: 1962, 1965).

Manusmṛti

Mānava Dharma-Śāstra. The Code of Manu. Original Sanskrit text edited by J. Jolly. London 1887.

Mūlamadhyamakakārikā of Nāgārjuna

Edited by Louis de la Vallée Poussin as *Mūlamadhyamakārikās de Nāgārjuna avec la Prasannapadā Commentaire de Candrakīrti*. St. Pétersbourg 1907-1912.

Nyāyasūtra

Edited by W. Ruben as *Die Nyāyasūtras. Text, Übersetzung, Erläuterung und Glossar.* Leipzig 1928.

Nirukta of Yāska

The Nighaṇṭu and the Nirukta: The Oldest Indian Treatise on Etymology, Philology, and Semantics. Edited and translated by Lakshman Sarup. Vols. I-III. Delhi: Motilal Banarsidass, 1967.

Nyāyakumudacandra of Prabhācandra

Edited by Pt. Mahendra Kumar Nyaya Shastri. Jaina Granthamālā, Vol. I. Bombay 1938.

Paramārthasāra of *Ādiśeṣa*

Edited and translated by H. Danielson as *Ādiśeṣa. The Essence of Supreme Truth* (*Paramārthasāra*). Leiden 1980.

Prajñāpradīpa of Bhāviveka

See Ames 1986, Kajiyama 1963.

Pramāṇasamuccaya of Dignāga

See Hattori 1968.

Prameyakamalamārtaṇḍa of Prabhācandra

Edited by Mahendra Kumar Shastri. Sri Garib Dass Oriental Series, No. 94.
3 ed. Delhi: Sri Satguru Publications 1990 (1 ed. 1912).

Prasannapadā of Candrakīrti

Edited and translated into French by J. May as *Candrakīrti Prasannapadā Madhyamakavṛtti.* Paris: Adrien Maisonneuve, 1959.

Ratnagotravibhāga
Edited by E.H. Johnston and T. Chowdhury. *Journal of the Bihar and Orissa Research Society* 36, 1950.

Ratnāvalī of Nāgārjuna
Edited by M. Hahn. Indica et Tibetica. Vol. 1. Bonn 1982.

Ṛgvedasaṃhitā
Edited by B.A. van Nooten & G.B. Holland as *Rig Veda. A Metrically Restored Text with an Introduction and Notes.* Harvard Oriental Series 50. Cambridge, Mass.: Harvard University Press, 1994.

Ṣaḍdarśanasamuccaya of Haribhadrasūri
Edited by L. Suali as *Ṣaḍdarśanasamuccaya by Haribhadra with Guṇaratna's Commentary Tarkarahasyādīpikā.* Calcutta 1905.

Sāṃkhyakārikā of Īśvarakṛṣṇa and commentary by Gauḍapāda
Les Strophes de Sāṃkhya (Sāṃkhya-Kārikā) avec le commentaire de Gauḍapāda. Texte Sanskrit et traduction annotée par Anne-Marie Esnoul. Paris: Collection Émile Senart 9, 1964.

Sāṃkhya-Vṛttị (V2)
Edited by Esther A. Solomon. Ahmedabad: Gujarat University, 1973.

Saṃyutta Nikāya
Edited by L. Feer. London: Pali Text Society. 5 vols., 1884-1898.

Syādvādamañjarī of Malliṣeṇa with the *Anyayogavyavacchedikā* of Hemacandra. Edited by A.B. Dhruva. Delhi 1933.

Śāstravārtāsamuccaya of Haribhadrasūri
Sanskrit text ed. by K. K. Dixit. Ahmedabad: L. D. Institute of Indology, 1969.

Śāstravārtāsamuccaya and *Dikpradā* of Haribhadrasūri
Śāstravārtāsamuccaya by Śrī-Haribhadra-Sūri with his own Commentary named Dikpradā. Bombay: Nirnaya-Sagar Press, 1929.

Satyaśāsanaparīkṣā of Vidyānandin
Edited By Gokul Chandra Jain. Bhāratīya Jñānapīṭha Mūrtidevī Jaina Granthamālā, No. 30, 1964.

Siddhasāra
The Siddhasāra of Ravigupta. Vol. I: The Sanskrit Text edited by R.E. Emmerick. Wiesbaden 1980. Vol. II: The Tibetan version edited and translated by R.E. Emmerick. Wiesbaden 1982.

**Skhalitapramathanayuktihetusiddhi* of Āryadeva
See Clark, Jamspal 1979.

Sphuṭārthāvyākhyā of Vasubandhu
Edited by D. Śastri as *Abhidharmakośa and Bhāṣya of Ācārya Vasubandhu with the Sphuṭārthā Commentary of Ācārya Yaśomitra.* Varanasi 1970-1973.

Suhṛllekha
Nāgārjuna's Letter to King Gautamīputra. Jamspal, V. L., et. al. Delhi 1978.

Syādvādaratnākara of Vādideva
Syādvādaratnākara of Vādideva. Delhi: Bhāratīya Vidyā Prakāśana, 1988.

Tattvabodhavidhāyinī of Abhayadeva
Edited by S. Sanghavi & J. Dosi as *Sanmatitarkaprakaraṇam by Siddhasena Divākara with Abhayadevasuri's commentary, Tattvabodhavidhāyinī.* Kyoto: Rinzen Book Co., 1984 (1 ed. Bombay: Nirnaya Sagara Press, 1923-1931).

Tattvasamāsasūtravṛtti
Edited by M.M.V. Prasāda Dvivedī. The Chowkhamba Sanskrit Series, nos. 246, 286 (work no. 50). Varanasi 1969.

Tattvasaṃgraha of Śāntarakṣita
Edited by D. Śāstri, with the Commentary "Pañjikā" of Kamalaśīla. 2 Vols. Varanasi 1982.

Upaniṣads
The Early Upaniṣads: Annotated Text and Translation. Edited by Patrick Olivelle. New York: Oxford University Press, 1998.

Vākyapadīya of Bhartṛhari
Edited by S. Iyer as *Vākyapadīya of Bhartṛhari with the Commentary of Helārāja. Kāṇḍa III. Part 1.* Poona: Deccan College Monograph Series, 1963.

Vākyapadīya of Bhartṛhari
Edited by W. Rau. Wiesbaden 1977.

Varṇārhavarṇastotra of *Mātṛceṭa*
See Hartmann 1987.

Yogabindu of Haribhadrasūri
Sanskrit text and translation by K. K. Dixit. Ahmedabad: Lalbhai Dalpatbhai Series 19, 1968.

Yogasūtra of Patañjali and *Yogasūtrabhāṣya* of Vyāsa
Yogasūtra of Patañjali with the Yogasūtrabhāṣya of Vyāsa and the Tattvavaiśāradī of Vācaspatimiśra. Poona: Ānandāśrama Sanskrit Series, 1932.

Yogasūtra of Patañjali and *Yogasūtrabhāṣya* of Vyāsa
Yogasūtra of Patañjali with the Yogasūtrabhāṣya of Vyāsa and the Tattvavaiśāradī of Vācaspatimiśra. Poona: Ānandāśrama Sanskrit Series, 1932.

Yuktidīpikā
Edited by Albrecht Wezler & Shujun Motegi as *The Most Significant Commentary on the Sāṃkhyakārikā.* Alt- und Neu-Indische Studien 44. Stuttgart: Franz Steiner Verlag, 1998.

Secondary Literature

A Critical Pāli Dictionary. Begun by V. Treckner, revised, continued, and edited by Dines Anderson, Helmer Smith, and Hans Hendriksen. Copenhagen: Royal Danish Academy of Sciences and Letters, 1924-.

Ames, W. 1986. *Prajñāpradīpa* (tr. and ed. of chs. 3-5, 23, 26). Unpublished Diss., University of Washington, Seattle.

Bhatt, Bansidhar. 1974. "Vyavahāra-naya and Niścaya-naya in Kundakunda's Work." *Zeitschrift der Deutschen Morgenländischen Gesellschaft*, Supplement II:279-291.

Bhattacharya, V. 1943. *The Āgamaśāstra of Gauḍapāda.* Calcutta.

Bossche, Frank van den. 2010. "God, the Soul and the Creatrix. Haribhadra Sūri on Nyāya and Sāṃkhya." *International Journal of Jaina Studies (Online)* 6/6:1-49.

Chakravarti, P. 1975. *Origin and Development of the Sāṃkhya System of Thought.* New Delhi: Mushiram Manoharlal.

Chemparathy, G. 1968/1969. "Two Early Buddhist Refutations of the Existence of Īśvara as the Creator of the Universe." *Wiener Zeitschrift für die Kunde des Süd- und Ost-Asiens* XII-XIII:85-100.

Cheng, Hsueh-li. 1982. *Nāgārjuna's Twelve Gate Treatise.* Studies of Classical India, Vol. 5. Dordrecht.

Clark, W.; Jamspal, L. 1979. "The Dialectic which Refutes Errors Establishing Logical Reasons." *The Tibetan Journal* 4/2:29-50.

Conze, E. 1973. *Materials for a Dictionary of the Prajñāpāramitā Literature.* Tokyo.

Danielson, H. 1980. *Ādiśeṣa. The Essence of Supreme Truth (Paramārthasāra).* Leiden.

Dayal, H. 1978. *The Bodhisattva Doctrine in Buddhist Sanskrit Literature.* Reprint: Delhi. (1 ed., New York 1932).

Dreyfus, Georges B. J. & Sara L. McClintock (eds.). 2003. *Svātantrika and Prāsaṅgika Distinction: what difference does a difference make?* Boston: Wisdom Publications.

Dvivedī 1969.
See *Tattvasamāsasūtravṛtti.*

Eckel, Malcolm D. 1978. "Bhāvaviveka and the Early Mādhyamika Theories of Language." *Philosophy East and West* 28/3:323-337.

Eckel, Malcolm D. 1980. *A Question of Nihilism. Bhāvaviveka's Response to the Fundamental Problems of Mādhyamika Philosophy.* Unpublished Diss., Harvard University.

Eckel, Malcolm D. 1987. *Jñānagarbha's Commentary on the Distinction between the Two Truths. An Eight Century Handbook of Madhyamaka Philosophy.* Albany: State University of New York Press.

Eckel, Malcolm D. 2008. *Bhāviveka and His Buddhist Opponents.* Harvard Oriental Series 70. Cambridge Mass. and London: Harvard University Press.

Ejima, Y. 1980. *Chūgan-Shisō no Tenkai-Bhāvaviveka Kenkyū.* Tokyo.

Frauwallner, Erich. 1933. "Dignāga und anderes." *Festschrift für M. Winternitz zum siebzigsten Geburtstag.* Leipzig, 237-242.

Frauwallner, Erich. 1958. "Zur Erkenntnislehre des klassischen Sāṃkhya-Systems." *Wiener Zeitschrift für des Kunde Süd- und Ostasiens* II:84-139.

Frauwallner, Erich. 1961. "Landmarks in the History of Indian Logic." *Wiener Zeitschrift für des Kunde Süd- und Ostasiens* V:125-148.

Frauwallner, Erich. 1973. *History of Indian philosophy.* Translated from original German into English by V. M. Bedekar. Vol. 2: The nature-philosophical schools and the Vaiśeṣika system. The system of the Jaina. The Materialism. Delhi: Motilal Banarsidass

[Original: Geschichte der indischen Philosophie. Salzburg: Otto Müller Verlag, 1956].

Garbe, R. 1917. *Die Sāṃkhya-Philosophie.* Leipzig.

Glasenapp, H. von. 1950. *Vedānta und Buddhismus.* Akademie der Wissenschaften und der Literatur. Abhandlungen der Geistes- und Sozial-wissenschaftlichen Klasse, Nr. 11. Wiesbaden.

Gokhale, V.V. 1963. "Masters of Buddhism Adore the Brahman through Non-Adoration." *Indo-Iranian Journal* V/4:271-275.

Gokhale, V.V. 1972. "The Second Chapter of Bhavya's *Madhyamakahṛdaya** (Taking the Vow of an Ascetic)." *Indo-Iranian Journal* XXIV/1-2:40-45.

Gokhale, V.V.; Bahulkar, S. S. 1985. "Madhyamakahṛdayakārikā Tarkajvālā. Chapter 1." Indiske Studier 5:76-108. København: Akademisk Forlag.

Granoff, Phyllis. 1999. "Refutation as Commentary: Medieval Jain Arguments against Sāṃkhya." *Asiatische Studien/Etudes Asiatiques* LIII/3:579-591.

Hacker, P. 1953. "Vivarta. Studien zur Geschichte der Illusionistischen Kosmologie und Erkenntnistheorie der Inder." Abhandlungen der Geistes- und Sozialwissenschaftlichen Klasse, Nr. 5:187-242. Wiesbaden.

Halbfass, W. 1979. "Observations on Darśana." *Wiener Zeitschrift für die Kunde Südasiens* XXIII:195-203.

Halbfass, W. 1981. "Darśana, Ānvīkṣikī, Philosophy." *India and Europe. An Essay in Understanding.* Albany: State University of New York Press, 296-327.

Harrison, Paul. 2014. "Earlier Inventories of Sanskrit Manuscripts in Tibet: A Synoptic List of Titles." *From birch bark to digital data: recent advances in Buddhist manuscript research.* Papers presented at the Conference Indic Buddhist Manuscripts: the state of the field, Stanford, June 15-19, 2009. Edited by Paul Harrison and Jens-Uwe Hartmann. Wien: Verlag der Österreichischen Akademie der Wissenschaften, 2014.

Hartmann, J-U. 1987. *Das Varṇārhavarṇastotra des Mātṛceṭa.* Göttingen.

Harzer, Edeltraud. 2006. *The Yuktidīpikā. A Reconstruction of Sāṃkhya Methods of Knowing.* Indologica Halensis. Gesiteskultur Indiens. Texte und Studien, Band 8. Edited by Walter Slaje. Aachen: Shaker Verlag.

Hattori, Masaaki. 1968. *Dignāga, On Perception, being the Pratyakṣapariccheda of Dignāga's Pramāṇasamuccaya.* Translated and annotated by Masaaki Hattori. Cambridge, Mass.: Harvard University Press.

Heitmann, Annette L. 1997. "Bibliographie zur Bhavya-Literatur." *Glimpses of the Sanskrit Buddhist Literature.* Kameshwar Nath Mishra (Ed.). Sarnath: Central Institute of Higher Tibetan Studies, 106-154.

Heitmann, Annette L. 2004. *Nektar der Erkenntnis. Buddhistische Philosophie des 6 Jh.: Bhavyas Tarkajvālā I-III.26.* Aachen: Shaker Verlag.

Hiriyanna, M. 1924a. "Bhartṛprapañca: An Old Vedāntin." *The Indian Antiquary* 53:77-85.

Hiriyanna, M. 1924b. "Fragments of Bhartṛprapañca." *Proceedings of the All Indian Oriental Conference* 3:439-450.

Hiriyanna, M. 1925. "Prapañcavilayavāda — A Doctrine of Pre-Śaṅkara Vedānta." *The Journal of Oriental Research* 1:109-117.

Hiriyanna, M. 1928. "Brahmadatta: An Old Vedāntin." *Journal of Oriental Research* 2:1-9.

Honda, Megumu. 1967. "Sāṃkhya Philosophy Described by his Opponent Bhavya." *Journal of Indian Buddhist Studies* 31:436-442.

Honda, Megumu. 1968. "Dharmapāla's Report on Sāṃkhya." *Journal of Indian Buddhist Studies* 33:439-445.

Hopkins, Jeffrey. 1996. "The Tibetan Genre of Doxography: Structuring a Worldview." *Tibetan Literature: Studies in Genre. Essays in honor of Geshe Lhundup Sopa.* Edited by José Ignacio Cabezón & Roger R. Jackson. Ithaca, N.Y: Snow Lion, 170-186.

Hopkins, Jeffrey. 2003. *Maps of the Profound. Jam-yang-shay-ba's Great Exposition of Buddhist and Non-Buddhist Views on the Nature of Reality.* Ithaca, New York, Boulder, Colorado: Snow Lion Publications.

Iida, S. 1966. "Āgama (Scripture) and Yukti (Reason) in Bhāvaviveka." *Kanakura Festschrift.* Kyoto: Heirakuji-Shoten, 79-96.

Iida, S. 1980. *Reason and Emptiness. A Study in Logic and Mysticism.* Tokyo.

Ingalls, D. H. H. 1952. "The Study of Śaṅkarācārya."*Annals of the Bhandarkar Oriental Research Institute* XXXIII:1-14.

Jacobi, Hermann. 1911. "The Dates of the Philosophical Sūtras of the Brahmans." *Journal of the American Oriental Society* 31:1-29.

Jacobsen, Knut. 1997. *Prakṛti in Sāṃkhya-Yoga: Material Principle, Religious Experience, Ethical Implications.* New York: Peter Lang.

Jacobsen, Knut. 2008. *Kapila: Founder of Sāṃkhya and Avatāra of Viṣṇu* (including a translation of the *Kapilāsurisaṃvāda*). New Delhi: Munshiram Manoharlal Publishers Pvt. Ltd.

Jaini, P.S. 1959. "The Sautrāntika Theory of Bīja." *Bulletin of the School of Oriental and African Studies* XXII/2:236-249.

Johansson, Rune E. A. 1979. *The Dynamic Psychology of Early Buddhism.* London.

Johnston, E. H. 1937. *Early Sāṃkhya. An Essay on its Historical Development according to the Texts.* London.

Jolly, J. 1977. *Indian Medicine.* New Dehli.

Jong, J.W. de. 1949. *Cinq Chapitres de la Prasannapadā.* Paris.

Kajiyama, Y. 1963. "Bhāvaviveka's Prajñāpradīpaḥ (1. Kapitel)." *Wiener Zeitschrift für des Kunde Süd- und Ostasiens* VII:37-62.

Kane, P. V. 1930."Vedānta Commentators before Śaṅkarācārya." *Proceedings and Transactions of the Fifth Indian Oriental Conference,* Vol. II. University of Panjab, Lahore, 937-953.

Keith, A. B. 1975. *A History of the Sāṃkhya Philosophy. The Sāṃkhya System.* Delhi: Nag Publishers. (1 ed. Calcutta/London 1918.)

Kent, Stephen A. 1982. "Early Sāṃkhya in the 'Buddhacarita'." *Philosophy East and West* 32/3:259-278.

King, Richard. 1995. *Early Advaita Vedānta and Buddhism: the Mahāyāna context of the Gauḍapādīyakārikā.* Albany: State University of New York Press.

Krasser, H. 2011. "How to teach a Buddhist monk to refute the outsiders. Text-critical remarks on some works by Bhāviveka." *Dhīḥ* 51:49–76.

Krasser, H. 2012. "Bhāviveka, Dharmakīrti and Kumārila." *Devadattīyam, Johannes Bronkhorst Felicitation Volume.* Edited by F. Voegeli, V. Eltschinger, D. Feller, M. P. Candotti, B. Diaconescu, M. Kulkarni. Bern, 535–594.

Krause, Charlotte. 1999. "Siddhasena Divākara and Vikramāditya." *German Jaina Śrāvikā Dr. Charlotte Krause. Her Life & Literature.* Volume I. Compiled by Hazarimull Banthia & Luitgard Soni. Varanasi: Pārśvanātha Vidyāpīṭha, 114-178.

Kværne, P. 1975. "On the Concept of Sahaja in Indian Buddhist Tantric Literature." *Temenos* 11:88-135.

Lamotte, É. 1949-1980. *Le Traité de la Grande Vertu de Sagesse de Nāgārjuna (Mahāprajñāpāramitāśāstra)*, I-V, Louvain.

Lamotte, É. 1980. "Conditioned Co-production and Supreme Enlightenment." *Buddhist Studies in Honour of Walpola Rahula.* Edited by Somaratna Balasooriya et. al. London: Gordon Fraser; Sri Lanka: Vimamsa.

Lang, Karen. 1986. *Āryadeva's Catuḥśataka. On the Bodhisattva's Cultivation of Merit and Knowledge.* Indiske Studier 7. København: Akademisk Forlag.

Larson, Gerald James. 1979. *Classical Sāṃkhya: An Interpretation of its History and Meaning.* Delhi: Motilal Banarsidass.

Larson, Gerald James & Ram Shankar Bhattacharya. 1987. *Sāṃkhya: A Dualist Tradition in Indian Philosophy.* Encyclopedia of Indian Philosophies. Princeton: Princeton U.P.

Larson, Gerald James; Bhattacharya, Ram Shankar. 2008. *Yoga: India's Philosophy of Meditation.* Encyclopedia of Indian Philosophies XII. Delhi: Motilal Banarsidass Publishers.

La Vallée Poussin, L. de. 1933 "L'auteur du Joyau dans la Main." *Mélanges Chinois et Bouddhiques* 2:60-67.

Lindquist, S. 1935. *Siddhi und Abhiñña.* Uppsala.

Lindtner, Christian. 1981. "Atiśa's Introduction to the Two Truths, and its Sources." *Journal of Indian Philosophy* 9:161-214.

Lindtner, Christian. 1982a. "Adversaria Buddhica." *Wiener Zeitschrift für die Kunde Süd-Asiens* XXVI:167-194.

Lindtner, Christian. 1982b. *Nagarjuniana. Studies in the Writings and Philosophy of Nāgārjuna.* Indiske Studier 4. København: Akademisk Forlag.

Lindtner, Christian. 1985a. "Remarks on the Gauḍapādīya-kārikā-s (GK)." *Indo-Iranian Journal* 28/4:275-279.

Lindtner, Christian. 1985b. "A Treatise on Buddhist Idealism. Kambala's Ālokamālā." Indiske Studier 5:109-221. København: Akademisk Forlag.

Lindtner, Christian. 1986. "Bhavya, the Logician." *Golden Jubilee Volume. The Adyar Library Bulletin* 50:58-84.

Lopez, D.S. 1987. *A Study of Svatāntrika.* Ithaca, New York: Snow Lion.

Maas, Philipp. 2006. *Samādhipāda: Das erste Kapitel des Pātañjala-yogaśāstra zum ersten Mal kritisch ediert.* Indologica Halensis Band 9. Hrsg. von Walter Slaje unter Mitwirkung von Jürgen Hanneder und Andreas Pohlus. Aachen: Shaker Verlag.

Malinar, Angelika. 1999. "Prakṛti as sāmānya." *Asiatische Studien/Etudes Asiatiques* LIII/3:619-643.

May, J. 1959. *Candrakīrti. Prasannapadā Madhyamakavṛtti.* Paris.

Mimaki, K. 1980. "Sur le rôle de l'antaraśloka ou du saṃgrahaśloka." *Indianisme et Bouddhisme: Mélanges Offerts à Mgr Étienne Lamotte.* Louvain-la-Neuve, 233-244.

Mimaki, K. 1982. *Blo gsal grub mtha'. Chapitres IX (Vaibhāṣika) et XI (Yogācāra) édités et Chapitre XII (Mādhyamika).* Kyoto.

Murakami, Shikan. 1999. "What is *Caitanya* – Eternal or Non-eternal?" *Asiatische Studien/Etudes Asiatiques* LIII/3:645-665.

Nakamura, H. 1983. *A History of Early Vedānta Philosophy.* Part One. Delhi: Motilal Banarsidass.

Nakamura, H. 2004. *A History of Early Vedānta Philosophy.* Part Two. Delhi: Motilal Banarsidass.

Norman, K.R. 1987. "An Epithet of Nibbāna." *Śramaṇa Vidyā. Studies in Buddhism. Prof. Jagannath Upadhyaya Commemoration Volume I.* Ed. by N.H. Samtani. Samyag—Vāk Series III. Sarnath: Central Institute of Higher Tibetan Studies, 23-31.

Oberhammer, G. 1960. "The Authorship of the śaṣṭitantram. *Wiener Zeitschrift für die Kunde Süd- und Ost-Asiens* IV:71-91.

Oetke, C. 1988. *"Ich" und das Ich. Analytische Untersuchungen zur Buddhistisch-Brahmanischen Ātmankontroverse.* Alt- und Neu-Indische Studien 33. Stuttgart 1988.

Parpola, Asko. 1981. "On the formation of the Mīmāṃsā and the problems concerning Jaimini, with particular reference to the teacher quotations and the Vedic schools." *Wiener Zeitschrift für die Kunde Südasiens* XXV:145-177.

Qvarnström, O. 1988. "Space and Substance. A Theme in Madhyamaka -Vedānta Polemics." *Studies in Central and East Asian Religions* 1:3-34.

Qvarnström, O. 1989. *Hindu Philosophy in Buddhist Perspective. The Vedāntatattvaviniścaya Chapter of Bhavya's Madhyamakahṛdaya-kārikā.* Lund: Almqvist Wiksell International.

Qvarnström, Olle. 1999. "Haribhadra and the Beginnings of Doxography in India." *Approaches to Jaina Studies: Philosophy, Logic, Rituals and Symbols.* Edited by O. Qvarnström & N. K. Wagle. Toronto: University of Toronto, 169-210.

Qvarnström, Olle. 2003. "Early Vedānta Philosophy Preserved by the Jain Tradition: The Vedavādadvātriṃśikā of Siddhasena Divākara." *Jainism and Early Buddhism. Essays in Honour of Padmanabh S. Jaini.* Parts 1-2. Ed. by O. Qvarnström. Berkeley: Asian Humanitics Press.

Qvarnström, Olle. 2005. "The Jain-Mīmāṃsā Debate on Omniscience." *Studies in Jain History and Culture. Disputes and Dialogues.* Routledge Advances in Jaina Studies. Edited by Peter Flügel. London & New York: Routledge, 89-106.

Qvarnström, Olle. 2012. "Sāṃkhya as portrayed by Bhāviveka and Haribhadrasūri. Early Buddhist and Jain criticisms of Sāṃkhya epistemology and the theory of reflection." *Journal of Indian Philosophy* 40(4):395-409.

Qvarnström, Olle. 2015. "The Niyatidvātriṃśikā ascribed to Siddhasena Divākara." *Jaina Scriptures & Philosophy. Festschrift William Bollée.* edited by Flügel, Peter & Olle Qvarnström. London: Routledge.

Ram, Kanshi. 1988. "Vijñānabhikṣu's Theory of Double Reflection." *Annals of the Bhandarkar Oriental Research Institute* 69:77-92.

Rukmani, T.S. 1988. "Vijñānabhikṣu's Double Reflection Theory of Knowledge in the Yoga System." *Journal of Indian Philosophy* 16:367-375.

Ruegg, D.S. 1980. "On the Reception and Early History of the dBu-ma (Madhyamaka) in Tibet." *Tibetan Studies in Honour of Hugh Richardson.* Warminster, 277-279.

Ruegg, D.S. 1981a. *The Literature of the Madhyamaka School in India.* A History of Indian Literature VII:1. Edited by Jan Gonda. Wiesbaden: Harrassowitz.

Ruegg, D.S. 1981b. "Autour du lTa ba'i khyad par de Ye śes sde." *Journal Asiatique* 269:207-229.

Ruegg, D.S. 1982. "Toward a Chronology of the Madhyamaka School." *Indological and Buddhist Studies: Volume in Honour of Professor J.W. de Jong on his Sixtieth Birthday.* Edited by L.A. Hercus, et al. Canberra Faculty of Asian Studies, 505-530.

Rüping, K. 1977. *Studien zur Frühgeschichte der Vedānta-philosophie. Teil 1. Philologische Untersuchungen zu der Brahmasūtra-Kommentaren des Śaṅkara und des Bhāskaras.* Wiesbaden.

Saito, Akira. 2011. "Bhavya's Critique of the Sāṃkhya Theory of pratibimba." *Studies in Indian Philosophy and Buddhism* 18:13-22.

Sāṅkṛtyāyana, R. 1937. "Second Search of Sanskrit Palm-leaf Mss. in Tibet." *Journal of Bihar and Orissa Research Society* XXXIII/1:1-55.

Sastri, K.S. 1924. "Bodhāyana and Dramidācārya, Two Old Vedāntins Presupposed by Rāmānuja." *Proceedings of the All Indian Oriental Conference* 3:465-473.

Solomon 1973.
See *Sāṃkhya-Vṛttị* (V2).

Solomon, Esther, A. 1974. *The Commentaries of the Sāṃkhya Kārikā — A Study*. Ahmedabad: Gujarat University.

Steinkellner, Ernst. 1999a. "Die ältesten Sätze zur Theorie der Wahrnehmung in Indien: Eine Sammlung von Fragmenten des klassischen Sāṅkhya-Systems." *Psychologie des Bewusstseins - Bewusstsein der Psychologie: Giselher Guttmann zum 65. Geburtstag.* Hrsg. von T. Slunecko, O. Vitouch, C. Korunka, H. Bauer, B. Flatschacher. Wien: Wiener Universitätsverlag, 247- 253.

Steinkellner, Ernst. 1999b. "The Ṣaṣṭitantra on Perception, a Collection of Fragments." *Asiatische Studien* 53(3):667-676.

Sørensen, P. K. 1986a. *Candrakīrti's Triśaraṇasaptati. The Septuagint on the Three Refuges.* Wiener Studien zur Tibetologie und Buddhismuskunde. Heft 16. Wien.

Sørensen, P. K. 1986b. *A Fourteenth Century Tibetan Historical Work: Rgyal-Rabs Gsal-Ba'i Me-Loṅ. Author, Date and Sources. A Case Study.* Fontes Tibetici Havnienses, Vol. I. København: Akademisk Forlag.

Tatia, Nathmal. 1951. *Studies in Jaina Philosophy.* Varanasi: P.V. Research Institute.

Vaidya, P. L. 1960. *Madhyamakaśāstra of Nāgārjuna with the Commentary Prasannapadā by Candrakīrti.* Buddhist Sanskrit Texts No. 10. Dharbanga.

Vetter, T. 1978. "Die Gauḍapādīya Kārikās: Zur Entstehung und zur Bedeutung von (A)dvaita." *Wiener Zeitschrift für die Kunde Südasiens* XXII:95-133.

Vetter, T. 1979. *Studien zur Lehre und Entwicklung Śaṅkaras.* Publications of the De Nobili Research Library. Oberhammer, G. (ed.). Indological Institute, University of Vienna. Vol. VI. Wien.

Walleser, Max. 1910. *Der Ältere Vedānta. Geschichte, Kritik und Lehre.* Heidelberg.

Wezler & Motegi 1998. See *Yuktidīpika.*

Winternitz, M. 1983. *A History of Indian Literature.* Vol. 2: Buddhist Literature and Jain Literature. A new authoritative translation by V. Srinivasa Sarma. Delhi: Motilal Banarsidass. (1 ed. *Geschichte der indischen Literatur,* Bd. 2, Leipzig 1920.)

Index to Sanskrit Verses